Get Set Procreate 5

A practical guide to illustrating on an iPad filled with tips, tricks, and best practices

Samadrita Ghosh

BIRMINGHAM—MUMBAI

Get Set Procreate 5

Copyright © 2022 Packt Publishing

All rights reserved. No part of this book may be reproduced, stored in a retrieval system, or transmitted in any form or by any means, without the prior written permission of the publisher, except in the case of brief quotations embedded in critical articles or reviews.

Every effort has been made in the preparation of this book to ensure the accuracy of the information presented. However, the information contained in this book is sold without warranty, either express or implied. Neither the author, nor Packt Publishing or its dealers and distributors, will be held liable for any damages caused or alleged to have been caused directly or indirectly by this book.

Packt Publishing has endeavored to provide trademark information about all of the companies and products mentioned in this book by the appropriate use of capitals. However, Packt Publishing cannot guarantee the accuracy of this information.

Group Product Manager: Rohit Rajkumar
Publishing Product Manager: Ashitosh Gupta
Senior Editor: Aamir Ahmed
Senior Content Development Editor: Rakhi Patel
Technical Editor: Saurabh Kadave
Copy Editor: Safis Editing
Project Coordinator: Sonam Pandey
Proofreader: Safis Editing
Indexer: Pratik Shirodkar
Production Designer: Aparna Bhagat
Marketing Coordinator: Teny Thomas

First published: September 2022
Production reference: 1150922

Published by Packt Publishing Ltd.
Livery Place
35 Livery Street
Birmingham
B3 2PB, UK.

ISBN 978-1-80056-300-1

www.packt.com

To my parents, who have tirelessly supported my dreams in a world that warned them otherwise, and my friends, who always saw more in me than I could see in myself.

– Samadrita Ghosh

Contributors

About the author

Samadrita Ghosh is self employed artist based in India. She has worked in the industry as an animator, illustrator, and pre-production artist since 2016 and has worked on several projects for diverse clients.

In 2020, she graduated with a bachelor's degree in design from **Indian Institute of Technology (IIT), Guwahati**, and is now pursuing an independent career in illustration. She has been using Procreate to illustrate professionally for over 2 years.

I want to thank my mother, Dr Barnali Ghosh, for giving me my first iPad, where it all started.

About the reviewers

Nadia Ramlan is a digital artist from Malaysia with 10 years of experience in illustration and comics who primarily provides pre-production assets and graphic art. She has worked with local and international clients in the animation and comics industry, including InfiniteMotion Sdn. Bhd. and Headlocked Comics.

Nang Saphoi Longphai is an artist working on honing her skills in commercial art. Her work consists of fanart and original illustrations inspired by games, anime, and fashion. Saphoi completed her bachelor's degree in design at IIT Guwahati and has been freelancing ever since. Hailing from Arunachal Pradesh, she wishes to showcase her culture through her work in the near future.

Table of Contents

Preface	**xvii**

Part 1: UI Overview

1

The Gallery – Organizing Your Files — 3

Creating a canvas	3	Sharing by dragging and dropping	9
Creating a canvas using Import	4	**Ordering, renaming, and stacking**	**10**
Creating a canvas using Photo	5	Ordering your canvases	10
Creating a custom canvas	6	Renaming a canvas	11
Sharing a canvas	6	Stacking canvases	12
Sharing a single canvas	6	**Selecting, duplicating, and deleting**	**14**
Sharing multiple canvases	8	**Summary**	**16**

2

Getting Started – Setting Up a Canvas — 17

Working from presets	17	Creating a custom canvas	23
Preset – Screen_Size	18	Custom preset – Usual Landscape	24
Preset – Square	19	Dimensions, resolutions, and layer limits	25
Preset – 4K	19	Dimensions	25
Preset – A4	20	Resolution	25
Preset – 4 x 6 Photo	21	Layer limits in Procreate	26
Preset – Paper	21		
Preset – Comic	22		

Choosing a color profile	27	Time-lapse and canvas properties	31
RGB	27	Time-lapse video	31
CMYK	28	Canvas properties	32
Importing your own color profile	30	**Summary**	**33**

3

Understanding Your Workspace 35

The top-right panel: painting tools	35	The Modify button	43
Paint	36	Undo and Redo	45
Smudge	37	**The top-left panel: Advanced Features**	**45**
Eraser	38	Gallery	46
Layers	39	Actions	46
The Colour button	39	Adjustments	50
The left panel: the sidebar	**42**	Selections	52
Brush size slider	42	Transform	52
Brush opacity slider	43	**Summary**	**53**

4

Using the Actions Menu 55

The Add menu	55	The Share menu	84
Insert a file	56	Share Image	85
Insert a photo	57	Share Layers	86
Take a photo	58	**The Video menu**	**89**
Add text	59	Time-lapse Replay	90
Cut, Copy, Copy Canvas, and Paste	62	Time-lapse Recording	91
The Canvas menu	**63**	Export Time-lapse video	92
Crop and Resize	63	**The Prefs (Preferences) menu**	**94**
Animation Assist	72	Interface toggles	95
Page Assist	73	Connect legacy stylus	98
Drawing Guide	74	Pressure and Smoothing	99
The Reference companion	75	Gesture controls	102
Flip Canvas	78	Rapid Undo Delay	102
Canvas Info	79	Selection Mask Visibility	103

The Help menu	104	Learn to Procreate	111
Restore purchases	105	Customer support	112
Advanced settings	105	Procreate Folio	112
What's new?	108	Write a Review	113
Procreate Handbook	110	**Summary**	**114**

5

Selecting and Transforming — 115

The Selections tool	115	The Transform tool	129
Automatic selection	116	Interface	130
Freehand selection	118	Freeform	133
Rectangle and Ellipse selection	120	Uniform	135
Add	121	Distort	136
Remove	122	Warp	138
Invert	123	Snapping	141
Copy & Paste	124	Flipping tools	143
Feather	125	Rotate 45°	143
Save & Load	126	Fit to Screen	144
Selection mask visibility	127	Interpolation	146
Selecting layer contents	128	Reset	147
Finalizing edits	129	Finalizing edits	147
		Summary	**147**

Part 2: Utility and an In-Depth Discussion of Utility and Features

6

Using Gestures and Shortcuts — 151

Understanding basic gestures	151	Three-finger scrub	155
Pinch	152	Three-finger swipe down	156
Double-tap undo	153	Four-finger tap	159
Three-finger tap redo	154	QuickShape	159
		Precise slider control	164

Using accessibility gestures	164	Customizing gestures	173
Activating single touch gestures	164	Painting gestures	174
Exploring layer gestures	**168**	Advanced feature gestures	176
		Full Screen gestures	181
Selecting layers	168	Layer content gestures	182
Pinch to merge layers	170	General gesture options	186
Two-finger tap for layer opacity	170	**Summary**	**188**
Two-finger swipe right for alpha lock	171		
Two-finger hold to select layer contents	172		

7

Organizing Your Layers — 189

The Layers interface	190	Clipping Mask	207
Create a new layer	191	Drawing Assist	209
Layer thumbnail	192	Invert	209
Layer name	192	Reference	210
Primary layer	192	Merge Down	210
Blend mode	193	Combine Down	210
Layer visibility	193	**Understanding blend modes**	**210**
Background color	193	Multiply	210
Layer Options menu	194	Darken	211
Organizing layers	**194**	Color Burn	212
Selecting layers	194	Linear Burn	213
Grouping layers	197	Darker Color	214
Moving layers	199	Lighten	215
Transferring layers between canvases	200	Screen	216
Lock, duplicate, and delete layers	202	Color Dodge	217
Exploring Layer Options	**204**	Add	218
Rename	204	Lighter Color	219
Select	205	Overlay	220
Copy	205	Soft Light	221
Fill Layer	206	Hard Light	222
Clear	206	Vivid Light	223
Alpha Lock	206	Linear Light	224
Mask	206	Pin Light	225
		Hard Mix	226

Difference	227	Luminosity	234
Exclusion	228	**Sharing layers**	**235**
Subtract	229	Drag and drop export	236
Divide	230	Share Layers menu	237
Hue	231	**Summary**	**237**
Saturation	232		
Color	233		

8

Painting Tools and the Brush Library – Using and Organizing Brushes — 239

The Paint, Smudge, and Erase tools	**239**	Brush Library basics	246
Paint	240	Recent and pinned brushes	256
Smudge	241	**The basics of Brush Studio**	**260**
Erase	242	Interface	262
Brush Size Memory	242	Advanced brush settings	264
The Brush Library	**244**	Brush attributes	267
Brush sets and brushes	245	**Summary**	**268**

9

Brush Studio Settings – Editing and Combining Brushes — 269

Exploring Brush Studio settings	**269**	Dynamics	304
Stroke path	269	Apple Pencil	306
Stabilisation	273	Properties	307
Taper	276	Materials	309
Shape	278	About this brush	310
Grain	291	**Dual Brushes**	**315**
Rendering	299	Creating a Dual Brush	316
Wet mix	301	Editing a Dual Brush	317
Color dynamics	302	**Summary**	**321**

10

Using Colour Tools — 323

Colour terms — 323
Hue — 324
Saturation — 324
Value — 326

The interface — 327
The Colours panel — 327
Active colour — 329
ColourDrop — 330
SwatchDrop — 333
Eyedropper — 335

Disc — 337
Interface — 337
Saturation disc controls — 337

Classic — 338
Interface — 339

Harmony — 340
Interface — 340
Reticles — 340
Modes — 341
Choosing colors — 342

Value — 342
Interface — 343

Palettes — 344
Swatches — 344
Palette library — 348
Palette Capture — 349
Importing and sharing palettes — 351

Summary — 352

11

Adjustments – Applying Image Effects — 353

Exploring the Adjustments interface — 353
The Adjustments menu — 354
The Layer and Pencil modes — 355
Adjustment actions — 358

Tweaking colors with color adjustments — 360
Hue, Saturation, and Brightness — 360
Colour Balance — 361
Curves — 363
Gradient Map — 368

Working with blur effects — 376
Gaussian Blur — 376
Motion Blur — 377
Perspective Blur — 378

Applying image effects — 383
Noise — 383
Sharpen — 387
Bloom — 388
Glitch — 391
Halftone — 399
Chromatic Aberration — 404

Warping an image with the Liquify tool — 407
Modes — 408

Settings	414	Duplicating objects with the Clone tool	416
Adjust and Reset	415	The Clone interface	416
		Summary	419

12

Using Assisted Drawing Tools — 421

Using the Drawing Assist interface	421	Realistic drawing with Perspective Guides	434
The Drawing Guides interface	427	The Perspective interface	438
Drawing squared grids with 2D Grid	428	Symmetrical drawing with Symmetry Guides	439
The 2D Grid interface	429	The Symmetry interface	441
Drawing technical graphics with the Isometric Grid	431	Guide Options	444
The Isometric interface	432	Summary	450

13

Using Animation Assist for 2D Animation — 451

Using the Animation Assist interface	451	Frame settings	458
Animation Assist interface	454	Appearance settings	459
Fine-tuning motion using animation settings	456	Editing frames with Frame options	460
Preview settings	457	Summary	465

14

Sketchbooking with Page Assist — 467

Using the Page Assist interface	467	Adjusting pages using Page options	471
Page Assist interface	469	Summary	473

15

Painting on 3D Models — 475

Opening a 3D model — 475
Importing a 3D model — 476
Importing Procreate's Model pack — 477

Understanding 3D models — 478
UV maps — 479

Using the 3D interface — 480
The workspace — 480
The Reference companion — 481
The 3D menu — 485
3D gestures — 488

Working with layers in 3D — 489
Texture sets — 489
Meshes — 491
Base Layer — 491
Additional Layers — 492
Materials — 493
Material options — 498

Transforming graphics on a 3D model — 499
Interface — 499
Advanced transformation — 504

Modifying the environment using Lighting Studio — 508
Overview — 509
Lighting — 510
Environment — 511

Exporting from a 3D canvas — 512
Share Model — 514
Share Image — 514
Share textures — 519

Summary — 520

Part 3: Illustration Tips

16

Rendering Objects Using Blend Modes — 523

Clock body — 524
Shading using Multiply mode — 525
Adding light using Screen mode — 528
Drawing specular reflections using Add mode — 530
Drawing dark shadows using Multiply mode — 532
Adding color effects using Hard Light mode — 534

Clock face — 537
Adding cast shadow using Multiply mode — 537
Adding light using Screen mode — 540

Metal parts — 542
Shading using Multiply mode — 542
Adding light using Add mode — 544

Finishing touches — 546
Adding reflection using Screen mode — 546

Summary — 551

Index	553
Other Books You May Enjoy	**568**

Preface

Procreate is a robust and industry-grade painting software that is an extremely versatile yet affordable alternative to subscription-based applications. *Get Set Procreate* is a comprehensive introduction to the latest version of the software, for those who are new to Procreate. Complete with step-by-step instructions, easy-to-follow descriptions, and practical guidelines, this guide will reveal the ins and outs of the application.

You will learn how to use the features of Procreate 5.2 to create beautiful illustrations, animations, 3D paintings, and much more. The book will take you through all the tools available on Procreate and explain how to use them effectively to create high-quality artworks.

By the end of the book, you will be able to confidently navigate the application to achieve the results you want.

Who this book is for

If you're a beginner who wants to start illustrating professionally on Procreate but doesn't know where to begin, this is the book for you. This book is also for experienced illustrators and animators accustomed to other software, like Photoshop, looking to pick up a new skill.

What this book covers

Chapter 1, *The Gallery – Organizing Your Files*, is where you will learn about the landing page of the application, called the Gallery. This will allow you to jump in as soon as you open the app.

Chapter 2, *Getting Started – Setting Up a Canvas*, will go over how to create a new canvas, both starting with a preset and starting a custom one from scratch to suit your specific needs. Using this knowledge, you will be able to choose your preferred settings, dimensions, color profiles, and much more.

Chapter 3, *Understanding Your Workspace*, will briefly map out the interface of Procreate, namely the toolbars and buttons visible in the workspace. For experienced artists, it will help you recognize and locate features you may already know from other software.

Chapter 4, *Using the Actions Menu*, goes into more detail about the Actions menu. It is a powerful set of tools that can be used to make changes to the canvas, interface, and so forth.

Chapter 5, *Selecting and Transforming*, is where we discuss the Selections tool and the Transform tool. Both of these tools are often used together to select and modify specific areas of an image.

Chapter 6, *Using Gestures and Shortcuts*, looks at how, by lowering UI complexity, Procreate leaves room for a variety of intuitive gestures. This chapter will give you a thorough overview of the different types of gestures and shortcuts available. If you are familiar with keyboard shortcuts on a computer, it will give you an alternative on the iPad.

Chapter 7, *Organizing Your Layers*, introduces you to how layers work in Procreate, including features such as layer options and blend modes.

Chapter 8, *Painting Tools and the Brush Library – Using and Organizing Brushes*, is where you will learn about the painting tools, namely the three types of brushes that are available. You will also learn how to organize, import, and share brushes using the Brush Library. Lastly, the chapter will introduce the basics of using the Brush Studio.

Chapter 9, *Brush Studio Settings – Editing and Combining Brushes*, is an in-depth discussion of the Brush Studio, covering all its features. It also explains how to combine two brushes into one Dual Brush.

Chapter 10, *Using Color Tools*, talks about how Procreate has a wide variety of color selection tools to suit your workflow. This chapter will go over each of those in detail.

Chapter 11, *Adjustments – Applying Image Effects*, is about the Adjustments menu. It consists of several layer adjustment tools to give your artwork an extra edge, using features such as image effects and color adjustments.

Chapter 12, *Using Assisted Drawing Tools*, talks about Drawing Assist, which is a set of tools that help you automate your drawing for accuracy when you need to follow perspective, symmetry, and other geometrical rules. The chapter will discuss the different types of assisted drawing tools available in Procreate.

Chapter 13, *Using Animation Assist for 2D Animation*, discusses how Animation Assist works, which is Procreate's very own animation tool.

Chapter 14, *Sketchbooking with Page Assist*, explains how to use Page Assist. This is a useful tool for maintaining multiple pages of art on a single canvas, just as you would with a sketchbook or comic book.

Chapter 15, *Painting on 3D Models*, is all about the fascinating 3D painting feature that allows you to paint directly on 3D models. It will introduce the basics of how 3D models are composed and how they can be painted on.

Chapter 16, *Rendering Objects Using Blend Modes*, sees you blend layers together to enhance the quality of your rendering. This chapter is a step-by-step walk-through of an illustration, with a special focus on using blend modes to render different types of materials.

To get the most out of this book

This book covers Procreate 5.2, specifically as used on an iPad Pro 12.9-inch (third generation). It is supported by the iPad models mentioned in the following table. To start using this book, you will need to have purchased and launched the Procreate application, which is available on the App Store, for a one-time price of 10 USD.

iPad models that support Procreate 5.2	Operating system requirements
iPad Pro 12.9-inch (first to fifth generation), iPad Pro 11-inch (first to third generation), iPad Pro 10.5-inch, iPad Pro 9.7-inch	iPadOS
iPad (fifth to ninth generation)	iPadOS
iPad mini (fifth and sixth generation), iPad mini 4	iPadOS
iPad Air (third to fifth generation), iPad Air 2	iPadOS

If you are new to Procreate, you will automatically find the latest version on the App Store. If you're a prior user, make sure the app is updated to Procreate 5.2.

While it's possible to use Procreate with multiple types of styluses, using an Apple Pencil is highly recommended to experience its full spectrum of features.

Download the color images

We also provide a PDF file that has color images of the screenshots and diagrams used in this book. You can download it here: `https://packt.link/UlHUL`.

Conventions used

There are a number of text conventions used throughout this book.

`Code in text`: Indicates code words in text, database table names, folder names, filenames, file extensions, pathnames, dummy URLs, user input, and Twitter handles. Here is an example: "From here, choose any `.swatches` file to import the Procreate palette directly into your app."

Bold: Indicates a new term, an important word, or words that you see onscreen. For instance, words in menus or dialog boxes appear in **bold**. Here is an example: "In the top right-hand corner of the **Layers** panel, you will spot a + icon."

> **Tips or important notes**
> Appear like this.

Get in touch

Feedback from our readers is always welcome.

General feedback: If you have questions about any aspect of this book, email us at `customercare@packtpub.com` and mention the book title in the subject of your message.

Errata: Although we have taken every care to ensure the accuracy of our content, mistakes do happen. If you have found a mistake in this book, we would be grateful if you would report this to us. Please visit www.packtpub.com/support/errata and fill in the form.

Piracy: If you come across any illegal copies of our works in any form on the internet, we would be grateful if you would provide us with the location address or website name. Please contact us at `copyright@packt.com` with a link to the material.

If you are interested in becoming an author: If there is a topic that you have expertise in and you are interested in either writing or contributing to a book, please visit `authors.packtpub.com`.

Share Your Thoughts

Once you've read *Get Set Procreate 5*, we'd love to hear your thoughts! Scan the QR code below to go straight to the Amazon review page for this book and share your feedback.

https://packt.link/r/1800563000

Your review is important to us and the tech community and will help us make sure we're delivering excellent quality content.

Part 1: UI Overview

In this first part of the book, you will gain a working knowledge of how the interface works. If you are experienced with other software, you can start illustrating right away.

This section comprises the following chapters:

- *Chapter 1, The Gallery – Organizing Your Files*
- *Chapter 2, Getting Started – Setting Up a Canvas*
- *Chapter 3, Understanding Your Workspace*
- *Chapter 4, Using the Actions Menu*
- *Chapter 5, Selecting and Transforming*

1
The Gallery – Organizing Your Files

The very first page you will see upon opening Procreate for the first time is what is called the **Gallery**. This is where all your files exist and where you can create, organize, and view your artworks. This feature sets Procreate apart from most other drawing software, in which the landing page takes you directly to a new canvas.

To begin, the gallery should already have some sample artworks included to give you an idea of the full extent of what the software is capable of. The gallery is where the application automatically saves all your work, much like cloud-based types of software such as Google Docs. This relieves you from having to continually save your progress while working.

In this chapter, let's look into the gallery and its functionality. By the end of the chapter, you will have learned how to navigate the gallery, make a new canvas, share and arrange your existing canvases, and edit your canvas information.

In this chapter, we're going to cover the following main topics:

- Creating a canvas
- Sharing a canvas
- Ordering, renaming, and stacking
- Selecting, duplicating, and deleting

Creating a canvas

There are several ways of creating a new canvas on Procreate. In the upper-right corner of the gallery, you will see four buttons. Out of those buttons, **Import**, **Photo**, and **+** are the options that let you create a canvas from different sources of your choice. There is some overlap between how those three work, but let's look at them one by one.

4 The Gallery – Organizing Your Files

Creating a canvas using Import

Import allows you to create a new canvas directly from an image, video, PSD, or Procreate file saved in the **Files** app on your iPad. This is ideal for when you have downloaded a file from somewhere else (such as an email or a cloud drive) and want to open it in Procreate.

Tapping on **Import** will take you directly to **Files**, as shown here:

Figure 1.1: Importing from Files

From here, you simply have to go to the location of the file you want and tap on it. Once you have chosen a compatible file to open, Procreate will automatically create a canvas using it for you to work on.

Procreate supports the following file types:

- `.procreate`
- `PSD`
- `JPEG`
- `PNG`
- `TIFF`

- `.PDF`
- `GIF`
- `.MP4`
- `HEVC`

Another way to quickly import a file into Procreate is by dragging and dropping it from **Files**. We'll go into more detail about that in the *Sharing by dragging and dropping* section. With that, you now know how to import images from **Files** to create a new canvas. Now, let's look at the other options we have.

Creating a canvas using Photo

Another avenue the application offers is to import an image from the **Photos** app. Tapping on **Photo** will take you to your iPad's gallery, from where you can pick an image of your choice. It will look like this:

Figure 1.2: Importing from Photos

Here, you have an option to choose either from the entire gallery of photos or your albums. Similar to **Import**, Procreate will automatically create a fresh canvas with the original image.

> **Important Note**
>
> A canvas created from an imported file from either **Files** (using **Import**) or **Photos** (using **Photo**) will have the same properties as the source, including dimensions, resolution, and color profile. For time-based files such as GIFs and videos, the canvas will automatically turn on **Animation Assist** at the same frame rate as the source.

Of course, in this case, dragging and dropping an image from the Photo Library also does the trick. You now know how to create a canvas using Photo.

Creating a custom canvas

Tap on the + icon in the upper-right corner to create a fresh blank canvas from the available presets. If you find that none of them fit your needs, you could always make one from scratch! In the next chapter, we will cover, in detail, the process of setting up a custom canvas.

Next, we will look at the different ways in which we can share a canvas on Procreate.

Sharing a canvas

Procreate lets you export a canvas directly from the gallery to several supported apps such as Google Drive, Twitter, and Instagram. There are two ways to do it: you can choose to either share a single canvas or share multiple canvases together.

Sharing a single canvas

To begin, perform the following steps:

1. Open the gallery and find the canvas you want to export.
2. Swipe left on it to reveal three buttons, **Share**, **Duplicate**, and **Delete**, as shown here:

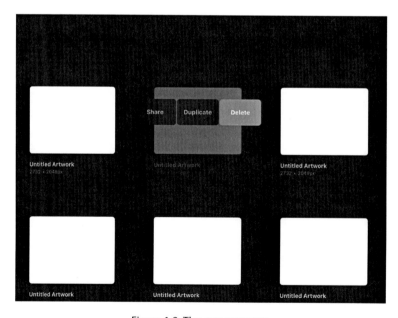

Figure 1.3: The canvas menu

3. Tap on **Share** to reveal this menu, which has all the possible formats your file can be exported as:

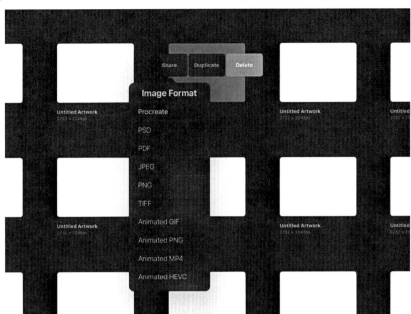

Figure 1.4: The export formats menu

4. Once you have chosen your desired format, a dialog box will open. From here, you can choose the destination of your exported file, as shown here:

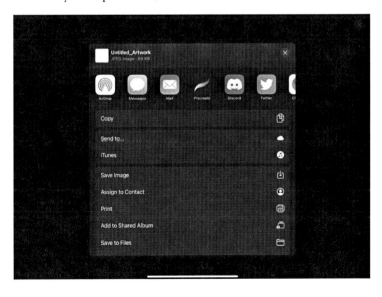

Figure 1.5: The Share menu

8 | The Gallery – Organizing Your Files

You can easily save the file to your device or send it to an app of your choice. It's worth noting that sharing to an app does not mean that the image is saved to your device. You have to do that separately.

Sharing multiple canvases

Procreate also lets you export multiple canvases at once:

1. From the gallery, tap on the **Select** option. A small circle will appear under each canvas.
2. Tap on a canvas to check the circle and select it.
3. Once you have selected all the canvases you want to export, you will notice that the upper-right menu has now changed, as shown here:

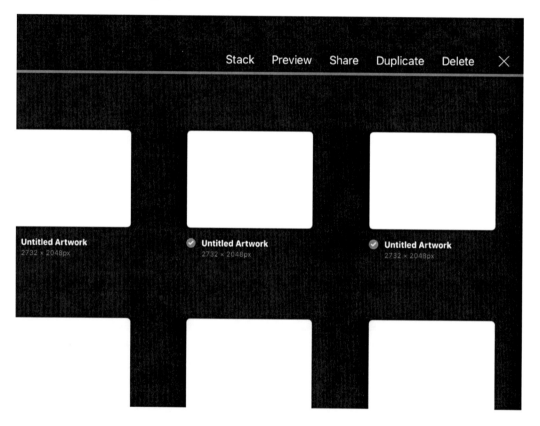

Figure 1.6: The canvas

4. Out of those options, select **Share**.

Similar to the previous process, choose a format and destination for your files to complete the process and bulk export the selected canvases.

Sharing by dragging and dropping

A quicker and easier way to export files is by dragging and dropping a canvas into the intended destination. For this, you will need to use the **Split View** feature of your iPad. To activate **Split View**, follow these steps:

1. Open Procreate.
2. Gently push up the horizontal white bar at the bottom of your screen to reveal the Tab bar. From there, press and hold the **Photos/Files** app icon (or wherever you want to export to).
3. Drag the icon to the left or right edge of the screen.
4. Your screen will automatically split, with the two apps on either side of the app divider line. You can adjust the position of this line to decide how much screen space to allot to each app:

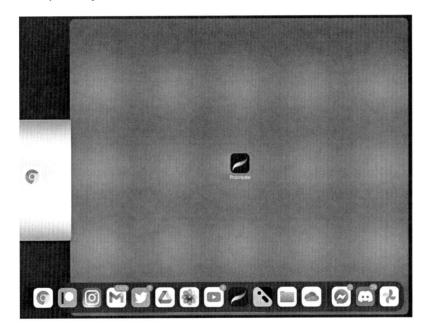

Figure 1.7: Activating the split view

5. Next, simply select the canvases you'd like to export using the **Select** button from the previous section, and drag them into your destination app to export them automatically.

> **Important Note**
>
> The format of a file exported using drag and drop depends on the destination app. You can edit this via **Open Procreate | Actions | Help | Advanced Settings | Drag and Drop Export**. By default, the file type is set to `.jpeg` when exporting to **Photos** and `.procreate` when exporting to **Files**.

Now that we know how to create and export canvases, it's useful to learn how to organize the gallery.

Ordering, renaming, and stacking

For artists working on several projects at once, it's important to be able to easily sort out their gallery to navigate it smoothly. There are many convenient ways to organize your canvases within the Procreate gallery.

Ordering your canvases

The gallery has no constraints about sorting canvases in chronological, alphabetical, or any other order. By default, every new canvas you create gets added to the left-hand side of the top row. Even so, you are pretty much free to arrange your files in whatever order you want them to appear. This is done by long pressing on a canvas thumbnail and dragging it to the desired position:

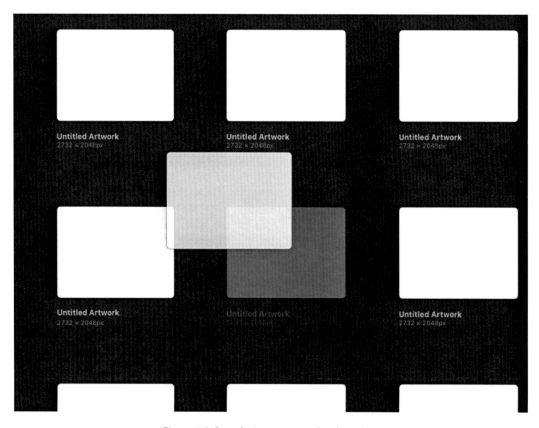

Figure 1.8: Reordering canvases by dragging

Renaming a canvas

The default name of a new canvas is `Untitled Artwork`. To edit this, simply tap on the canvas name and it will pop out as a text editor bar, where you can type in the name you want. Tapping on the **x** mark (the cancel icon) on the right-hand side of the text editor will reset it to the default setting. This is how it will look:

Figure 1.9: Renaming a canvas

Right off the bat, you will notice, that Procreate allows you to have multiple canvases with the same name without marking them, such as **painting and painting(1)**. You are also free to use special characters in any order. Note that it's a slightly different feeling from, perhaps, naming files on your computer:

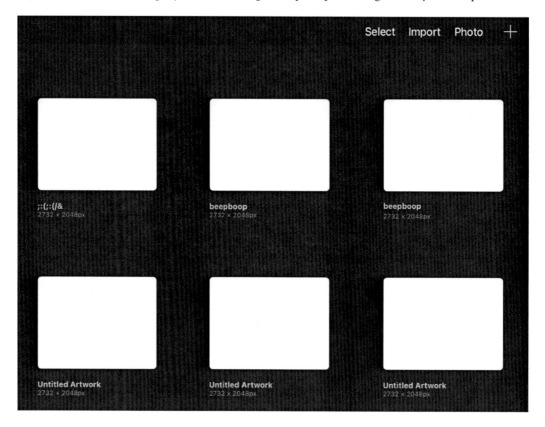

Figure 1.10: No naming conventions

Stacking canvases

Stacking is the feature you can use when you want to group together similar canvases. It's like creating a "folder" on your computer. Each one of these groups is called a stack.

To stack two canvases, drag one canvas thumbnail over the other and wait for a blue box to appear over the one on the bottom. Then release it to create a stack:

Ordering, renaming, and stacking 13

Figure 1.11: Creating a stack

A stack is named `Stack` by default. You can rename it in the same way as renaming a canvas: by tapping on the name and editing the it.

Adding an existing canvas to a stack can be done in the following ways:

- Drag and hold the stack over the canvas. A blue box will appear over the canvas, and a blue circle with the current number of canvases in the stack will appear in the upper-right corner. Once this happens, release the stack. This will reset the stack name to the default setting, irrespective of what it was named before. The canvas added will be found at the very bottom of the stack.
- Drag and hold the canvas over the stack. Don't release it until a blue box blinks over the stack and it opens up to show all the canvases inside. Place the canvas in the position you'd like before releasing it. This method lets you keep whatever name the stack originally had.
- You can also choose the canvases you want to stack using the **Select** feature, which is covered in the next section.

> **Important Note**
> You cannot create a stack within a stack. Additionally, one stack cannot be stacked with another using drag and hold.

To move a canvas out of a stack, drag it over to the stack name. Then, hold it until the name turns blue and blinks, and the gallery appears. Place the canvas where you'd like.

Selecting, duplicating, and deleting

There are many more actions you can perform on your canvases from the gallery. These features are useful when you want to execute an action in bulk on several canvases. Tap on **Select** in the upper-right corner of the gallery to begin:

Selecting, duplicating, and deleting   15

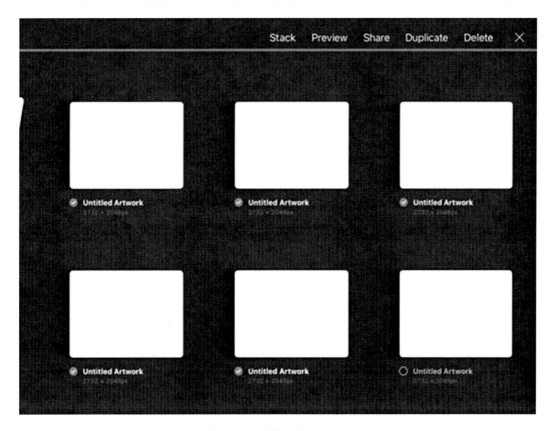

Figure 1.12: The select menu

Once you have selected your desired canvases, you can perform the following actions on them:

- **Stack**: Create a stack with all the selected canvases and stacks.
- **Preview**: This will open up a slideshow with all the selected artworks in fullscreen mode, which you can swipe through. For canvases that have **Animation Assist** turned on, the preview will play the animated video.
- **Share**: You can bulk export all of the selected canvases in the same way that we discussed earlier, including dragging and dropping to your preferred destination.
- **Duplicate**: Create copies of each selected canvas.
- **Delete**: This is self-explanatory. This cannot be undone, so be careful when using it.

> **Important Note**
>
> While in the gallery, pinch out of a canvas thumbnail to automatically activate the **Preview** mode and swipe through all your artworks in fullscreen, without having to load the individual canvases.

Summary

Hopefully, you're now comfortable with how the landing screen of Procreate 5 functions, and you've got the hang of using all these features to organize your gallery. Try using your newly learned skills to group together all the sample artworks into a stack, because in the next chapter, it will be time to create your own custom canvas.

2
Getting Started – Setting Up a Canvas

While making a new canvas, Procreate offers you a default set of canvas presets to choose from. Your canvas specifics will largely depend on the artwork you want to make. For instance, a thumbnail you want to post to Instagram and a poster you want to print out for your bedroom wall need separate settings to work in the way they are intended. The size they will be viewed in, where, and in what format they will be displayed are among the factors you need to consider while choosing your canvas settings.

If you find that the default options don't cover your precise needs, you can easily create a fresh canvas manually. This allows you to have a lot more control over parameters such as size and resolution. Since Procreate automatically records a time-lapse video, the canvas settings also include time-lapse settings.

Open Procreate and tap on the + icon in the upper-right corner of the screen. This will open up the **New canvas** menu, which we will focus on for this chapter.

In this chapter, we're going to cover the following main topics:

- Working from presets
- Creating a custom canvas
- Dimensions, resolutions, and layer limits
- Choosing a color profile
- Time-lapse and canvas properties

Working from presets

The first thing you will notice once you open the **New canvas** menu is a list of canvas presets. They are included in Procreate by default and can be quite convenient when used properly. In this section, we will look at each preset, what they're most suited for, and how to edit/delete them. Note that the exact presets you have available might differ based on your device.

Preset – Screen_Size

The very first option available is **Screen_Size**. Depending on the model of your iPad, it will create a canvas that has the same size and resolution as your screen. This preset is *not editable*.

The specifics of this preset are as follows (**3rd generation 12.9-inch iPad Pro**):

- Dimensions: The same as the screen (2732 x 2048 px)
- **Dots per Inch (DPI)**: 132
- Color profile: Display P3
- Layers available: 91
- Video settings: 1080p (H.264):

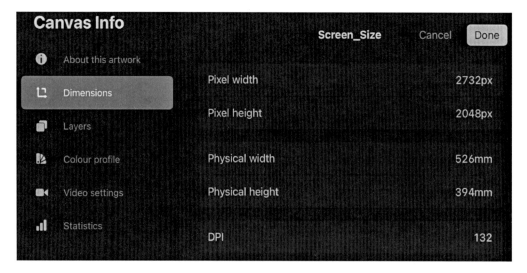

Figure 2.1: The Screen_Size preset

This preset is great if you're designing an image that will only be viewed on screens. For example, images such as website headers and social media layouts are good places to use the Screen_Size canvas.

> **Important Note**
>
> You can edit a preset by swiping left on it and tapping on **Edit**. This is also a handy way to check the properties of a canvas before using it since there are some things you can't edit once a canvas has been created (such as the color profile and time-lapse settings).
>
> Please note that **Screen_Size** is the only preset that cannot be edited.
>
> Once you edit a preset, it will have the settings you assign it every time it's used, until you edit it again.

Preset – Square

Square is the first item on the list. As per its name, it creates a square canvas with the following specifics:

- Dimensions: 2048 x 2048 px
- DPI: 132
- Color profile: sRGB IEC6 1966-2.1
- Layers available: 124
- Video settings: 1080p (H.264):

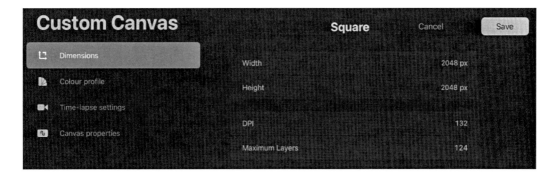

Figure 2.2: The Square preset

Square is a great preset to use when you want to make images for Instagram slides, social media marketing, or generally anywhere on the internet.

Preset – 4K

Next on the list is **4K**, which is a canvas for a high-resolution film:

- Dimensions: 4096 x 1714 px
- DPI: 132
- Color profile: sRGB IEC6 1966-2.1
- Layers available: 72

- Video settings: 1080p (H.264):

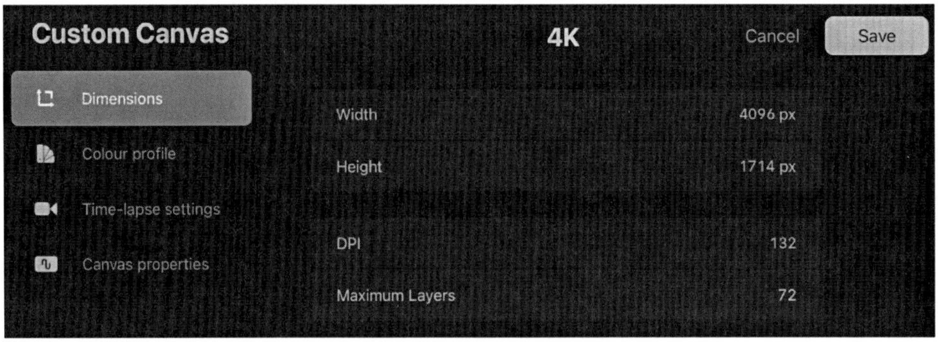

Figure 2.3: The 4K preset

This is an especially useful preset for making an animation film, specifically when you are planning to zoom into a single frame. The large dimensions of the **4K** preset allow you to work both in a wide angle setting and close up (or even for extreme close-ups), without the loss of quality.

Preset – A4

A4 is a universally useful format. On Procreate, it comes with the following settings:

- Dimensions: 210 x 297 mm
- DPI: 300
- Color profile: sRGB IEC6 1966-2.1
- Layers available: 57
- Video settings: 1080p (H.264):

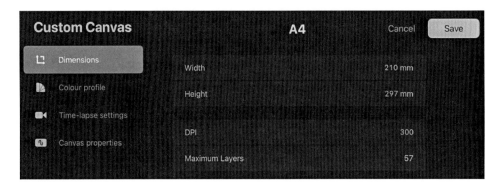

Figure 2.4: The A4 preset

This preset is useful for making print-ready documents, brochures, flyers, and more. Combined with Procreate's text editing tools, it also offers you a convenient way to design and format your own documents within the app. The DPI value of 300 means your file will be ready for print right off the bat.

Preset – 4 x 6 Photo

4 x 6 Photo is another preset that is optimized for printing, with the following settings:

- Dimensions: 6" x 4"
- DPI: 300
- Color profile: sRGB IEC6 1966-2.1
- Layers available: 244
- Video settings: 1080p (H.264):

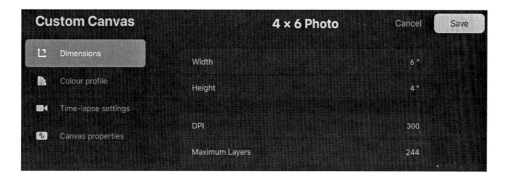

Figure 2.5: The 4 x 6 Photo preset

This preset's 3:2 aspect ratio is made to mimic traditional film photographs. It's great for making small-sized prints.

Preset – Paper

Paper is commonly called US Letter. On Procreate, it comes with the following settings:

- Dimensions: 11" x 8.5"
- DPI: 300
- Color profile: sRGB IEC6 1966-2.1
- Layers available: 59

Getting Started – Setting Up a Canvas

- Video settings: 1080p (H.264):

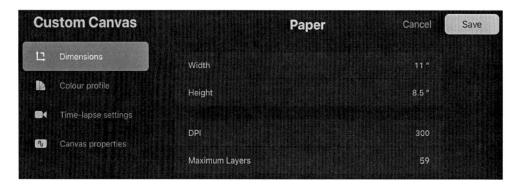

Figure 2.6: The Paper preset

This preset is optimized for printing in standard North and South American paper sizes.

Preset – Comic

As the name suggests, the **Comic** preset is designed for making graphic novels. The preset settings are as follows:

- Dimensions: 6" x 9.5"
- DPI: 400
- Color profile: Generic CMYK profile
- Layers available: 54
- Video settings: 1080p (H.264):

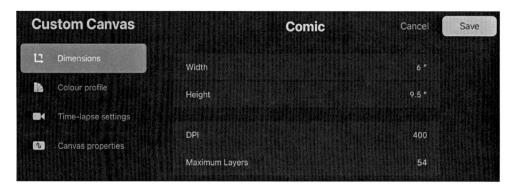

Figure 2.7: The Comic preset

You will notice that this is the only preset that uses a CMYK (Cyan, Magenta, Yellow, and Key) profile. Color profiles and their uses will be described in more detail later. For now, it's enough to know that CMYK means the canvas is optimized for color accuracy during printing.

Creating a custom canvas

Now that you are familiar with the available presets, you are ready to learn how to create a canvas from scratch:

1. Tap the + button in the upper-right corner of the gallery.
2. Once the **New canvas** menu opens up, tap the box with a + icon to enter the **Custom Canvas** screen. It looks like this:

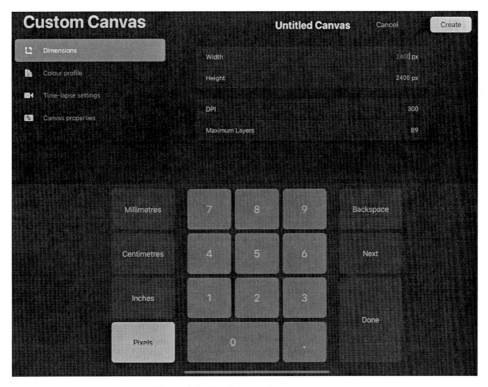

Figure 2.8: The Custom Canvas screen

3. Tap on the canvas name to edit it.

This will serve as the preset title (as explained next), not the name of the individual file! By default, the canvas created will still be named `Untitled Artwork`. What you are naming here is your own fresh preset, in case you want to open a similar file again later:

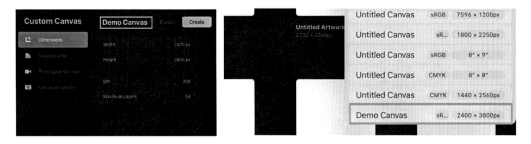

Figure 2.9: Every new canvas is saved as a preset

> **Important Note**
>
> Every time you create a new canvas, it automatically gets saved in the list of presets with the name `Untitled Canvas`. Even if you create the same canvas twice, it will be saved as two identical presets.
>
> So, it is a good practice to notice and rename custom canvases that you frequently use, and open them directly from the presets. Otherwise, your list can become repetitive and confusing in no time.

With that, you're all set to create your own custom canvas.

As an artist, I have my own favorite canvases that I have customized for my work. Here is one I use most frequently:

Custom preset – Usual Landscape

Usual Landscape is a generally versatile preset that I use to make most of my landscape orientation artworks. The preset settings are listed as follows:

- Dimensions: 7.5" x 6"
- DPI: 300
- Color profile: Display P3
- Layers available: 128
- Video settings: 1080p (H.264):

Figure 2.10: The Usual Landscape preset

Dimensions, resolutions, and layer limits

To set up a custom canvas, the first items of information you need to enter are the dimensions and resolution (DPI). Procreate sets a limit of maximum layers depending on those values. Let's look at each of those terms and what they mean.

Dimensions

Dimensions refers to the physical size of your canvas. It can be entered in inches ("), centimeters (cm), millimeters (mm), or pixels (px). On Procreate, it's written in the width x height format.

As you can see in the following screenshot, the first value you enter will be for the width (horizontal) of the canvas, and the second one will be for the height (vertical):

Figure 2.11: Canvas Dimensions

Resolution

The term "resolution" refers to how densely the pixels are arranged on a canvas. It is measured in DPI, as shown in the following screenshot:

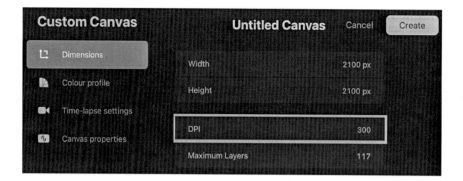

Figure 2.12: The canvas resolution in DPI

This tells us how many digital pixels or ink dots (for printing) fit into one physical inch of the canvas. Naturally, the value of the pixel dimensions of the canvas will depend on the DPI you choose.

As a rule of thumb, it's safe to use 300 DPI or higher when working for print. Usually, screens work on 72 or 96 **PPI** (**Pixels per Inch**, as used in the digital context), so higher resolution images get compressed to match that value.

Layer limits in Procreate

For every canvas that you create, Procreate sets a limit on the maximum number of layers you can use. The limit depends on a set of factors, including the dimensions and resolution of your canvas along with the RAM of your device. Adjust the canvas properties to see how it changes the layer limit:

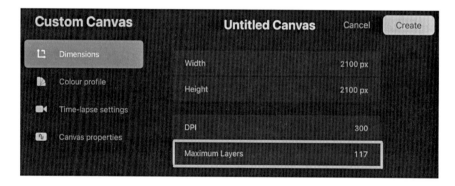

Figure 2.13: The layer limit

For a smooth illustrating experience, adjust your canvas to have at least 100 layers available to you.

Next, we will look at color profiles and how to use them.

Choosing a color profile

The color profile of a canvas dictates how it manages color. Select the **Color profile** tab in the **Custom Canvas** screen, as shown in the following screenshot:

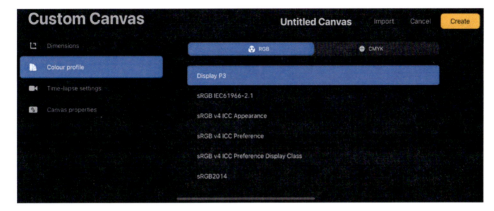

Figure 2.14: Canvas Color profile

Procreate allows you to work with RGB or CMYK. They are the most widely used profiles and have their separate uses. Let's look at them in more detail.

RGB

RGB stands for **Red**, **Green**, and **Blue**; the three colors of light that most screens display. These colors are emitted in varying combinations to make different colors in a way that the maximum values of all three together produce white light:

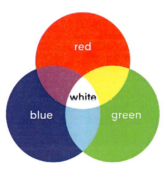

Figure 2.15: RGB combines light

RBG color profiles allow you to use a large range of colors, including brighter, highly saturated versions. They are best used when you are designing for screens, such as publishing on the internet or for a film.

CMYK

CMYK stands for **Cyan**, **Magenta**, **Yellow**, and **Key** (**Black**). These are the four colors of ink that most printers combine to print different colors. In theory, cyan, magenta, and yellow combined in the same quantities produce black ink, as shown in the following diagram. In reality, black ink is used separately while printing and is referred to as key:

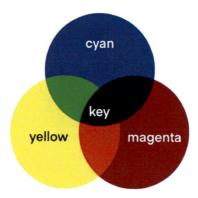

Figure 2.16: CMYK combines ink

The range of colors you can use here is narrower, limited to what can realistically be printed. That's why it is always a good idea to use CMYK profiles when your work is intended for print. Trying to print an image with an RGB profile can result in unpredictable color inaccuracies.

Here is a comparison of the colors available for each context:

Figure 2.17 (a): The color range in RGB; (b): The color range in CMYK

You will notice that highly saturated colors toward the right edge are eliminated from the CMYK color square since they are impossible to print.

> **Important Note**
>
> Once you have created a canvas, you cannot switch between the RGB and CMYK profiles. However, you can choose from different versions of the same profile available.
>
> To view the same image under another color profile, create a separate canvas that has the color profile you want, and import the image into it.

It's a good practice to open your RGB artworks in a CMYK canvas to get a quick idea of how they will look when printed. This is so that you can tweak the colors for accuracy if necessary. For example, take a look at the following:

Figure 2.18 (a): The image viewed in RGB; (b): Identical image viewed in CMYK

After making some edits, the following is closer to the intended colors:

Figure 2.19: The CMYK image adjusted for color accuracy

Importing your own color profile

There are subtle differences between the options available under both RGB and CMYK. Not all RGB profiles are identical, and neither are all CMYK profiles.

If you are looking for a specific profile that isn't available on Procreate by default, you can import your own using the **Import** button in the upper-right corner of the **Color profile** tab:

Figure 2.20: Importing a color profile

The slight differences between all the different versions of color profiles are best explored at your own pace. Now, we will move on to our last two settings, that is, **Time-lapse settings** and **Canvas properties**.

Time-lapse and canvas properties

The final settings we will look at when creating our custom canvas are related to the time-lapse video and the canvas background.

Time-lapse video

One of the most interesting features of Procreate is that a full-length time-lapse video is recorded for every canvas by default. The **Time-lapse settings** tab allows you to specify the quality in which you want your time-lapse video to be recorded. These are the resolution choices you have:

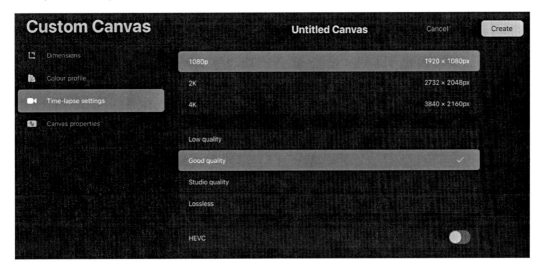

Figure 2.21: The time-lapse properties

HEVC is a relatively newer format suitable for transparent videos. If it's toggled on, your file size will increase.

> **Important Note**
>
> Once a canvas has been created, you can't change the time-lapse quality. However, you can still edit the preset, which will apply to any later canvases you create with it.
>
> Changing the color profile midway while working on a canvas can also affect time-lapse quality.

Canvas properties

The **Canvas properties** tab lets you decide the kind of background you want your canvas to have. This is how the editor looks:

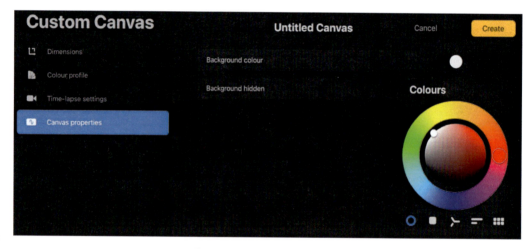

Figure 2.22: Canvas properties

The **Background color** option lets you specify the color of the background layer. Additionally, you can toggle **Background hidden** on if you'd like to create a canvas with a transparent background. You don't have to worry too much about these two settings because they are not permanent and can easily be changed at any point.

Once you are happy with your preferences, tap on **Create** to instantly make and load a new canvas (as well as a preset). Inversely, tap on **Cancel** if you want to discard your changes and return to the **New canvas** menu.

Summary

By the time you reach this point, you should have the skills necessary to create a new canvas from presets or from scratch. You will have understood the uses and advantages of each preset. You should also be familiar with the terms **Dimensions**, **Resolution**, **Layer Limit**, **Color Profile**, and **Time-lapse**.

Moving forward, we'll cover the last bit of information that will bring you up to speed with the interface of Procreate. In the following chapter, you will learn how to navigate the tools available when a canvas is opened on the app.

3
Understanding Your Workspace

Now that you have learned how to create a canvas, we are ready to look at how to navigate the Procreate workspace. Tap on a canvas thumbnail to load the canvas. Once the canvas is open, you will immediately notice that the interface looks much *emptier* than other painting software that you usually find. This is because a lot of tools are packaged away into the toolbars surrounding the drawing area, giving you a clean, uncluttered space to work in.

In this chapter, you will learn how to access the most common tools and features that you will be using while drawing. All the tools I discuss here will be explained at length individually in later chapters. If you'd like to explore the interface on your own, this chapter will offer you the groundwork to start from.

We're going to cover the following broad topics here:

- Painting tools (top right)
- The sidebar (left)
- Advanced features (top left)

The top-right panel: painting tools

The top right-hand side of the canvas interface has a row of tools, as shown in the following figure, which you will be using for painting.

Figure 3.1: Painting tools

This section has the **Paint**, **Smudge**, and **Erase** tools, along with **Layers** and **Colour**. Let's look at them one by one.

Paint

The brush-shaped icon, also called **Paint**, is the tool you will be using to draw. Unlike most illustration software, Procreate doesn't crowd your screen space with separate buttons for each brush. Tapping on the **Paint** tool again while it's already selected will open up **Brush Library**, as shown in the following figure. From here, you can go on to choose the brush you want.

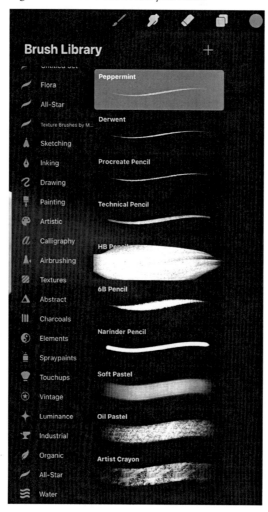

Figure 3.2: The Brush Library pop-over

We will discuss the Brush Library and Brush Studio in detail in *Chapter 8, Painting Tools and the Brush Library – Using and Organizing Brushes*.

Tap anywhere outside the pop-over or the icon itself to close the library.

Smudge

To the right of the **Paint** tool, you will spot an icon that looks like a finger. This is the **Smudge** tool. It emulates the action of smudging an artwork with your fingertips by distorting the pixels on a layer in the direction that it is applied in. Similar to **Paint**, if you tap on it twice, a pop-over similar to the **Brush Library** appears, as shown:

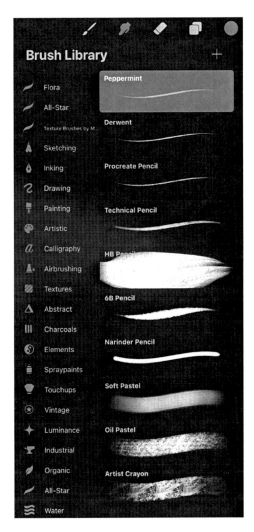

Figure 3.3: The Smudge Brush Library pop-over

Your **Smudge** tool will essentially behave like a *smudging brush*, according to the brush selected.

Eraser

The **Erase** tool works similarly to **Paint** and **Smudge**. Tapping the eraser icon to the right of the **Smudge** tool will activate the eraser, and tapping it again will bring up the **Brush Library** pop-over for it. From here, you can pick an eraser that matches your brush or a completely different type.

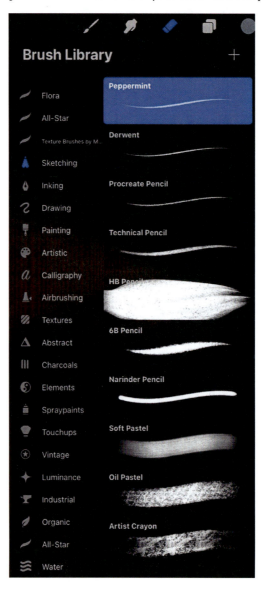

Figure 3.4: The Eraser Brush Library pop-over

Your **Erase** tool will essentially behave like an *erasing brush*, according to the brush selected.

Layers

To the right of the **Erase** tool is the **Layers** icon. It looks like two overlapping boxes. Tapping this will open up your layers. We will learn more about layers and how to work with them in *Chapter 7, Organizing Your Layers*.

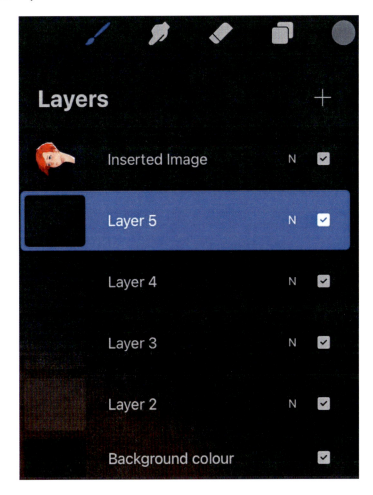

Figure 3.5: The Layers pop-over

The Colour button

The last icon on the painting tools list is the **Colour** button in the top right-hand corner of your drawing screen. Tapping on it will invoke the Colour editor. There are various handy interfaces that Procreate offers while choosing Colours. Jump to *Chapter 10, Using Colour Tools,* to learn about all the colour adjustment tools.

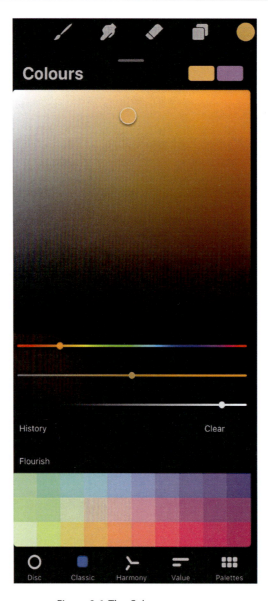

Figure 3.6: The Colours pop-over

The **Colour** button also functions as the bucket fill tool. Drag and drop the **Colour** button to any point on the canvas to flood-fill it with the selected colour.

Figure 3.7: Bucket fill

Next, we will look at the features available on the sidebar to the left.

The left panel: the sidebar

The sidebar consists of the panel of tools available along the left edge of your screen. It has two sliders, one square-shaped icon, and two curved arrow icons, as shown here:

Figure 3.8: The sidebar

Let's see what these controls are used for.

Brush size slider

The first slider is used to change the size of the brush/eraser/smudge tool that you are using. You can tap anywhere on the slider to jump to a brush size or manually slide it up and down.

Figure 3.9: Size slider

Procreate also allows you to save specific brush sizes that you frequently use. This feature is called **Brush Size Memory**, and it's discussed in *Chapter 8, Painting Tools and the Brush Library – Using and Organizing Brushes*.

Brush opacity slider

The second slider works in the same way but for brush opacity, which is how solid or transparent each stroke will be.

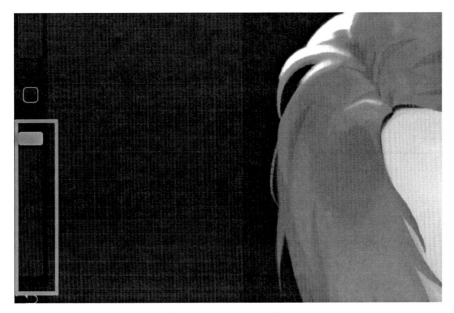

Figure 3.10: Opacity slider

> **Important note**
> It's possible to make even finer adjustments using sliders. Place your finger on the slider button, swipe to the side, and move your finger up and down without lifting it. You will notice that the slider is now moving slower than usual. This gesture helps you fine-tune the brush size or opacity.

The Modify button

The square-shaped icon in between the size and opacity sliders is known as the **Modify** button. It invokes the Eyedropper tool, which lets you select a colour directly from your canvas.

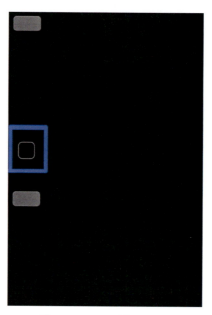

Figure 3.11: Modify button

Drag the Eyedropper over the colour you want and release it to select it. Alternatively, hold the **Modify** button and tap anywhere on your artwork to pick the colour from there, as shown:

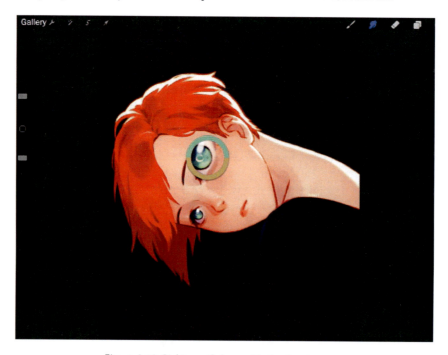

Figure 3.12: Picking a Colour with the Eyedropper

You can edit the **Modify** button to perform different actions depending on your preference. This will be covered in more detail in the *Actions* section of this chapter.

Undo and Redo

Right below the opacity slider are the buttons for Undo and Redo, as shown here:

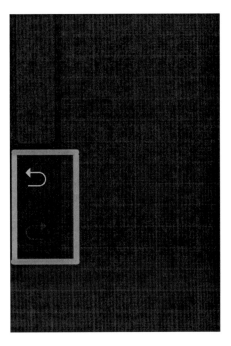

Figure 3.13: Undo and Redo buttons

If you're experienced with using other painting software, you will be aware of the functions of these buttons. The **Undo** button lets you reverse the last action you did, while the **Redo** button re-performs the action that you just undid. It's possible to undo up to 250 actions on Procreate.

Procreate offers shortcuts to Undo and Redo, without using these buttons. This is done through gestures. More information about gestures can be found in *Chapter 6, Using Gestures and Shortcuts*.

With the sidebar figured out, we will be moving on to the last set of tools in the Advanced Features menu.

The top-left panel: Advanced Features

In the top-left corner, you will find a row of buttons, referred to as Advanced Features. This is a versatile set of features that you will be using very often while drawing.

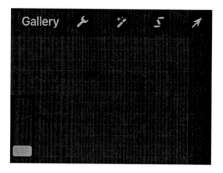

Figure 3.14: Advanced Features menu

Let's elaborate on each of these.

Gallery

On the extreme left, you will see an option called **Gallery**. Tapping this will close your canvas and take you back to the Procreate Gallery. The app auto-saves your progress, so you won't have to worry about manually saving your work.

Actions

The wrench-shaped icon to the right of **Gallery** is called the **Actions** menu. This menu has most of the features you would need with regard to the canvas as a whole.

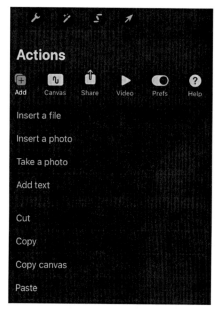

Figure 3.15: Actions menu

Broadly, these are the features available under **Actions**:

- **Add**: Use this menu to insert an external image into your artwork. It also has a clipboard, which can be used for cut, copy, and paste actions.

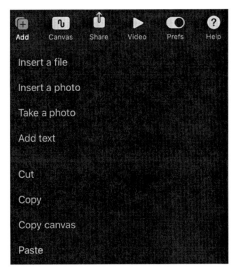

Figure 3.16: Add menu

- **Canvas**: Alter the properties of the whole canvas using this menu, including dimensions and orientation, as well as toggle-assisted drawing and animation tools. You can also view detailed technical information about your canvas from this menu.

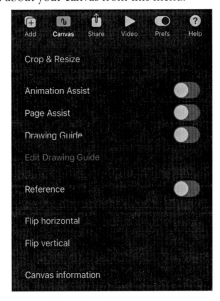

Figure 3.17: Canvas menu

- **Share**: Use the **Share Image** menu to select the preferred format to export your canvas as. The **Share Layers** menu is used when exporting the separate layers as a single PDF, PNG files, or videos and GIFs for animation.

Figure 3.18: Share menu

- **Video**: This menu lets you watch and export the process of your artwork as a time-lapse video. You could either export the full length of your process or a shortened 30-second version. You can also toggle off **Time-lapse Recording** if you don't want it to be recorded.

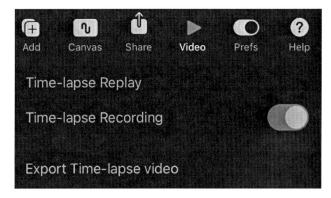

Figure 3.19: Video menu

- **Preferences (Prefs)**: Fine-tune Procreate to fit your needs. This menu will help you customize your workspace, gestures, and interface according to what works best for you. This menu is explained in more detail in *Chapter 6, Using Gestures and Shortcuts*.

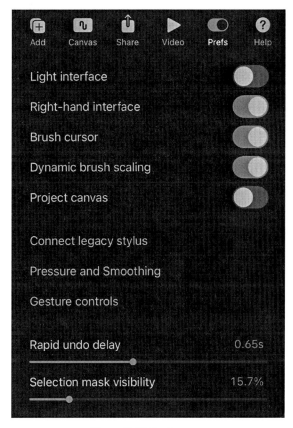

Figure 3.20: Prefs menu

- **Help**: This menu lets you access any assistance you might need with respect to using the application, such as **Procreate Handbook** and leaving a review.

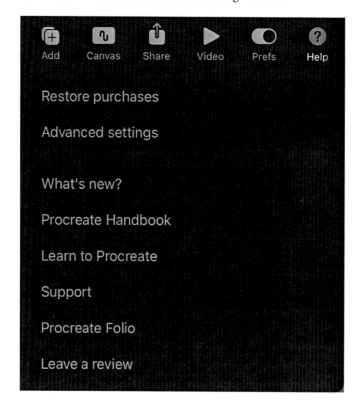

Figure 3.21: Help menu

Refer to *Chapter 4, Using the Actions Menu*, for a detailed overview of this menu.

Adjustments

Right next to the **Actions** menu is a magic wand shaped icon. Tapping on this icon will bring up the **Adjustments** menu. This is a list of image effects and colour adjustments that can be applied to the selected layer.

To learn about these effects in detail, refer to *Chapter 11, Adjustments – Applying Image Effects*.

The top-left panel: Advanced Features 51

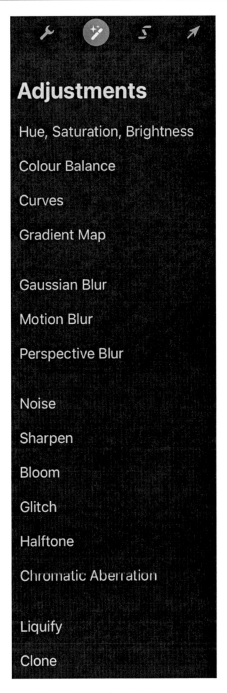

Figure 3.22: Adjustments menu

Selections

The S-shaped icon next to **Adjustments** invokes the Selection tool, which allows you to select sections of the layer to work upon. This tool will be covered in detail in *Chapter 5, Selecting and Transforming*.

Figure 3.23: Selection tool

Transform

The last tool on the **Advanced Features** tab is the arrow-shaped icon called **Transform**. This tool is used to move, resize, warp, or otherwise edit the selected area. We'll look at the Transform tool in *Chapter 5, Selecting and Transforming*.

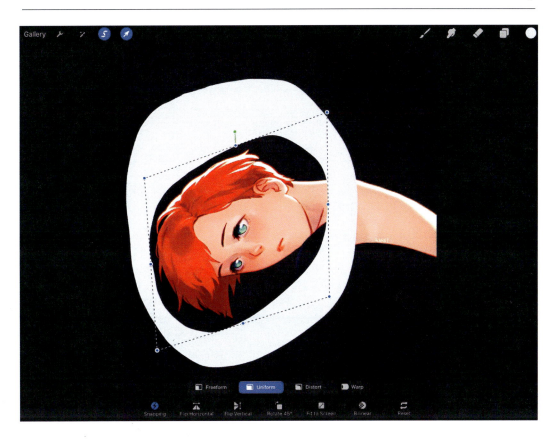

Figure 3.24: Transform tool

Summary

This chapter has been a broad overview of the Procreate interface. You have learned about the range of features available on your workspace, what their functions are, and where to locate them on your screen on the three panels. At this point, you can jump right into drawing.

This chapter should enable you to explore Procreate's tools further. Additionally, there are several sub-options to each feature that let you streamline your process, which we will describe as we get into the later chapters.

4
Using the Actions Menu

A lot of the most commonly used tools in Procreate are available on the **Actions** menu. We briefly touched upon it in the previous chapter while discussing Advanced Features. Tapping on the wrench-shaped tool in the top-left corner of your workspace will bring up the **Actions** menu.

Actions is a widely used menu from where you can make changes that will affect a canvas as a whole. From here, we will elaborate on these functions further.

We're going to cover the following broad topics in this chapter:

- The **Add** menu
- The **Canvas** menu
- The **Share** menu
- The **Video** menu
- The **Prefs** menu
- The **Help** menu

The Add menu

This is the first submenu under **Actions**. **Add** allows you to import any kind of image file or text into your canvas. Additionally, clipboard tools such as **Cut**, **Copy**, and **Paste** are also available here. The **Add** menu looks like this:

Figure 4.1: The Add menu

This menu has several options, which we will look at in the following subsections.

Insert a file

This option allows you to import an image from **Files**. When you tap on it, the **Files** app on your iPad will open up, as shown in *Figure 4.2*. From here, you can locate the specific image you want to insert and select it. The imported file will be added to your Procreate canvas as a new layer on top of your currently selected layer:

Figure 4.2: Insert a file

If you want to import a file but don't want it to appear on your time-lapse video, you can swipe left on **Insert a file** to reveal a button that says **Insert a private file**. If you tap this button, any image file you insert will not show up on the time-lapse video.

Insert a photo

Similar to the previous option, **Insert a photo** lets you import an image from the **Photos** app. Tapping on this option will open up the image gallery on your iPad, as shown in the following screenshot, from where you can choose which photo to insert. The selected image will be added as a new layer on top of the currently selected layer:

Using the Actions Menu

Figure 4.3: Insert a photo

Similar to the last option, swipe left on **Insert a photo** and tap on **Insert a private photo**, which won't show up on your time-lapse.

Take a photo

This option allows you to take a photo using your camera and insert it directly into your canvas. Tapping on **Take a photo** will automatically open your iPad's camera, from where you can snap a photograph.

Here, too, you can swipe left on **Take a photo** and tap on **Take a private photo** to make sure that the photo doesn't appear on your time-lapse.

Add text

Procreate offers you a convenient way to add and edit text in your artwork. When you tap on **Add text**, it creates a textbox on a new text editing layer, as shown here:

Figure 4.4: Add text

To edit text in Procreate, follow these steps:

1. Tap on the textbox to edit the text.
2. Double-tap anywhere on the textbox to invoke the text selection and formatting tools, as shown here:

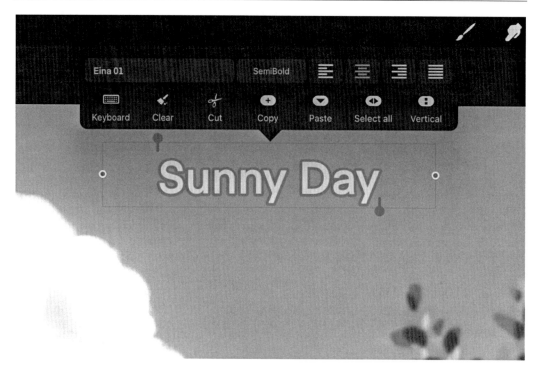

Figure 4.5: Text selection

3. Tap on any option on the top row to bring up the advanced text editor, as shown in *Figure 4.6*.
4. You can use the advanced text editor to select a font and change the style, design, and attributes of your text, as shown here:

The Add menu 61

Figure 4.6: The advanced text editor

5. Use the **Import Font** option, as shown in the previous screenshot, to add an external font to Procreate from **Files**.

> **Important Note**
>
> You can scale, resize, and rotate a textbox using the Transform tool without needing to rasterize it. The font size will change automatically to accommodate resizing. However, in case of a non uniform transformation (like **Distort** and **Warp**), a text layer is automatically rasterised.
>
> To learn more about the Transform tool, refer to *Chapter 5, Selecting and Transforming*.

Cut, Copy, Copy Canvas, and Paste

Next, we will look at the cluster of options commonly called clipboard tools, which are shown here:

Figure 4.7: Clipboard tools

These functions are common to most software. Let's briefly explain them:

- **Cut**: Using **Cut** clears the current layer or selected area, which can be reapplied on another layer using **Paste**.

- **Copy**: Applying **Copy** to a layer or a selected area will create a duplicate of it wherever **Paste** is applied.

- **Copy canvas**: This function works similarly to **Copy**, but instead of just the selected area or layer, it copies the contents of the entire canvas as a flattened image while keeping your layers intact. This feature is useful when you want to duplicate the complete artwork onto a layer without merging the layers or having to export and reinsert it.

- **Paste**: Use the **Paste** option to insert the content that you have cut or copied as a new layer on top of the current layer.

There are gesture-based shortcuts you can use to invoke the clipboard tools menu. We will look at all such functions in *Chapter 6, Using Gestures and Shortcuts*.

With the **Add** menu, you can try importing files from different locations to get the hang of it. Additionally, you can use the clipboard tools to perform **Cut**, **Copy**, and **Paste** actions, as well as a Procreate-specific **Copy Canvas** action.

With that, let's move on to the next set of tools in the **Actions** section – **Canvas**.

The Canvas menu

The **Canvas** menu is right next to the **Add** menu. The functions available in this menu are used to make sweeping changes to a whole canvas. This means that choices made in the **Canvas** menu affect the canvas as a whole and alter its properties. It looks like this:

Figure 4.8: The Canvas menu

The functions of this menu will become clear once we look at it in detail. There are several sub-options available. We will look at them in the following sections.

Crop and Resize

This is where you can edit the dimensions, aspect ratio, and resolution of the canvas. Tapping on **Crop and Resize** will bring you to this screen:

Figure 4.9: Crop and Resize

You will see four options in the top-right corner, namely **Cancel**, **Settings**, **Reset**, and **Done**. The **Settings** button will help you tweak the attributes of your canvas, such as size and resolution. A grid will appear over the canvas, as well as a **Settings** popover with editable fields. You can stretch the corners or edges of the grid to make your new canvas, like this:

Figure 4.10: Crop settings

In the popover, you can see and edit the values to alter canvas dimensions and **Dots Per Inch** (**DPI**), which is shown here:

Using the Actions Menu

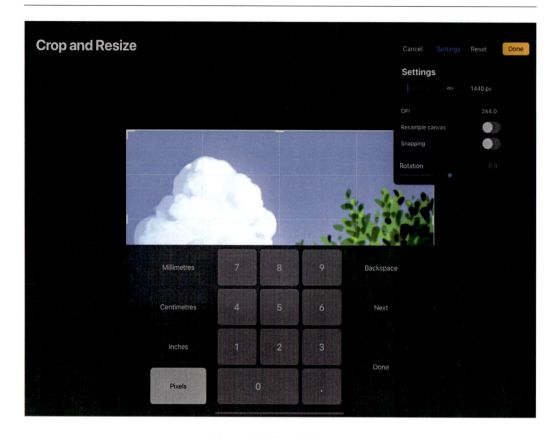

Figure 4.11: The Add menu

Tapping on the chainlink symbol will enable **Aspect Lock**. That means editing the height will proportionately change the width. In short, this allows you to *uniformly scale the canvas boundaries without scaling its contents.*

You can also edit the **DPI** value of your canvas. You should note that changing the DPI will proportionately alter the dimensions to fit the same number of pixels into your canvas. Note how the height and width values change depending on the DPI in these images:

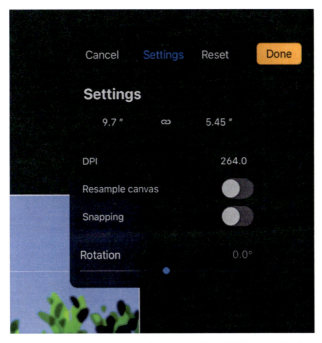

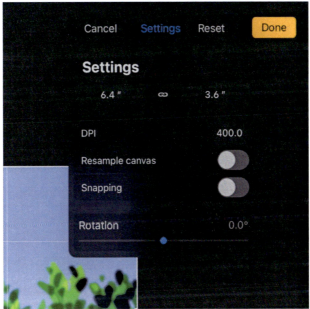

Figure 4.12: Dimensions with 264 DPI versus 400 DPI

The most versatile function available here is **Resample canvas**. Simply put, it helps you to scale an entire image up and down. Here are the ways to use it:

- **Dragging and scaling the grid overlay**: Doing this allows you to keep the dimensions of the canvas the same while choosing which part you want to keep inside the grid. For example, let's use a **9.7"** x **5.45"** canvas. Now, let's resample it, as shown here:

Figure 4.13: Resample canvas

Once we've done so, the final canvas will still be **9.7"** x **5.45"** but only have the portion visible in the grid. This will be the result:

Figure 4.14: The result of resampling

In short, this allows you to *uniformly scale the contents without resizing the canvas boundaries*.

- **Entering values**: If you would prefer to change the physical size of your canvas, tap on the numbers to edit them, as shown here:

Figure 4.15: Resampling dimensions

This will change the dimensions of your artwork to fit into the overlay grid, which now has the size 6" x 3.38". This essentially means scaling the entire canvas up or down, which can cause a loss of pixel information.

In short, this allows you to *uniformly scale both the canvas and its contents together.*

> **Important Note**
>
> Toggling **Resample** automatically enables **Aspect Lock**. If you would like the new canvas to have a different aspect ratio, edit the dimensions first and then hit **Resample**.

The next option under **Settings** is **Snapping**. Enabling this option will make the overlay grid snap to the edges, corners, or center of the present canvas, as shown in *Figure 4.16*:

The Canvas menu   71

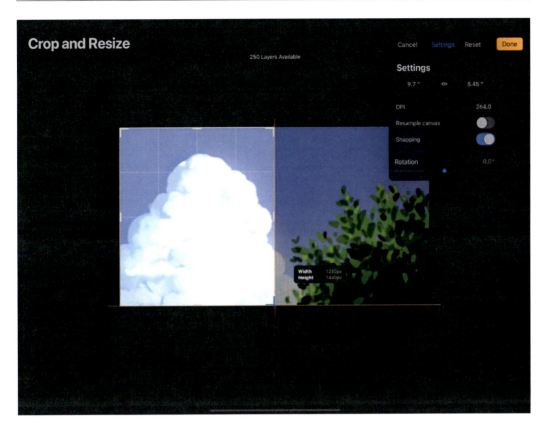

Figure 4.16: Snapping

This is a handy tool to extend your canvas to make a uniform border or trim it evenly from all sides. You can also use it to extend the canvas toward one side or diagonally.

The last setting option is called **Rotation**. Move the slider to rotate the canvas up to 45° on each side, with respect to the grid, as shown here:

Using the Actions Menu

Figure 4.17: Rotation

Once you are happy with the resizing, tap on **Done** to finalize your adjustments. If you'd like to start over, tap on **Reset** to revert the canvas to the original settings. To discard your resizing, tap on **Cancel**.

Animation Assist

The next option in the menu is called **Animation Assist**. As the name suggests, it helps you to make animations on Procreate. When **Animation Assist** is toggled on, it transforms the interface into one suited for animation, as shown in the following screenshot. Refer to *Chapter 12, Using Assisted Drawing Tools*, for a detailed rundown of this feature:

The Canvas menu 73

Figure 4.18: Animation Assist

Page Assist

This is the next option, called **Page Assist**, which turns your canvas into a multi-page structure. With this toggled on, you can create pages like that of a sketchbook or comic book, as shown in the image below:

Fig. 4.19: Page Assist

For more information about this feature, refer to *Chapter 14, Sketchbooking with Page Assist*.

Drawing Guide

Drawing Guide is used when you want to draw precisely within constraints such as perspective, symmetry, or grids. When toggled on, you can tap on the option called **Edit Drawing Guide** right below it to customize the kind of drawing tools you need, as shown in the following screenshot. *Chapter 12, Using Assisted Drawing Tools*, explains this tool in further detail:

Figure 4.20: Edit Drawing Guide

The Reference companion

Using the **Reference** feature allows you to view an image separately over your canvas, in a floating window. The **Reference** companion looks like this:

Figure 4.21: The Reference companion

There are several sources you can choose to reference from, namely **Canvas**, **Image**, and **Face**, as explained here:

- **Canvas**: Use your canvas itself as a reference. This saves you the trouble of having to zoom in and out repeatedly, since you can view the whole canvas separately while drawing or look at one part of the drawing while you work on a different part. You can also pick colors from the reference window using the eyedropper tool. The **Reference** window looks like this:

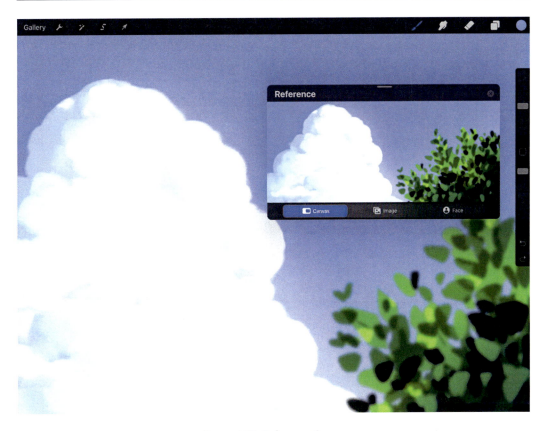

Figure 4.22: Reference Canvas

- **Image**: Import a different image from your gallery to use as a reference without having to use **Split View** or a separate layer for it. Tap on **Import Image** to select a reference picture from **Photos**, as shown here:

Figure 4.23: A reference image

Tap on **Clear** to remove the current reference image. Here too, you can use the eyedropper to pick colors directly from the reference image.

- **Face**: On supported iPad models, you will find another button that says **Face**. This feature lets you use Augmented Reality to *"draw on your face"* using FacePaint. This will turn on your front camera inside your reference window and automatically detect your face. Whatever you draw on the canvas will now appear on your face, similar to a camera filter.

Use the light gray horizontal bar on the top edge of the reference window to move it around. To resize the window, simply place your finger on any of its four corners and drag.

Flip Canvas

The next two options are **Flip Canvas Horizontally** and **Flip Canvas Vertically**, which are used to flip your canvas about these two axes.

> **Important Note**
> Flipping your canvas affects how your exports look. The exported image will have the same orientation as the flipped canvas. However, the time-lapse of the canvas will still retain the original orientation. Hence, the image and the time-lapse may look like flipped versions of each other.

Canvas Info

The last option on the menu is **Canvas Info**. This is where you can access all the specific information about your canvas. This data is sectioned as follows:

- **About this artwork**: Here, you can add personal information such as a profile image, name, and signature that will be embedded into your Procreate file. You will also be able to view the file's date of creation and latest modification, as shown here:

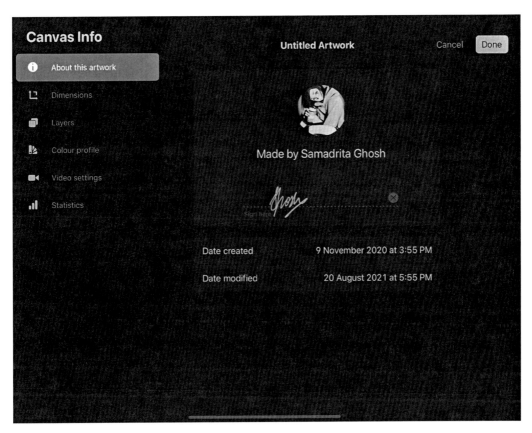

Figure 4.24: About this artwork

- **Dimensions**: This tab lets you check the height/width of a canvas in pixels as well as physical units of measurement, as shown here:

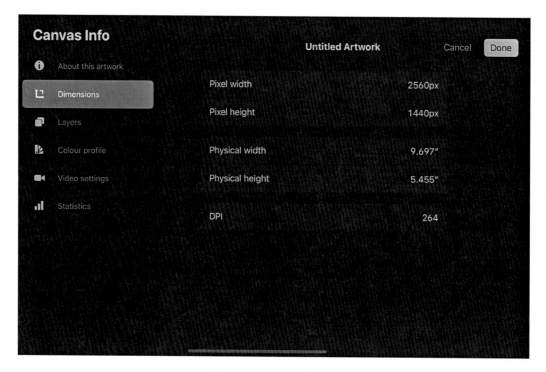

Figure 4.25: Dimensions

The DPI of your canvas can also be checked here. Refer to *Chapter 2, Getting Started – Setting Up a Canvas*, to learn more about dimensions and DPI.

- **Layers**: Check the layer limit of your canvas, how many layers you have already used, the number of layers still available to be added, and the number of assisted layers, clipping layers, layer masks, and layer groups that are currently in use:

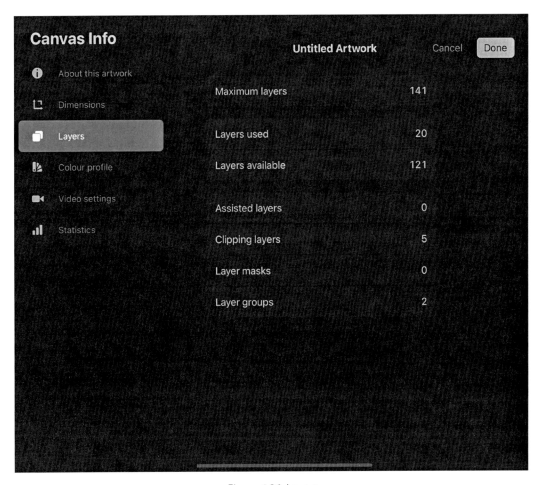

Figure 4.26: Layers

Find detailed information about the different properties of layers in *Chapter 7, Organizing Your Layers*.

- **Colour profile**: This tab lets you check which color profile you chose for the canvas while creating it.

Using the Actions Menu

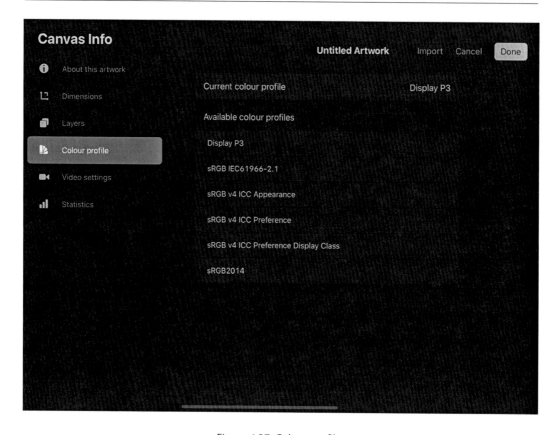

Figure 4.27: Colour profile

Color profiles determine how your canvas treats color when printed or viewed on screens. Refer to *Chapter 2, Getting Started – Setting Up a Canvas*, to learn more about color profiles and their uses.

- **Video settings**: Check the time-lapse video settings from this tab, as shown here:

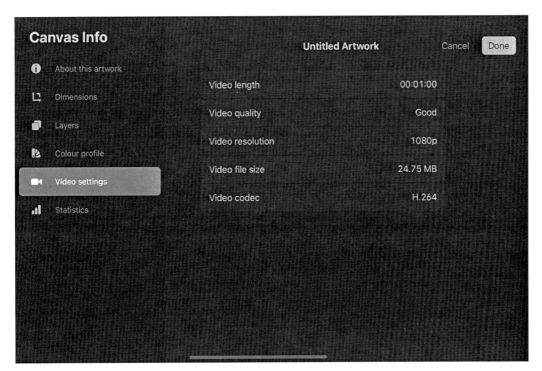

Figure 4.28: Video settings

Video length refers to the length of the time-lapse video recorded from the artwork. **Video quality** and **Video resolution** determine how large and high-definition the time-lapse video will be respectively. **Video file size** is the size of the time-lapse video once it is exported. **Video codec** is the type of compression your video uses.

> **Important Note**
> Video quality and resolution cannot be edited in the middle of drawing, but you can choose your preferred settings while making a new canvas.

- **Statistics**: As the name suggests, this tab has data about your artwork such as **Total strokes made**, which is the number of strokes you have made; **Tracked time**, which is the total span of time the canvas has been open for; and **Total file size**, which is the size of your Procreate file in MB (megabytes):

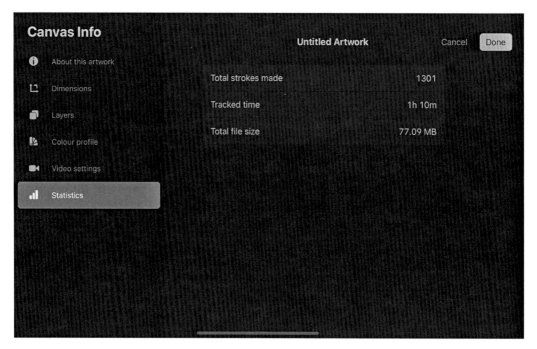

Figure 4.29: Statistics

This has been a discussion of the **Canvas** menu, used to make broad, sweeping changes to your canvas. It's a crucial menu, so it's recommended that you explore these features and get used to them at your own pace.

The next topic we will look at is the **Share** menu.

The Share menu

To the right of **Canvas**, you will find a tab called **Share**. This menu has all the options you will need to export your artwork. It can be seen in the following screenshot:

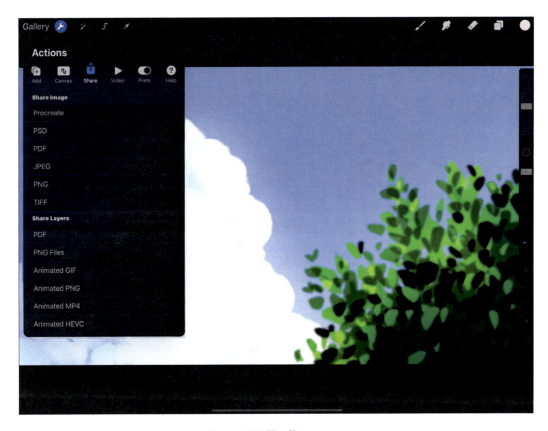

Figure 4.30: The Share menu

There are two broad ways Procreate treats your canvas while exporting. Let's elaborate on each.

Share Image

If you want your export to show how the canvas looks as a whole, in the form of a single image or file, you can do so using the **Share Image** menu. The following options are available for image export:

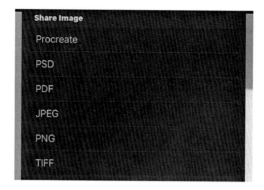

Figure 4.31: The Share Image options

Out of these, Procreate and PSD files will retain your layer information, which will let you work on the exported file using painting software on another device.

Share Layers

Share Layers treats the visible layers of your canvas as separate images while exporting. The following are the options available under it:

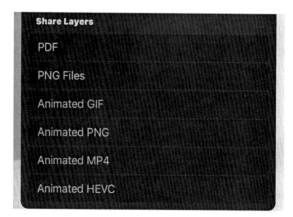

Figure 4.32: The Share Layers menu

Each of these options handles layers differently. Let's look at them one by one:

- **PDF**: This option is not to be confused with the **PDF** option under **Share Image**, which exports the canvas as a whole as a single-page PDF. Conversely, choosing the **PDF** option under **Share Layers** exports every visible layer as a separate page of a multi-page PDF file.

  Once you tap on **PDF**, a screen will appear asking you to choose your preferred file quality. Remember that higher quality means a larger file size.

- **PNG Files**: This option exports all your visible layers as separate transparent PNG files.
- **Animated GIF/Animated PNG/Animated MP4/Animated HEVC**: The last four options are used to export animations from Procreate. These exports types treat each ungrouped layer and layer group as a separate frame of animation and then export the animated result in the chosen format. Learn more about animation in *Chapter 12, Using Assisted Drawing Tools*.

After you have chosen your preferred method of exporting, a popup like this will appear:

Figure 4.33: Export options

At the very top, you will see the details of what you are exporting. This includes the name of the file, its format, and its size. The next row will feature the apps you commonly export to or have used recently. On the row below that will be the list of apps that you can export to. This list can be edited to your requirements by clicking on the button titled **More**, as shown here:

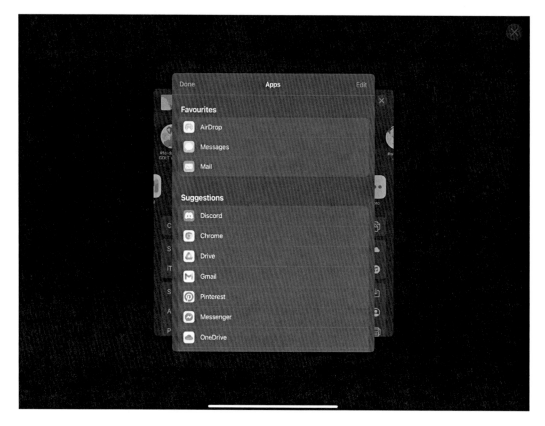

Figure 4.34: More apps

Next, you will see a list of actions you can perform to complete the export. The action I choose is usually **Save Image/Video**, which exports my artwork straight to **Photos**. If you've changed your mind, you can tap on the **X** icon in the top-right corner of the popup to cancel the export. When you do so, a screen will appear, informing you that the export was unsuccessful, as shown here:

Figure 4.35: Export unsuccessful

You now know how to export your artwork in any format, be it a still image, GIF, or video, and send it to a destination folder or app of your choice.

We will now move on to the next tab on the **Actions** menu, which is **Video**.

The Video menu

A great feature of Procreate is that it automatically records a stroke-by-stroke time-lapse video of your artwork. The **Video** menu is where you can view or otherwise manage this video and how it's recorded:

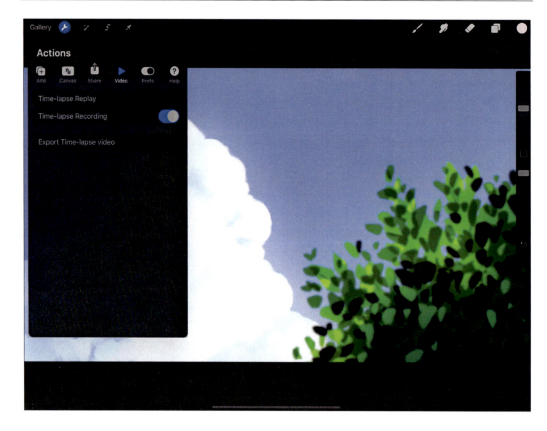

Figure 4.36: The Video menu

In the following sections, we will cover the options available under the **Video** menu.

Time-lapse Replay

As the name suggests, tap on **Time-lapse Replay** to play back the entire time-lapse that has been recorded up to this point. The screen looks like this while the video plays:

Figure 4.37: Time-lapse Replay

The progress bar at the top of the screen shows you how much of the video has been played. You can place your finger anywhere on the screen and move it to the left or right to skim through the video quickly. Dragging your finger to the right will fast-forward the playback, while dragging it to the left will rewind it. Dragging and holding your finger in one place will pause the playback until your finger is lifted again.

At the top right, you can see the total runtime of the time-lapse. Next to it is a button that says **Done**, which will close the time-lapse replay and take you back to the drawing interface.

Time-lapse Recording

Next, you will see an option called **Time-lapse Recording**, which can be toggled on and off. When toggled on, your document will record a time-lapse, and when toggled off, it will stop recording it for all the edits you make after that. **Time-lapse Recording** is toggled on by default when you make a new canvas.

You can disable it anytime, at which point Procreate gives you a **Purge Video?** option, like this:

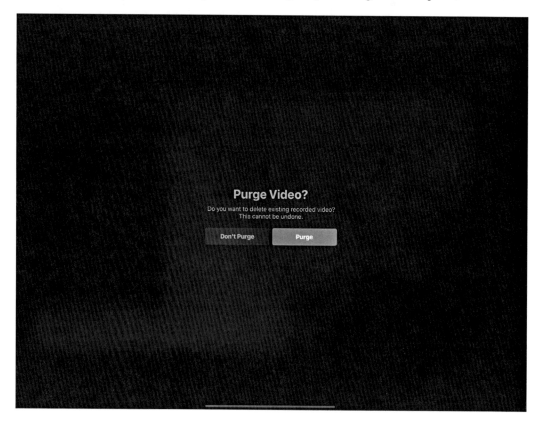

Figure 4.38: Purge Video?

If you tap on **Purge**, the whole time-lapse recorded up to this point will be permanently deleted. Alternatively, you can choose **Don't Purge**, which will retain the preceding time-lapse and then stop recording beyond it.

You can turn this setting back on whenever you like.

Export Time-lapse video

The last option on the **Video** menu allows you to export the time-lapse of your artwork. You can either export the full-length process video or a shorter 30-second version:

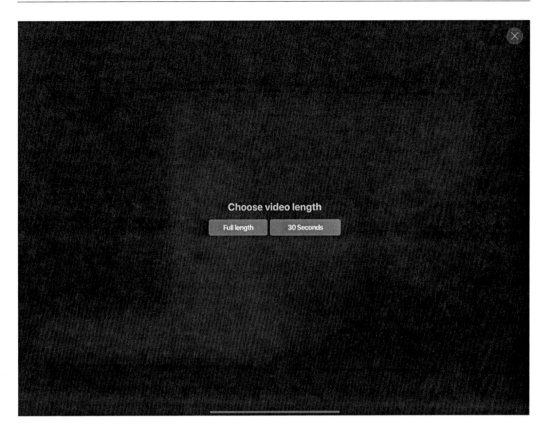

Figure 4.39: Exporting a time-lapse video

Once you select your preference, an export window similar to the one we discussed for **Share** will appear. From here, you can specify the destination of the exported time-lapse video:

Figure 4.40: Saving a time-lapse video

Now that we have learned all about the time-lapse feature, you'll be able to test it out for yourself. Play around with different quality settings and export lengths to figure out what works best for you.

Next, we will look into customizing your experience with the **Prefs** menu.

The Prefs (Preferences) menu

Procreate is a very versatile piece of software that can be tweaked to match a user's requirements. The **Prefs** menu has everything you need to personalize the interface, gestures, and sensitivity of Procreate to suit your needs:

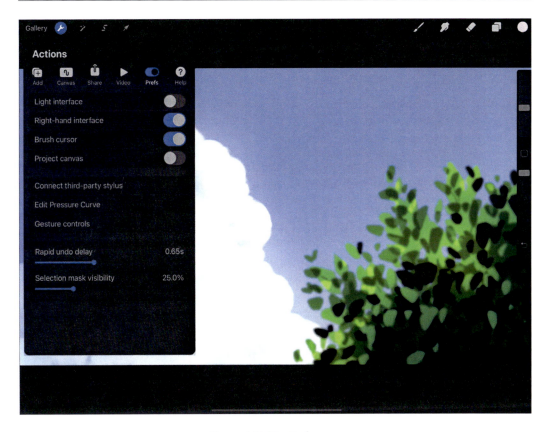

Figure 4.41: The Prefs menu

In the following sections, we will learn about the options in the **Prefs** menu.

Interface toggles

The first four options you will see on this menu are a few ways you can edit the look of your interface. All of these can be toggled on and off. The following are the interface preferences available:

- **Light interface**: Switch between light and dark mode using this button:

Using the Actions Menu

Figure 4.42: Light interface versus dark interface

- **Right-hand interface**: When toggled on, the sidebar will appear on the right edge of the screen, which is more suited to left-handed users. When toggled off, the sidebar appears on the left edge, aiding right-handed users:

Figure 4.43: Right-hand interface versus left-hand interface

- **Brush cursor**: Using this option, you can choose whether or not your brush cursor will be visible while you draw. The brush cursor is an outline of your brush, showing its shape and size when you draw, as shown here:

Figure 4.44: Visible brush cursor

- **Dynamic brush scaling**: By default, this toggle is on. This means that your brush size changes when you zoom in and out of the canvas, ensuring that the brush affects the same number of pixels on the canvas no matter the zoom. This means that the brush appears "larger" when you zoom in and vice versa. Turn off this toggle if you want your brush size to stay constant with respect to the screen, irrespective of zoom.
- **Project canvas**: This enables you to connect a second display using AirPlay or a cable, which shows your entire canvas in fullscreen mode without the interface or zoom.

Connect legacy stylus

Procreate supports a number of third-party stylus types. Through this option, you'll be able to connect any stylus that you see mentioned:

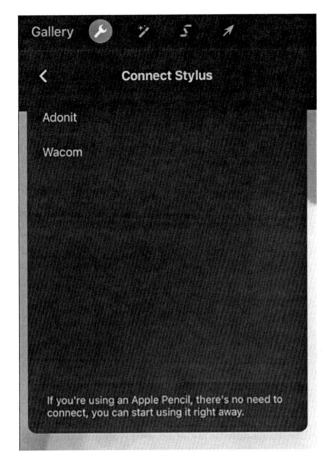

Figure 4.45: Connect legacy stylus

If you're using Apple Pencil, this step is not required, as it connects automatically via Bluetooth.

Pressure and Smoothing

This option affects how brushes respond to inputs from Apple Pencil. Its interface is shown in the following screenshot:

Figure 4.46: Pressure and Smoothing

Let's look at all these options:

- **Stabilisation/Motion Filtering**: These settings smoothen out brushstrokes to minimize shakiness. It's useful as an accessibility tool for artists who experience hand tremors. This is a global setting, which means it applies to brushes as a whole. To learn more about the specifics of stabilization and motion filtering, refer to *Chapter 9, Brush Studio Settings – Editing and Combining Brushes*.

- **App Pressure Sensitivity**: Apple Pencil offers a wide range of pressures to work with. The **App Pressure Sensitivity** graph allows you to adjust how the size and opacity of your brush will change with pressure.

> **Important Note**
> Apple Pencil supports all types of pressure and gesture settings in Procreate. This is because it was specifically created to be used in sync with the iPad. Procreate does support other stylus brands, but often certain features, such as pressure sensitivity, are not supported on some of them. It is highly recommended that you use Apple Pencil to fully enjoy the features of this program.

The horizontal axis is for pressure and the vertical axis is for brush response. The graph is a straight diagonal line by default. You can edit this curve as per your preference by adding up to six control points or handles, as shown here:

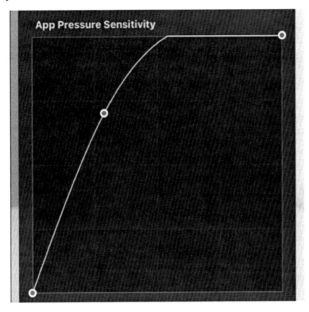

Figure 4.47: An edited pressure curve

This pressure curve applies to all brushes, but you can edit each brush's pressure curve from the Brush Studio, explained in *Chapter 9, Brush Studio Settings – Editing and Combining Brushes*.

The leftmost point on the horizontal axis pertains to zero pressure, and the rightmost point is the highest pressure your stylus can register. The topmost point on the vertical axis pertains to the highest size and opacity response of the brush.

The steeper the curve is, the quicker your brush will respond to light pressure. This is great if you want to consistently draw thick, bold lines without having to apply pressure constantly.

Inversely, the flatter the curve is, the more pressure you will need to apply to make your brush respond. This is applicable if you prefer drawing with thin, light lines.

- **Reset**: Tap on this button to revert back to the default curve.

Gesture controls

Procreate offers a range of gesture inputs that make it easier to perform certain actions in the app. If you are familiar with computer-based painting software, these will sound similar to *keyboard shortcuts*. The **Gesture controls** menu is used to assign your preferred gesture shortcuts to each applicable action, in the following way:

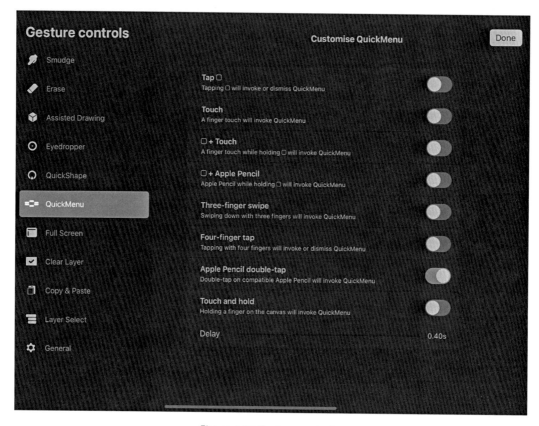

Figure 4.48: Gesture controls

There is a lot to be said when it comes to gestures on Procreate, all of which we cover in more detail in *Chapter 6, Using Gestures and Shortcuts*.

Rapid Undo Delay

Pressing down on the Undo button (on the sidebar), or the undo gesture (a two-finger tap by default) for a set interval of time activates what is called "rapid undo", which means your actions will be rapidly undone in quick succession until you release the button. The **Rapid Undo Delay** slider lets you decide how long you have to long-press the **Undo** button or gesture to activate rapid undo. This interval can be anywhere between no delay to 1.5 seconds.

Selection Mask Visibility

Whenever the **Select** tool is used to select an area of the canvas, the area outside the selection is overlaid by moving gray diagonal lines, which are usually semi-transparent. This overlay is called the selection mask. The **Selection Mask Visibility** slider lets you adjust the opacity of the selection mask.

Positioning the slider at different points can make a visual difference in the selection mask, as shown here:

Figure 4.49: The selection mask at 25% opacity versus 80% opacity

Using the Actions Menu

You can now go ahead and select your preferred settings from **Prefs**. It might take a bit of trial and error to fine-tune certain options, but sorting it out early can save you a lot of time later.

We are moving closer to the end of this chapter, now that almost all of the functions of the **Actions** menu have been discussed. The last menu we will cover is **Help**.

The Help menu

The last tab to be found in **Actions** is titled **Help**. As the name suggests, here's where you will find any kind of guidance required to operate the app. The following options are available on this menu:

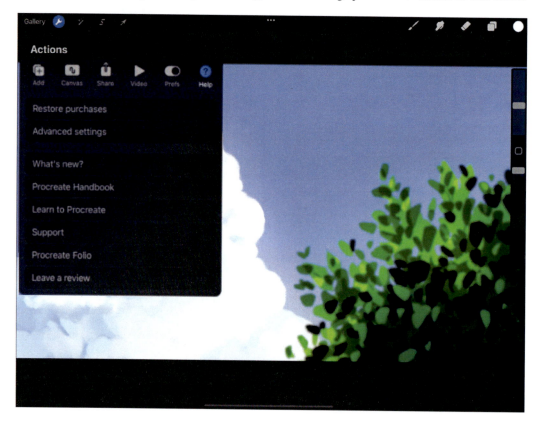

Figure 4.50: The Help menu

Procreate has a simple but extremely useful Help menu where the developers have linked the user to various kinds of external assistance and communities. Let's cover these options one by one.

Restore purchases

Procreate currently has no in-app purchases, but some of its older versions did. This option helps you restore any purchases you might have made while using those versions. If Procreate 5 is the first version you are using, then it will not apply to you.

Advanced settings

Tapping on this option will take you to **Settings** on your iPad, specifically the app settings tab of Procreate, which looks like this:

Figure 4.51: Advanced settings

There are the following broad types of settings:

- **ALLOW PROCREATE TO ACCESS**: Using these options, you can toggle which apps Procreate can access. Some of these are important to the functioning of Procreate. For instance, the app must have access to **Photos** to be able to import and export images from it.

- **Document Storage** decides where your Procreate files are backed up. You can choose your iPad or iCloud. Using iCloud is recommended, since it can be accessed from all your Apple devices.

- **Procreate Settings**: Adjust in-app settings using the next few options.

    Canvas Orientation Memory lets you choose whether Procreate will remember the orientation (rotation) you left your canvas at when you last closed it.

    Fit Canvas Inside Interface, when toggled on, means that when you load a canvas, it will fit border to border within the drawing area, like this:

Figure 4.52: Fit Canvas Inside Interface

When toggled off, the canvas will fit the whole screen, with some part of it overlaid by the Procreate interface, as shown here:

Figure 4.53: The canvas overlaid by interface

- **Palm Support™ level**: Palm Support is a feature of Procreate that lets you rest your palm on the screen while drawing, which will not be interpreted as drawing input. There are two sensitivity levels available. Use **Standard** mode for bigger hands and **Fine** mode for smaller hands. It is also possible to disable Palm Support completely.

- **Disable Time-lapse**: Toggle this setting on or off to decide whether you'd like every new canvas to have time-lapse enabled by default.

- **Simplified Undos**: When you perform a **Transform** or **Adjustments** action in Procreate, the whole transformation or adjustment is registered as a single action. Hence, when you hit undo, your layer reverts back to the original state in a single step, without going through the intermediate stages of transformation. This is called a Simplified Undo. Disabling it lets you register each individual change you make in a single transform or adjustments session as a separate step, allowing you finer control. However, this also means that you will exhaust your undos faster and won't be able to reach as far back into your process. It is toggled on by default.

- **Maximum Speed Distance**: Some brushes have a speed-based setting, which means that after a stroke is drawn beyond a certain distance, its speed registers as 100%. This makes subtle changes to the brush to better mimic how brushes work in real life. The **Maximum Speed Distance** slider helps you fine-tune the distance your brush must run before hitting maximum speed. If you find the current settings too slow or too rushed, then adjust the slider accordingly.

- **Drag and Drop Export**: Select your preferred file format and preferred image format when performing drag and drop export. We covered drag and drop export in more detail in *Chapter 1, The Gallery – Organizing Your Files*.

What's new?

This option takes you through the new features added to the application with Procreate 5.2. Tap this to open this screen:

Figure 4.54: What's new?

Tap on **Model pack** to import Procreate's own pack of 3D models. We will discuss this in more detail in *Chapter 15, Painting on 3D Models*.

Keep tapping on the **Next** button as each screen tells you more about Procreate's new features, as shown in the following screenshots:

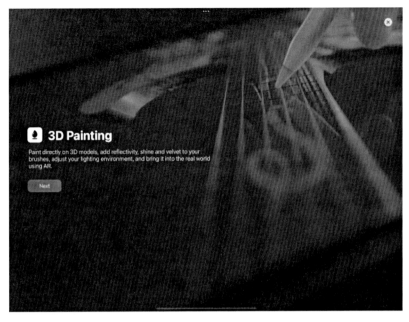

Figure 4.55: (a) 3D Painting, and (b) accessibility

The last screen sports a button labeled **Start Using Procreate**, which will exit this demo and take you back to the drawing interface, as shown in the following screenshot:

Figure 4.56: The end screen

At any point, you can tap the **x** icon in the top-right corner of the screen to exit the demo.

Procreate Handbook

This option will take you to the official instructional handbook on Procreate's website, which has a comprehensive breakdown of all their features with examples, including "Pro-tips," which are shown here:

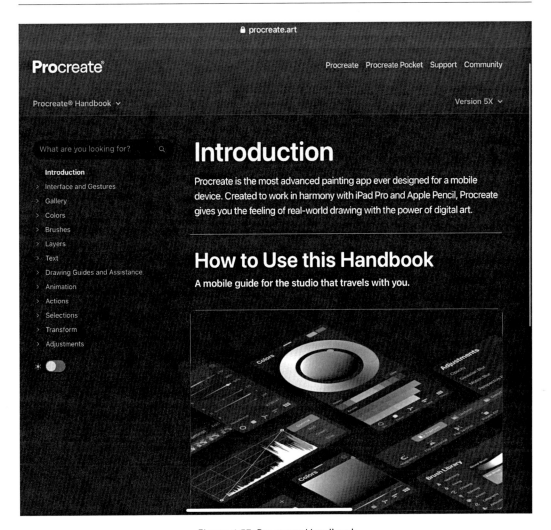

Figure 4.57: Procreate Handbook

This handbook is an excellent resource to keep handy, to understand the full extent of Procreate's functionality.

Learn to Procreate

Access a playlist from Procreate's official YouTube channel, which has live demonstrations of its features in a series of videos. The playlist, titled *Learn to Procreate*, has 50+ short videos, as shown in the following screenshot. It's a great way to learn the software at your own pace:

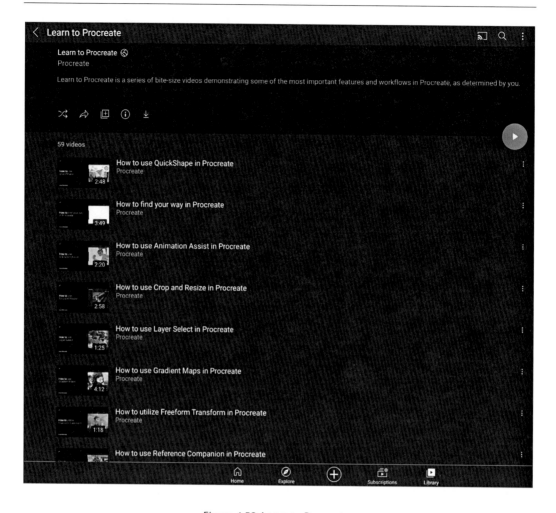

Figure 4.58: Learn to Procreate

Customer support

Directly get in touch with Procreate's customer support from their website using this option.

Procreate Folio

Procreate Folio is an online community of creators who use Procreate, where they can create an account and showcase their art. Tapping on **Procreate Folio** will take you to its website, as shown here:

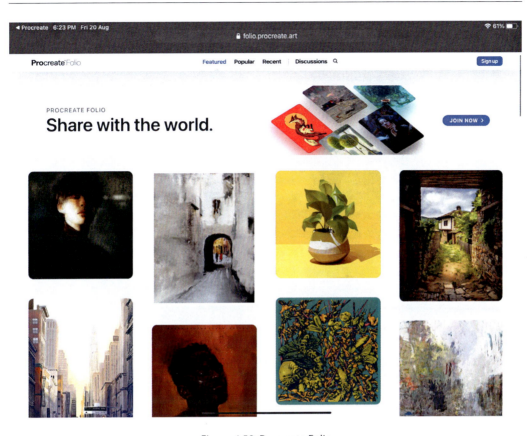

Figure 4.59: Procreate Folio

Write a Review

Tap on this option to visit the App Store and leave a review for the Procreate app, as shown here:

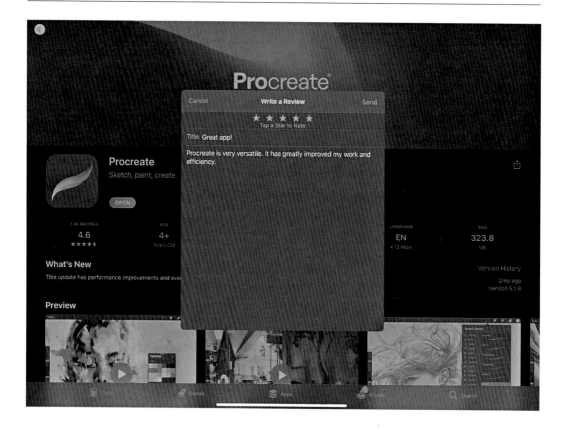

Figure 4.60: Write a Review

With that, we have covered all of the **Actions** menu. Let's summarize.

Summary

The **Actions** menu is one of the most robust sets of features offered by Procreate. In this chapter, we covered how to add images and text using **Add**, how to make sweeping changes to your document using **Canvas**, and how to export your artwork in your desired format using **Share**. You also learned how the time-lapse feature of Procreate works in **Video**, and how you can export or disable it.

Additionally, you were introduced to tweaking the interface to suit your needs using **Preferences**, where we briefly touched upon gesture controls.

Lastly, you now know how to access technical know-how, external support, and advanced settings using the **Help** menu.

With this, we are ready to move on to **Select** and **Transform**, a combination of feature-rich tools in Procreate, which we will cover in the next chapter.

5
Selecting and Transforming

In this chapter, we are going to learn about the **Selections** and **Transform** tools. They are the last two buttons found on the **Advanced Features** tab at the top-left corner of your workspace. The **S**-shaped icon is for the **Selections** tool and the arrow-shaped icon is for the **Transform** tool. Both of these tools are often used together, to demarcate and edit specific parts of your artwork. This allows you to have better control.

The **Selections** tool is used to isolate the area of interest, and the **Transform** tool is used to make further modifications to this selected area. In this chapter, we will look closely into how these tools help you to select and adjust sections of your image while leaving the rest untouched.

We're going to cover the following broad topics in this chapter:

- The Selections tool
- The Transform tool

The Selections tool

As its name suggests, the **Selections** tool helps you select your working area and confine all edits to that area only. This is helpful when you need to work on a certain region, or a particular element on a layer, without making any changes to the other areas. Tap on the **S**-shaped icon to invoke the tool, like this:

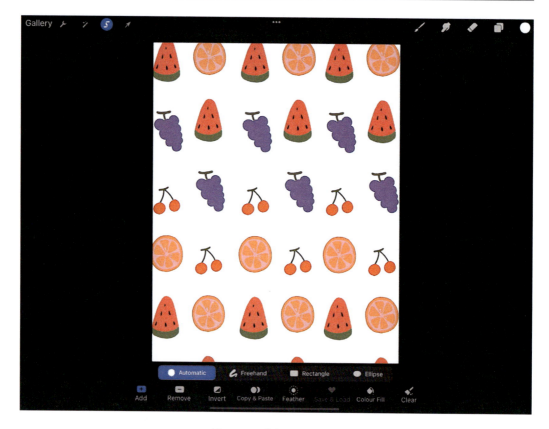

Figure 5.1: Selections tool

You will notice that there are several options available in the **Selections** tool. Let's look at them one by one. The first row consists of four options called **selection modes**, and the second row has **secondary tools**.

Automatic selection

This option allows you to select chunks of your art with a single tap. It's especially useful for artworks containing separate shapes. We can select each bunch of grapes with a single tap, as shown here:

Figure 5.2: Automatic selection

You can change the threshold of the selection. The threshold is a value that can be increased or decreased to include more or fewer pixels surrounding your current selection. It usually takes into account transparency or similar colored pixels.

To activate the selection threshold:

1. Tap and hold on a spot you want to select.
2. Without lifting your finger/Apple Pencil, slide it to the left or right until you've arrived at your preferred threshold.

Freehand selection

Freehand allows you to manually demarcate the area you want to select by drawing around that area by hand. Use this type of selection for more complex shapes. When you start selecting using **Freehand**, the starting point of the selection appears as a gray circle. When you're done selecting, you can tap this circle again to create a closed space, which is now a new selection. This is shown in the following two screenshots:

Figure 5.3: (a) open Freehand selection, (b) closed Freehand selection

An interesting feature of the **Freehand** selection tool is that you can create polygonal selections by tapping on each corner successively. Each point you tap on gets connected to the previous with a straight line, as shown here:

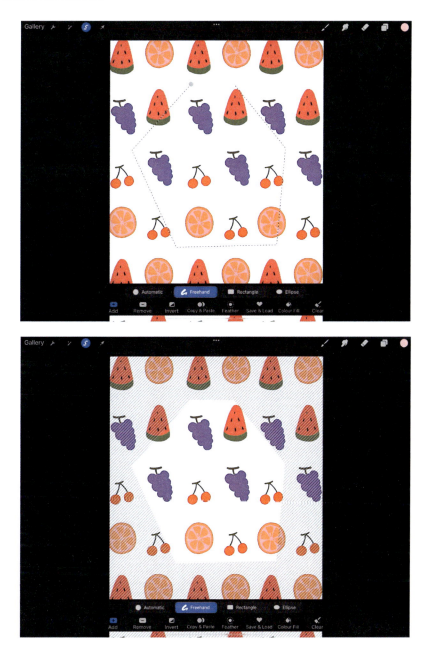

Figure 5.4: Polygonal selection using Freehand

Rectangle and Ellipse selection

The last two types of selection tools are **Rectangle** and **Ellipse**. As their names suggest, they allow you to select rectangular or elliptical areas. This is done by dragging the selection shape into the desired configuration, as shown here:

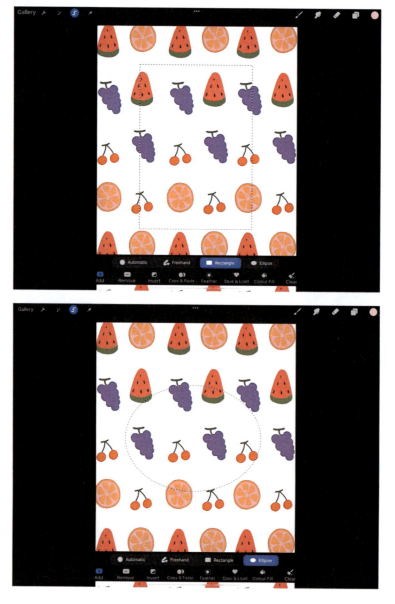

Figure 5.5: (a) Rectangle selection, (b) Ellipse selection

These are the four selection modes. You can switch between selection modes while a selection is active to fine-tune your selected area. You can also zoom in and out of your canvas or rotate it.

To fully understand the functions of the **Selections** tool, we will now look at the rest of the interface, specifically the bottom row of the panel. This consists of the **Add, Remove, Invert, Copy & Paste, Feather, Save & Load, Color Fill**, and **Clear** tools. We will cover them in the following sections.

Add

Add is the first button on the second row of the **Selections** toolbar and is toggled on by default. This button is used to add more area to your selection. It saves you the hassle of selecting the whole area perfectly in one go since you can always go back in and add more. For instance, say we want to add more area to the selection of this lemon in **Freehand** mode:

Figure 5.6: (a) Adding area, (b) area added to current selection

122 Selecting and Transforming

Doing this will let you update your selection to include more space.

Add behaves differently depending on which selection mode you're using. Let's look into the different ways it can work:

- While using **Freehand**, tapping **Add** automatically closes any open selections, and you can continue drawing and selecting more area.
- While using **Rectangle** and **Ellipse**, it works similarly. Once you tap **Add**, you can continue making more shapes and adding to your selection.
- While using the **Automatic** selection mode, **Add** is automatically included in its features, so it is grayed out. To add to your selection, simply tap.

Remove

Remove works the same way as **Add**, but it's used to "unselect" parts of your existing selection in case you have selected too much area. **Remove** is also useful for carving out spaces within a selection, or to fine-tune its edges. For instance, say this time you want to deselect a chunk in the middle of this lemon:

Figure 5.7: (a) Removing area, (b) area removed from the current selection

Evidently, this will let you remove the selection from only the middle of the lemon and make a donut-shaped selection.

Invert

Invert is used to switch the area selected with the rest of the layer area that is not selected. You can switch back and forth as many times as needed. The following screenshots will help demonstrate how this happens:

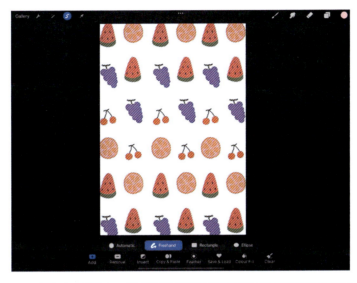

Figure 5.8: (a) Original selection, (b) inverted selection

In the first screenshot, you will notice that the white space surrounding the fruits is selected. Once the selection is inverted in the second screenshot, the fruit shapes will be selected instead. This is how the **Invert** tool functions.

Copy & Paste

If you'd like to edit your selection on a separate layer, tap **Copy & Paste**. This will duplicate the selected area onto a new layer above the current one, called **From selection**, as shown here:

Figure 5.9: (a) Selection copied, (b) duplicated to a new layer

Feather

Feather brings up a slider that lets you blur the edges of your selection. By default, a selection has sharp edges, but you can use this tool to soften those edges as per your needs. This will result in a selection with a diffused border. The degree of diffusion depends on how far along the slider is pushed. The following screenshots demonstrate the use of the **Feather** tool:

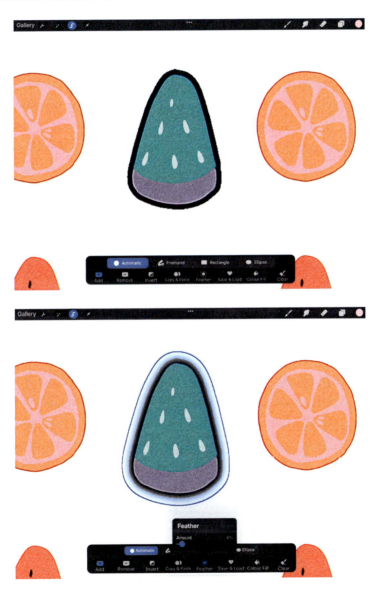

Figure 5.10: (a) Original selection, (b) feathered selection

Save & Load

The heart-shaped icon next to **Feather** is called **Save & Load**. This is an extremely useful feature for when you need to make the same selection again and again. This feature allows you to save your commonly used selections, which can be loaded at any time.

To save a selection, follow these steps:

1. Make a selection that you want to save for later.
2. Tap **Save & Load** and then tap the + icon to save the selection, as shown here:

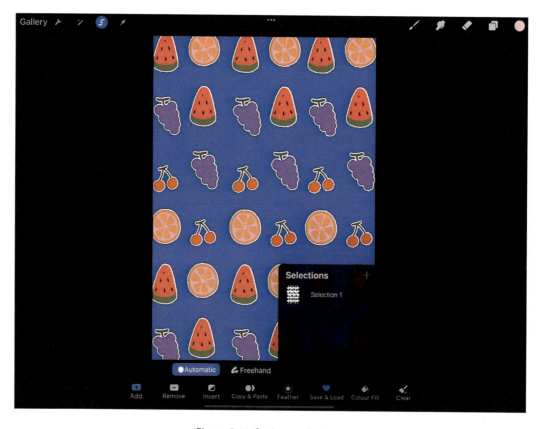

Figure 5.11: Saving a selection

To load a saved selection, follow these steps:

1. Tap **Save & Load**. This will bring up the list of all your saved selections, with a thumbnail next to their names showing their shapes.
2. Tap on the selection you want, which will activate it.

When you don't need a saved selection anymore, simply swipe left on it and tap on **Delete**.

> **Important Note**
> Saved selections are only available within the canvas from which they are created. A selection saved in one canvas cannot be loaded in another.

You can also long-press the **Selections** tool to reload the previous closed selection you had made.

Selection mask visibility

Whenever the **Select** tool is used to select an area of the canvas, the area outside the selection is overlaid by moving gray diagonal lines, which are usually semi-transparent. This overlay is called the **selection mask**. It's possible to adjust how transparent this mask will appear using the **Selection mask visibility** slider.

To adjust it, follow these steps:

1. Tap on **Actions**, which is the wrench-shaped icon in the top-left corner of the screen.
2. Select the **Prefs** submenu, shown in the following figure.
3. Under **Prefs**, you will spot a slider called **Selection mask visibility**. Positioning the slider at different points will change the opacity of the selection mask:

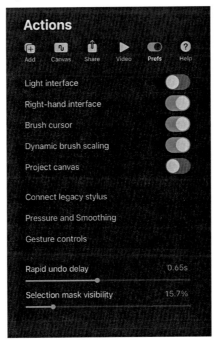

Figure 5.12: Selection mask visibility slider

128 | Selecting and Transforming

To learn more about the **Actions** menu and the **Prefs** submenu, refer to *Chapter 4, Using the Actions Menu*.

Selecting layer contents

You can select all the non-transparent pixels on a layer with a single tap, using this feature. To use it, follow these steps:

1. Tap on the **Layers** icon in the top-right-hand corner of the screen. This will open the **Layers** popover.
2. Tap on the layer you want to select the contents of.
3. Tap on it once more to bring up the layer options, as shown here:

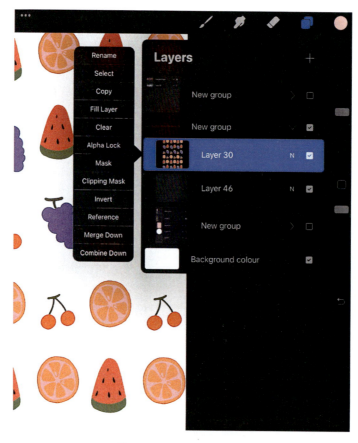

Figure 5.13: Layer options

4. Tap on **Select**.

Doing so will automatically activate selection mode and you can start drawing right away. To make edits to the selection, long-press the **Selections** button to invoke all its tools. To learn more about using layers and layer options, refer to *Chapter 7, Organizing Your Layers*.

Finalizing edits

Once you are happy with the edits you have made, simply tap on any other tool, such as **Paint** or **Erase**, to exit selection mode and continue drawing.

We have now explored the **Selections** tool in detail. You learned about the four different selection modes and the array of secondary functions you can use within this tool. Next, we will learn about the **Transform** tool, which is often used in conjunction with the former.

The Transform tool

To the right of **Selections**, you will find an arrow-shaped icon. This is the **Transform** tool. This tool is used to make size adjustments and distortions to your artwork or to reposition parts of it. Although it's commonly used together with **Selections**, it can also be used independently. In the following screenshot, you can see the interface of **Transform**:

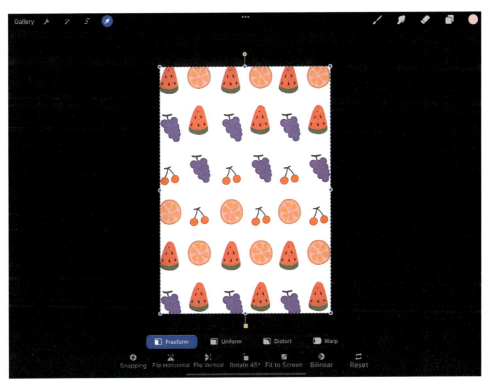

Figure 5.14: Transform tool

As you can see, tapping on the arrow icon automatically detects the contents of the current layer, encloses them in a bounding box, and brings up its toolbar. Alternatively, it's possible to select a section using the **Selections** tool and then tap on **Transform**, in which case, all the transformations will apply to the selected area only.

On the top row of the toolbar, there are four different methods of transforming, and on the bottom row are the sub-options available for each style. Let's try to understand each element of the **Transform** tool in more detail.

Interface

Once the **Transform** button is tapped, the interface of the tool gets activated. There are several elements of this interface that we must note:

- **Bounding box**:

    The selection, or contents of the layer, gets enclosed by a box of moving dashed lines. This is the bounding box. It is the exact height and width of the image being transformed, as shown:

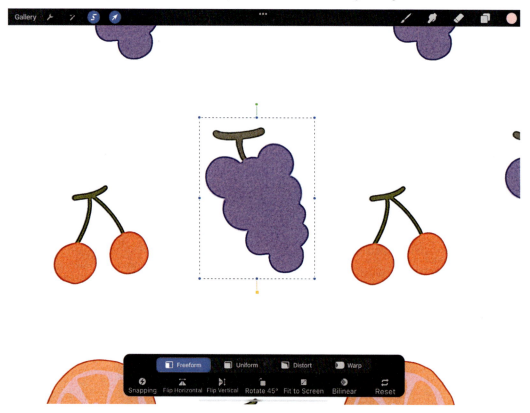

Figure 5.15: Bounding box

Once you see the bounding box, you can touch anywhere on the screen and drag to move the selection around. You can also pinch inside the box to zoom and rotate it, as shown in this screenshot:

Figure 5.16: Pinch-zoomed and rotated selection

- **Transformation nodes**:

    The bounding box has small blue points on each corner and the midpoint of each edge. These are called transformation nodes. You can use them as handles to transform the shape and size of the selection.

- **Bounding box adjust node**:

    The yellow node at the bottom of the bounding box can be used to rotate it around the selected content. At each orientation, the bounding box will fit the dimensions of the selection, as shown in the following screenshot. This feature allows you to transform along any angle:

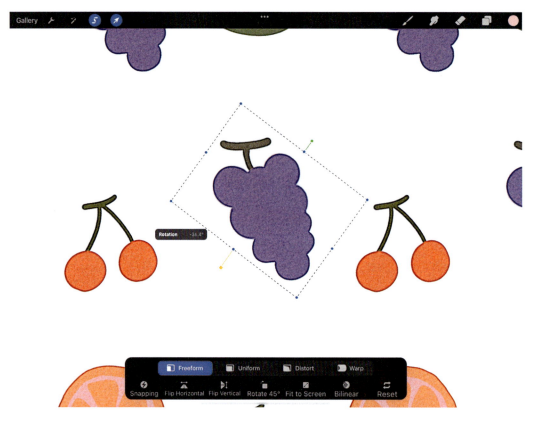

Figure 5.17: Adjusted bounding box

- **Rotation node**:

    The green node at the top of the bounding box is the rotation node. As the name suggests, you can rotate the selected content about its midpoint using this node, like this:

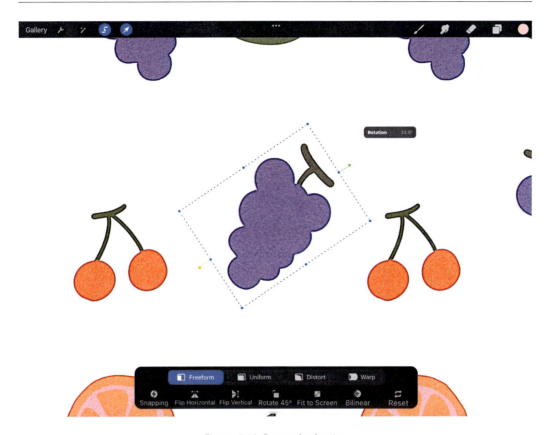

Figure 5.18: Rotated selection

All these elements of the interface behave differently depending on which transformation method you are using. We will now learn about these transformation methods one by one.

Freeform

The first option on the top row of the toolbar is **Freeform**. This method allows you to stretch or squash your selection along its height or width. You can adjust using the nodes on the edges of the bounding box to transform just one dimension, while keeping the other constant, like this:

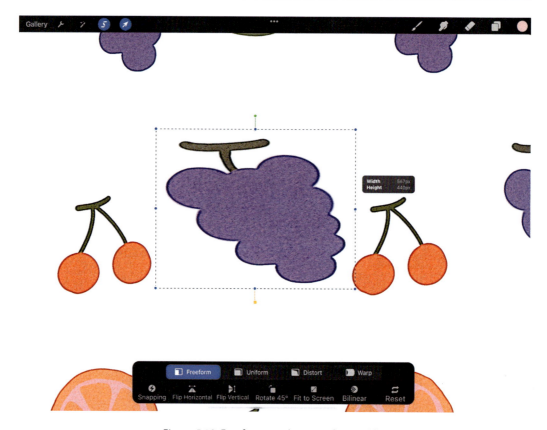

Figure 5.19: Freeform used to stretch one side

Alternatively, adjust using the corner nodes to transform both the height and width at the same time, as shown here:

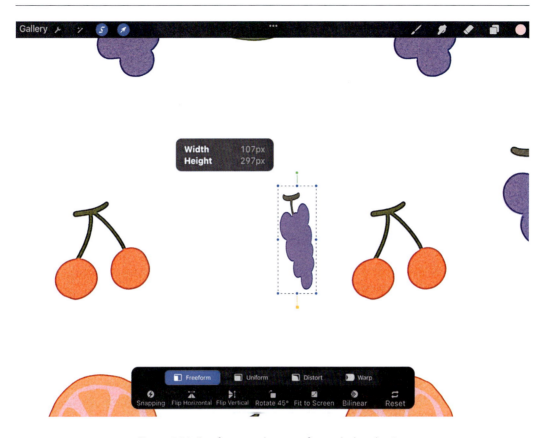

Figure 5.20: Freeform used to transform whole selection

Uniform

Uniform is the next transformation method, which allows you to scale your selection up and down uniformly while keeping the height-width ratio locked. No matter which node you adjust by, the rest of the image will automatically scale to keep the aspect ratio constant:

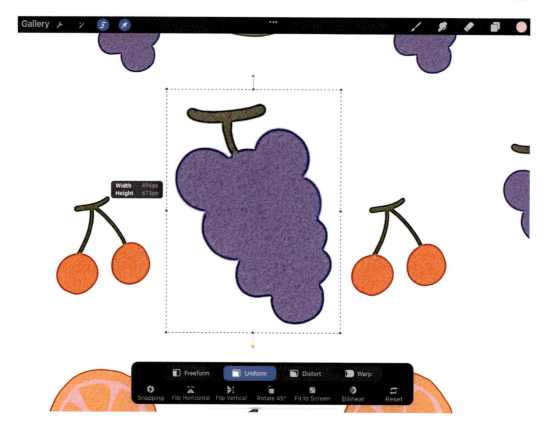

Figure 5.21: Uniform transformation

Distort

Distort allows you to deform the selection using all of the transformation nodes. Just like **Freeform**, it doesn't lock the aspect ratio and makes it possible to freely transform. It's useful when you want to align an image to perspective. Distorting a selection using the corner nodes makes these perspective-like transformations, as in this screenshot:

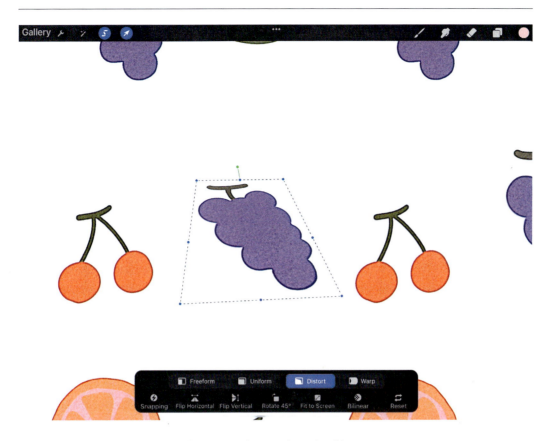

Figure 5.22: Perspective using Distort

Using the nodes on the midpoints helps stretch and shear the selection, as shown here:

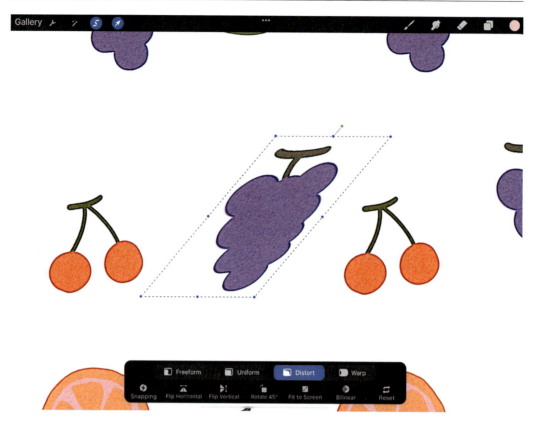

Figure 5.23: Shearing using Distort

Warp

The last option on the list of transformation methods is **Warp**. This tool places a mesh over the selection, which can be distorted by dragging anywhere on the selection area. The following screenshot demonstrates how it works:

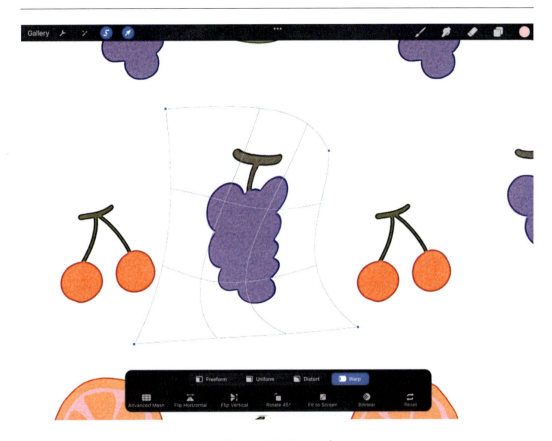

Figure 5.24: Warp tool

Warp is a special mode since it makes a new option appear on the second row of the toolbar. This option is called **Advanced Mesh**, shown as follows:

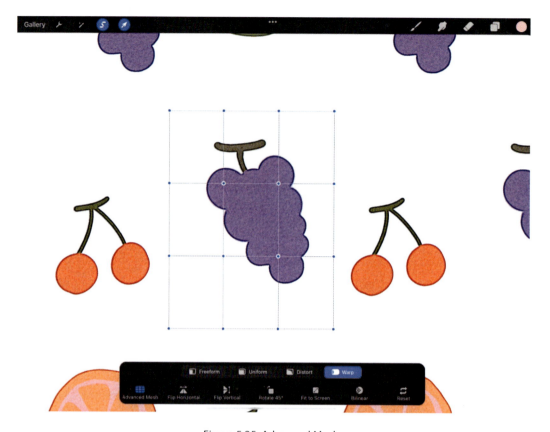

Figure 5.25: Advanced Mesh

This is a "power-up" for the **Warp** tool, where individual nodes appear on the mesh. These nodes can be transformed independently to make dramatic distortions to the image. **Advanced Mesh** is especially useful for overlaying designs on cloth, to mimic the flow of fabric.

We have covered all four methods of transformation and how they have their own specific areas of use. These tools are flexible, and you can switch between modes anytime during a transformation, allowing you finer control.

Now we can dive into the second row of tools available on the **Transform** toolbar. These remain mostly constant and apply to all of the aforementioned transformation modes. They are **Snapping**, **Flip**, **Rotate 45°**, **Fit to Screen**, **Interpolation**, and **Reset**.

Snapping

Snapping is a useful feature of the **Transform** tool. It helps to place a selection in alignment with the center of the canvas, or with respect to objects on other layers. It is the first tool on the bottom row of the toolbox. There are two types of snapping tools available:

- **Magnetics**: When this is toggled on, you can move the bounding box in a certain direction, be it vertically, horizontally, or at an angle. This feature locks the direction of movement and shows you a blue guide line along that axis. Refer to the following screenshot to get a better idea:

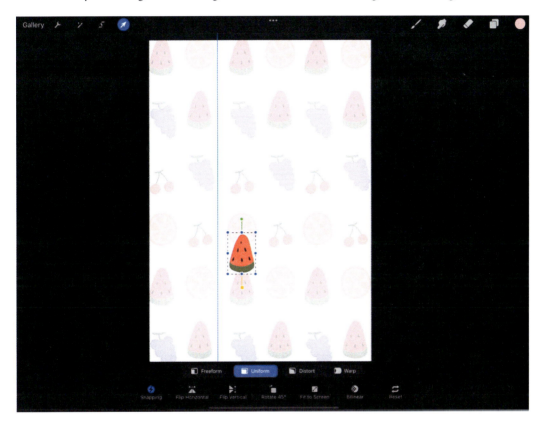

Figure 5.26: Direction locking in Magnetics

The same thing happens for rotation, where the selection snaps to 45° increments.

- **Snapping**: When toggled on, this tool detects the center and edges of the canvas, as well as objects on other layers, and snaps your bounding box to help align with them. Axes pertaining to the entire canvas show up as yellow guide lines, such as here, where the image has been snapped to the center of the canvas:

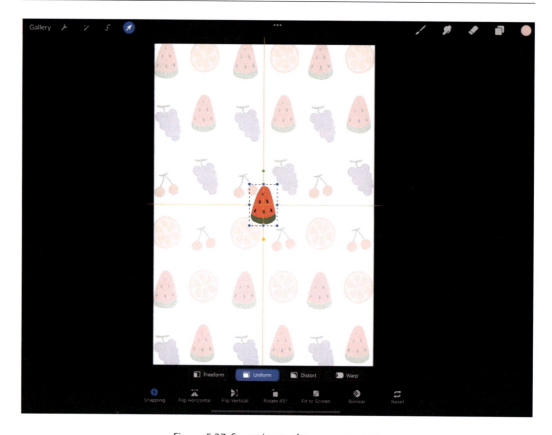

Figure 5.27: Snapping to the canvas center

Axes snapping to elements on the canvas are indicated by blue guide lines running through the element of reference. In the following screenshot, you can see how this happens when one watermelon is aligned with another:

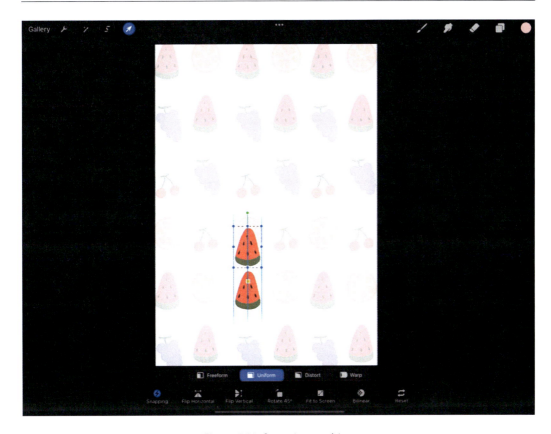

Figure 5.28: Snapping to object

After this, we come to a common but essential feature that makes transforming more efficient.

Flipping tools

The next two tools you will spot on the bottom row are **Flip Horizontally** and **Flip Vertically**. As their names suggest, they are used to flip your selection along these two axes. It's worth noting that these actions flip only the selected content and not the whole canvas. To learn about flipping the canvas, refer to *Chapter 4, Using the Actions Menu*.

The next option provides a quick and accurate way to rotate your selection at specific angles.

Rotate 45°

The next option, **Rotate 45°**, is used to make clockwise rotational increments of 45° to your selection. The cherries rotate about their center, as shown here:

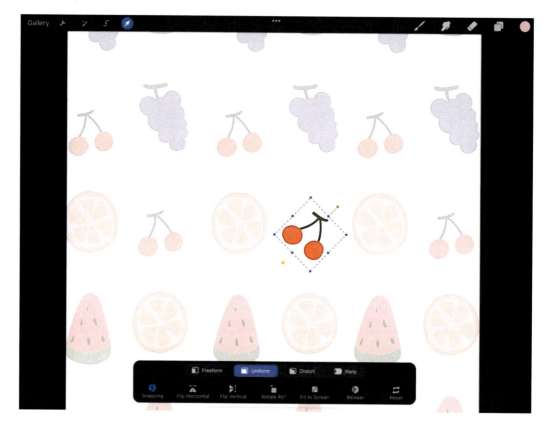

Figure 5.29: Rotation by 45°

The option we will look at next is useful for filling the screen with the selection.

Fit to Screen

When you want to scale your selection to fit edge-to-edge inside your canvas, use the **Fit to Screen** feature. Normally, tapping this button will scale the selection as large as it can go without cropping any part of it, as shown here:

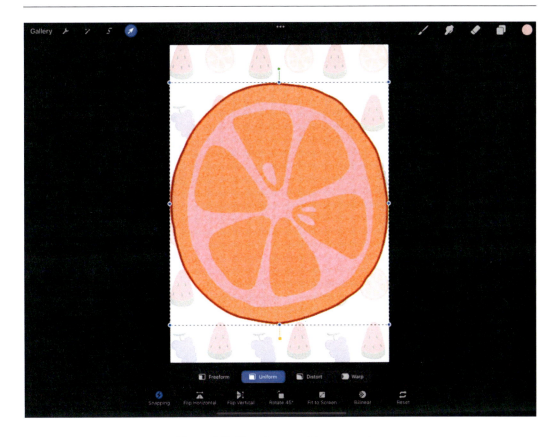

Figure 5.30: Fit to Screen without cropping

However, if **Magnetics** is toggled on, **Fit to Screen** scales the selection for maximum coverage. In this case, some part of it can spill out of the canvas area, like this:

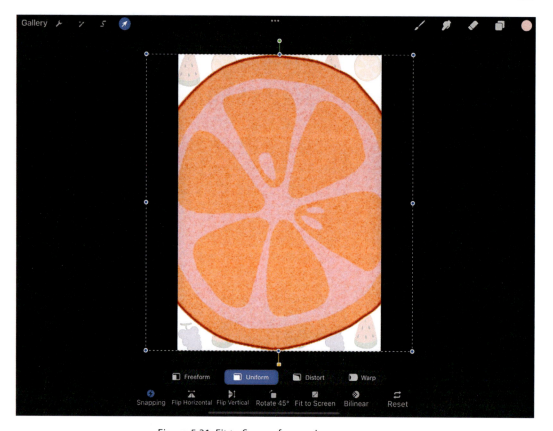

Figure 5.31: Fit to Screen for maximum coverage

> **Important Note**
> Once a part of the transformed selection is cropped out of the canvas, it's lost permanently. It is a useful practice to have a copy of the layer (or the whole canvas) handy, in case you're not sure about cropping.

Next, we will look at the engine that makes sure transformations are done with pixel-perfect accuracy.

Interpolation

The small circular icon second from the right is responsible for interpolation. When a selection is resized, rotated, or deformed, new pixels must be created or existing pixels need to be readjusted to facilitate that. However, the pixel grid making up the canvas stays the same. **Interpolation** is a feature that controls how this readjustment is done.

By default, this icon is labeled **Nearer**. Tap on it to bring up a popover that has more options. These are the three different ways interpolation can happen:

- **Nearest Neighbor**: This is the simplest form of interpolation where the engine just takes into account the nearest pixel while transforming. In other words, it makes sure your image has sharp edges even after multiple transformations. In some cases, the result may appear jagged, but it works fine for smaller selections.
- **Bilinear**: This method uses a 2x2 area of pixels around the edge of the selection when calculating new pixels. It is slower but more accurate than the previous option. Bilinear is the most versatile mode for both small and large artworks.
- **Bicubic**: The sharpest and most accurate type of interpolation is the **Bicubic** type, which considers an area of 16 pixels around the edge of the selection. Preference is given to the pixels nearer to the edge, giving a more accurate result than the other two modes. However, smaller images may appear blurry with this kind of interpolation.

Reset

The last option on the **Transform** toolbox is the icon with two arrows, called **Reset**. This button basically undoes all the transformation actions performed up until this point and makes it revert back to the original state.

Finalizing edits

Once you are happy with the transformation you have made, simply tap on any other tool, such as **Paint** or **Erase**, to exit transform mode and continue drawing.

Summary

To summarize, in this chapter, we learned about the **Selections** and **Transform** tools. Both of these are essential in terms of demarcating a specific work area (using **Selections**) and manipulating its size, shape, and position (using **Transform**).

By now, you should be familiar with how to choose the correct selection mode to suit your needs: **Automatic** for large chunks, **Freehand** for complex shapes, and **Rectangle** or **Ellipse** for specific shapes. You will also be familiar with all the other functions you can do while selecting, including adding, removing, inverting, and color-filling selections, among others.

Under **Transform**, we covered the four methods of transformation: **Freeform** for stretching and squashing along the two axes, **Uniform** for scaling up and down uniformly, **Distort** for applying perspective-like effects, and **Warp** for complex deformations. In this tool's other functions, we learned about its interface, and how to flip, rotate, align, and much more.

In the next chapter, we will start our exploration of one of the most crucial parts of using Procreate: gestures.

Part 2: Utility and an In-Depth Discussion of Utility and Features

This second part of the book will go over the most useful features in detail, explaining use cases in order for us to gain familiarity with the software quicker.

This section comprises the following chapters:

- *Chapter 6, Using Gestures and Shortcuts*
- *Chapter 7, Organizing Your Layers*
- *Chapter 8, Painting Tools and the Brush Library – Using and Organizing Brushes*
- *Chapter 9, Brush Studio Settings – Editing and Combining Brushes*
- *Chapter 10, Using Color Tools*
- *Chapter 11, Adjustments – Applying Image Effects*
- *Chapter 12, Using Assisted Drawing Tools*
- *Chapter 13, Using Animation Assist for 2D Animation*
- *Chapter 14, Sketchbooking with Page Assists*
- *Chapter 15, Painting on 3D Models*

6
Using Gestures and Shortcuts

Looking at the interface of Procreate, you'll realize that it is compact and lightweight, designed to put maximum focus on the work area. Most of the tools are packaged away into menus and sub-menus, most of which we learned about in the preceding chapters. While this design is greatly effective, it might get in the way of speed.

This is where gestures come in. Gestures are simple, easy-to-perform actions that act as shortcuts to perform specific functions. They save you the time and effort of having to go through multiple steps every time you want to do a task. Gestures also play a huge role in making the software intuitive and more natural to use. Having a grasp of Procreate's various gestures and their functions can greatly speed up your workflow.

We will start this chapter by learning what gestures are, and which ones are the most commonly used. Then we'll discuss a special set of gestures that makes Procreate accessible for more people. The next topic will introduce specifically layer-related gestures. Finally, we will talk about how to customize gestures to fit your needs.

We're going to cover the following broad topics in this chapter:

- Understanding basic gestures
- Accessibility gestures
- Layer gestures
- Customizing gestures

Understanding basic gestures

Basic gestures are the ones you will be using most frequently to perform simple fundamental actions. It is crucial to learn these at the earliest stages of using the software for a smooth experience. We will explore these gestures one by one in the following sections.

Pinch

The pinch is an extremely useful gesture. It helps to zoom, rotate, and reposition your canvas. The following are the types of pinch gestures:

- **Pinch to zoom**: You might already be familiar with this function. With two fingers, pinch out to zoom into your canvas:

Figure 6.1: Pinch out to zoom in

Similarly, you can pinch in to zoom out as shown in the following screenshot:

Figure 6.2: Pinch in to zoom out

- **Pinch and twist to rotate**: You can pinch your canvas and twist your hand in any direction to rotate the canvas in that direction.
- **Quick pinch**: Pinch your canvas briefly in a quick motion to resize it to fit the screen, as it was when you opened the canvas.

Double-tap undo

By default, tapping the screen with two fingers performs the undo function:

Figure 6.3: Double-tap to undo

You can also double-tap and hold your fingers to the screen to activate rapid undo. This will undo your actions rapidly in quick succession.

Three-finger tap redo

Similar to the previous section, tapping the screen with three fingers will redo the action that you last undid. Tap and hold with three fingers to activate rapid redo:

Understanding basic gestures | 155

Figure 6.4: Three-finger tap to redo

There are more three-finger actions, which are discussed in the next few sub-sections.

Three-finger scrub

This gesture is performed by using three fingers to quickly rub the screen from left to right, called a scrub:

Figure 6.5: Three-finger scrub to clear layer

By default, this clears all the contents of the current layer.

Three-finger swipe down

Swiping down with three fingers is used to bring up a floating menu called **Copy & Paste**:

Figure 6.6: Three-finger swipe down

This menu has clipboard tools (**Cut**, **Copy**, **Paste**, and so on), as shown in the following screenshot:

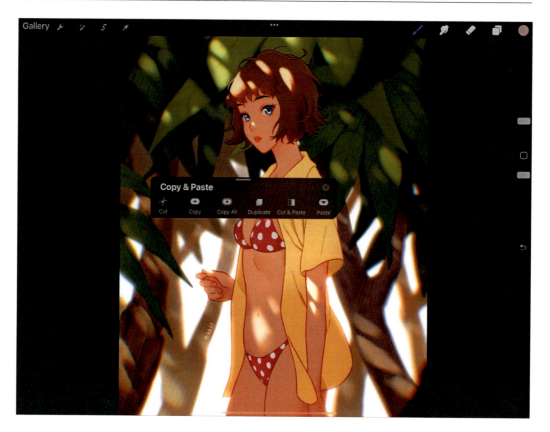

Figure 6.7: Copy & Paste menu

This menu can be used on the current layer or selection. The following options are available here:

- **Cut**: This is used to clear the contents of the layer or selection, while still having it available on your clipboard to be pasted later.
- **Copy**: This is used to copy the contents of the layer or selection into your clipboard without clearing the original.
- **Copy All**: This is used to copy the whole canvas as a single image, which you can then paste.
- **Duplicate**: This is used to perform the **Copy** and **Paste** functions in one go. The selection or layer will be duplicated onto a new layer titled `From Selection` or `Inserted Image` (when the whole layer is duplicated).
- **Cut & Paste**: This is used to perform the **Cut** and **Paste** functions together. The selection or layer will be cleared and transferred to a new layer titled `From Selection` or `Inserted Image` (when the whole layer is cut and pasted).
- **Paste**: This is used to re-insert your cut or copied selection as a new layer titled `From Selection` or `Inserted Image` (when the whole layer is pasted).

Four-finger tap

When the screen is tapped with four fingers, as shown in the following screenshot, it hides the interface and gives you a fullscreen view of your canvas:

Figure 6.8: Four-finger tap to enter fullscreen mode

Tap with four fingers once again to restore the interface. In the next section, we will discuss QuickShape, a great tool for accuracy.

QuickShape

This feature allows you to quickly create regular shapes from freely drawn strokes. Draw a freehand shape and hold your Apple Pencil down on your screen without lifting it. Your drawing will turn into the closest regular shape, such as a straight line, arc, circle, rectangle, and many more.

To use the QuickShape feature, follow these steps:

1. Draw a freehand shape. For this exercise, let's go with a wonky circle, as shown here:

Figure 6.9: Hand-drawn circle

2. Without lifting your pencil, press and hold until the shape turns into a regular ellipse. At the top of the screen, you will see a notification pop up, which says **Ellipse created**. You can stretch, rotate, and resize the shape by dragging your pencil without lifting it, as shown here:

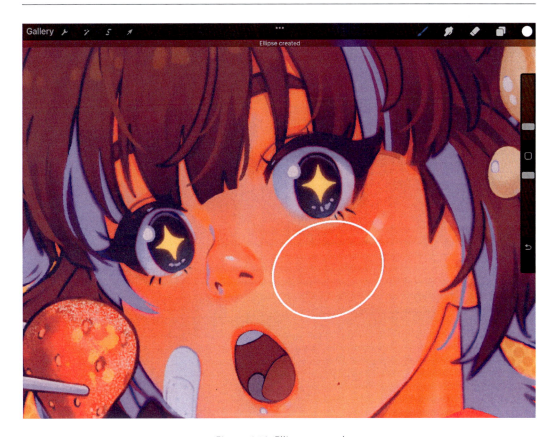

Figure 6.10: Ellipse created

3. As soon as you lift your pencil, you will see another notification at the top of the screen: a button that says **Edit Shape**. Once you tap on it, you will be given options to either make your shape an **ellipse** or a **circle**. At this point, four blue dots will also appear on your shape, as shown in the following screenshot:

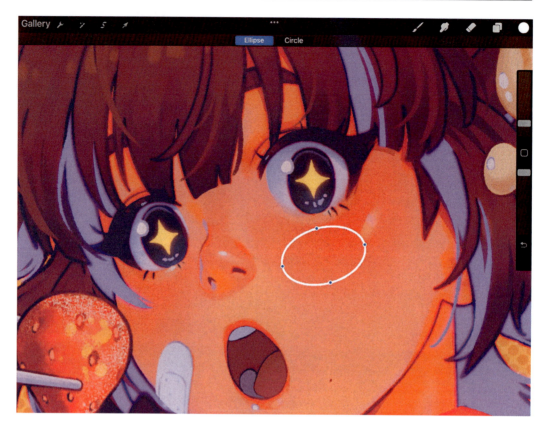

Figure 6.11: Edit shape and handles

These are called handles, which you can manually use to stretch and squash it.

4. For this exercise, we shall choose to tap on **Circle**. The shape will immediately become a regular circle, like this:

Understanding basic gestures 163

Figure 6.12: Circle created

5. You will notice that the blue handles are still present. You can use them to stretch the shape back into an ellipse.

6. To make the shape uniformly bigger or smaller, place your pencil anywhere between two handles on the outline of the shape, and drag.

7. To reposition the shape, place your pencil anywhere on the screen and drag it in any direction.

8. Once you are happy with the changes, tap on any tool, such as **Paint** or **Erase**, to commit and exit QuickShape.

In your own time, try drawing other kinds of shapes such as straight lines, arcs, rectangles/squares, polygons, and so on. It will help you become familiar with how each of their controls works.

Precise slider control

In *Chapter 3, Understanding Your Workspace*, we learned about the sidebar, which has the size and opacity sliders. These sliders help you change the size and opacity of your brush. It's possible to make finer adjustments than normal using sliders, with a simple gesture.

Place your finger on the slider button, swipe to the side, and move your finger up and down without lifting it. You will notice that the slider is now moving more slowly than usual. This gesture helps you fine-tune the brush size or opacity.

This section dived into all the major types of gestures that you will frequently use while drawing in Procreate. In the next section, we'll learn about the accessibility tools that the app has to offer.

Using accessibility gestures

There is a set of gestures that make Procreate more convenient to use with a single hand. It is one of the many ways the software takes accessibility into account, by accommodating users according to their needs.

This is done using what is called single touch gestures, which can be activated when required. It is a floating menu with the **Undo**, **Redo**, **Zoom**, **Move**, and **Fit Canvas** buttons. We will see this in the next section.

Activating single touch gestures

The single touch gesture menu can be activated by following these steps:

1. Go to your iPadOS **Settings**.
2. Select **Procreate**.
3. Find the option called **Single Touch Gestures Companion** and toggle it on:

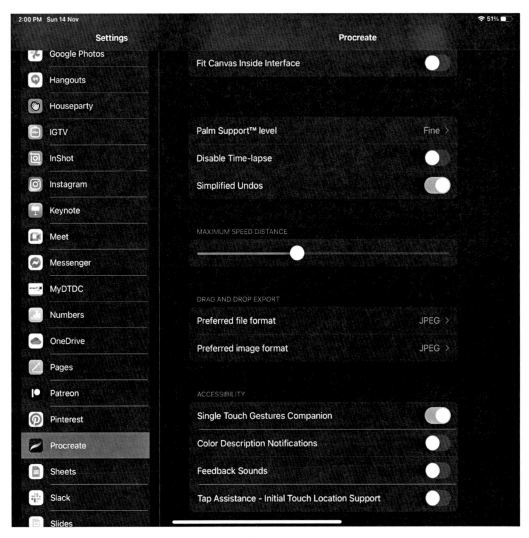

Figure 6.13: Single Touch Gestures Companion toggled on

The menu will now be available whenever you use the app until it is toggled off, as seen in the following screenshot:

Figure 6.14: Single touch gestures menu

Let's now look at how each of these buttons works in the following sections.

Undo and Redo

The first two buttons on the menu are **Undo** and **Redo**. By default, undo is performed with a two-finger tap, and redo with a three-finger tap. In the single touch menu, these are simplified to a single tap of the **Undo** and **Redo** buttons respectively.

Zoom

Zoom is the next button, which allows you to zoom in and out of your artwork and rotate it, without using the default pinch-and-twist gesture.

Follow these steps to use this feature:

1. Select **Zoom**. On doing so, the icon will turn blue, indicating that it has been selected.
2. Place your pencil anywhere on the canvas. You will see that a blue line is now joining that point with the center of the canvas.

3. Drag your pencil across the screen to see how the canvas zooms and rotates with the blue line:

Figure 6.15: Single touch zoom

4. To exit **Zoom** mode, tap on the **Zoom** button again to deselect it.

> **Important Note**
>
> Initially, when you tap on the screen to set a point of control, it's always a good idea to choose a point that is neither too close nor too far away from the center of the canvas. This ensures that you get a decent amount of control while both zooming and rotating it.
>
> Tapping close to the center gives you more scope for scaling but makes rotation difficult to moderate. Inversely, when your point of control is far away from the center, it is easier to rotate, but limits scaling. It's important to strike a balance that works best for you.

Move

Move is the fourth option on the menu. It is used to reposition the canvas on the screen. By default, this action is performed using the two-finger drag gesture.

Follow these steps to use this feature:

1. Select **Move**. On doing so, the icon will turn blue, indicating that it has been selected.
2. Place your pencil anywhere on the screen and drag it in any direction to move the canvas around.
3. To exit **Move** mode, tap on the **Move** button again to deselect it.

Fit Canvas

The last option on the menu is **Fit Canvas**. It is used to fit your canvas inside the interface for a full view. By default, this action is performed using the quick pinch gesture.

In this section, we covered how Procreate can be made easier to use with single touch gestures. The next section will introduce you to specific gestures that are used to work with layers.

Exploring layer gestures

Procreate uses layers to facilitate making art. Layer gestures are a set of handy shortcuts to make using layers more convenient. These gestures simplify commonly used layer tasks into easy-to-perform actions.

To use layer gestures, you must tap on the **Layers** icon in the top right-hand corner of the interface, so that the **Layers** popover is open. Let's look at the different gestures available in the following sections.

Selecting layers

Tap on a layer to select it as the primary layer, on which you will be able to draw and make edits.

To select more than one layer, select any one of them as the primary layer, then swipe right on all the other layers you wish to select, as shown in the following screenshot:

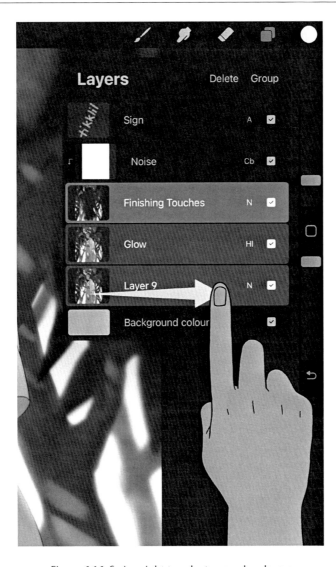

Figure 6.16: Swipe right to select secondary layers

The primary layer is indicated in light blue and the secondary layers in dark blue. After this, you can group, delete, or transform them together.

While multiple layers are selected, you will only be able to draw and perform adjustments on the primary layer. However, selections and transformations will apply to all selected layers as a whole. To learn more about layers, refer to *Chapter 7, Organizing Your Layers*.

Pinch to merge layers

Place two fingers on two layers and pinch to merge them and all layers in between into a single layer:

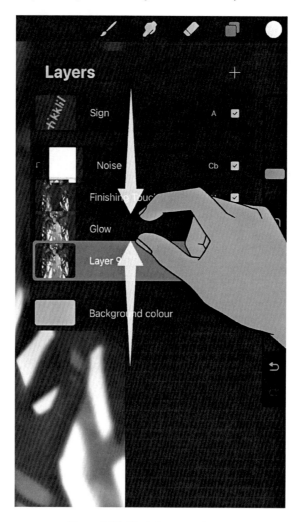

Figure 6.17: Pinch to merge layers

Two-finger tap for layer opacity

On the **Layers** panel, tap on a layer with two fingers to select it and activate opacity controls. The current opacity of the layer will appear as a blue slider at the top of the screen, as shown here:

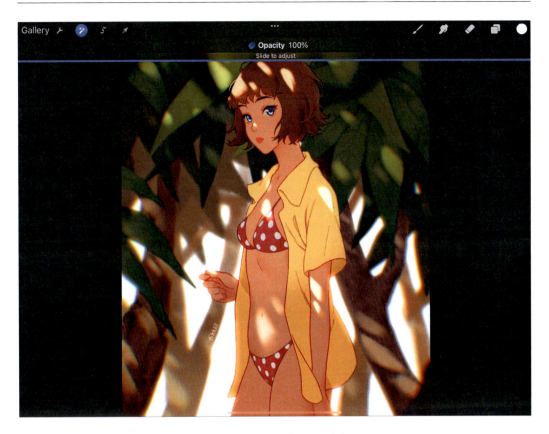

Figure 6.18: Layer Opacity slider

Once the controls have been activated, scrub the screen with your finger to the left to decrease the opacity of the layer, and to the right to increase it.

Two-finger swipe right for alpha lock

On the **Layers** panel, swipe right on a layer with two fingers to alpha lock it:

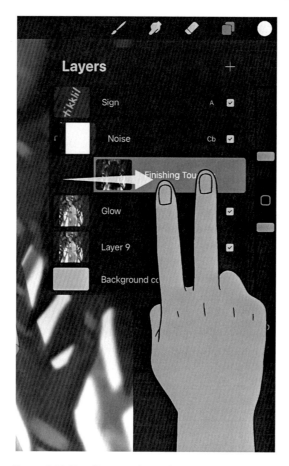

Figure 6.19: Two-finger swipe right to toggle alpha lock

This means that you can no longer paint on the transparent pixels of the layer. Swipe right once again to turn off the alpha lock.

Two-finger hold to select layer contents

On the **Layers** panel, use two fingers to touch and hold a layer. This will activate **Selections** and select the contents of that layer. Transparent pixels will not be selected.

You can modify the selection in various ways, such as by painting, adjusting, or transforming it. To learn more about the **Selections** tool, refer to *Chapter 5, Selecting and Transforming*.

This section discussed layer gestures in detail. In the next and final section, you will learn how to take gestures into your own hands and customize the experience you have with them.

Customizing gestures

There are many ways to customize your experience with gestures. This can be done using the **Gesture Controls** menu. You can use this menu to assign shortcuts of your choice to certain actions, and even enable certain features that are not toggled on by default.

Follow these steps to access the **Gesture Controls** menu:

1. Tap on **Actions**, which is the wrench-shaped icon in the top left-hand corner of the interface.
2. Go to the sub-menu titled **Prefs**.
3. Tap on **Gesture Controls**.

    This will bring you to the **Gesture controls** panel, shown here:

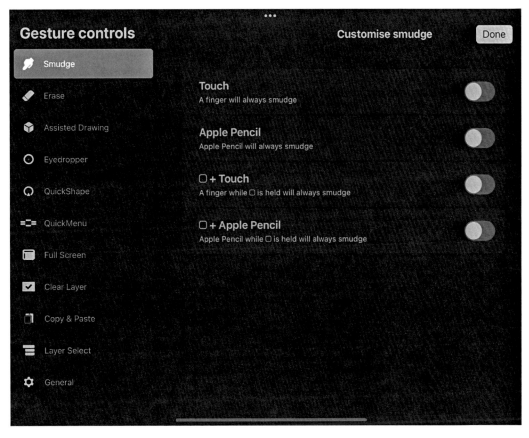

Figure 6.20: Gesture controls

In the left column, you will see a list of actions for which you can customize gestures. On the right are the possible gestures you can designate each. You may assign different shortcuts to the same action, but the same shortcut can't be used for different actions. If this situation arises, you will see a yellow warning flash up next to the feature in question.

Let's dive into each of these features and how to customize gestures for each.

Painting gestures

The first three features on the list are **Smudge**, **Erase**, and **Assisted Drawing**. Let's discuss them one by one:

- **Smudge**: You have the option to toggle any of these four options on:

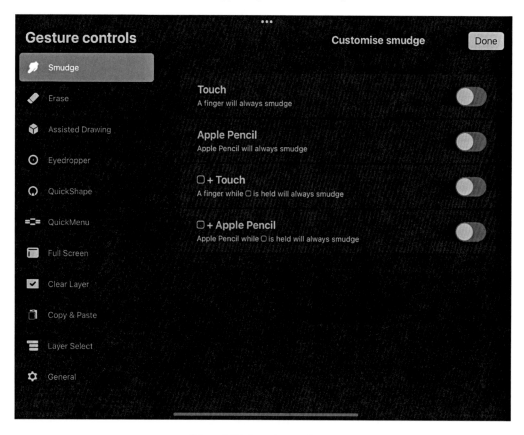

Figure 6.21: Smudge gestures

Doing so will ensure that input through that particular method will always smudge, no matter which tool is selected. For example, if **Touch** is toggled on, touching the screen with your finger will always perform the smudge action, even if the **Erase** tool is selected.

- **Erase**: Similar to the last option, you have the option to toggle any of these four options on:

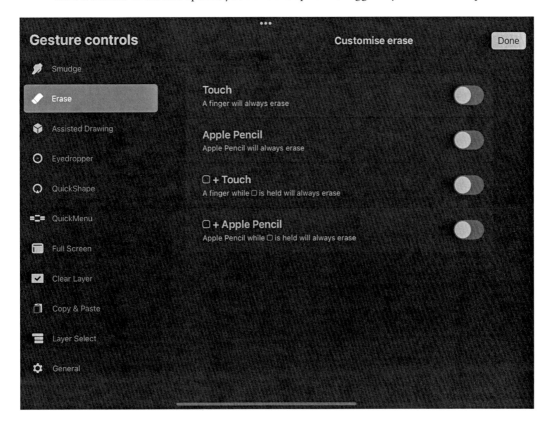

Figure 6.22: Erase gestures

Doing so will ensure that input through that particular method will always erase, no matter which tool is selected. For example, if **Apple Pencil** is toggled on, drawing with your Apple Pencil will always perform the erase action, even if the **Smudge** tool is selected.

- **Assisted Drawing**: You can choose the gesture that will turn on Drawing Assist on the current layer – either by tapping the **Modify** button or by double tapping on your gen 2 Apple Pencil:

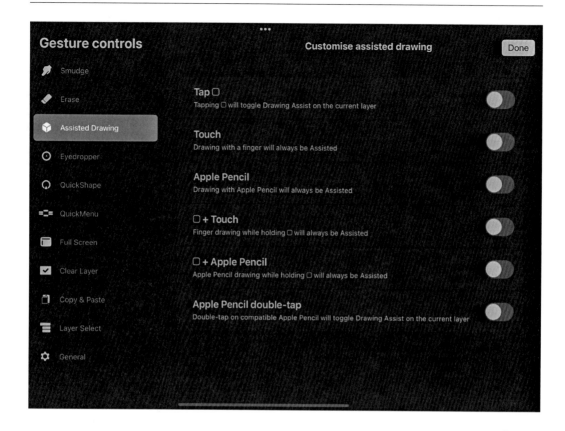

Figure 6.23: Assisted Drawing gestures

Similar to the two previous options, you have six gesture options to choose from, which will ensure that drawing using that particular method will always be assisted.

To learn more about Drawing Assist, refer to *Chapter 12, Using Assisted Drawing Tools*.

Advanced feature gestures

Eyedropper, **QuickShape**, and **QuickMenu** fall under advanced feature gestures. Let's explore the gestures available for each:

- **Eyedropper**: The following screenshot shows the gestures available for invoking the **Eyedropper** tool. You can toggle on as many as you like, as long as the same gestures are not assigned to any other feature.

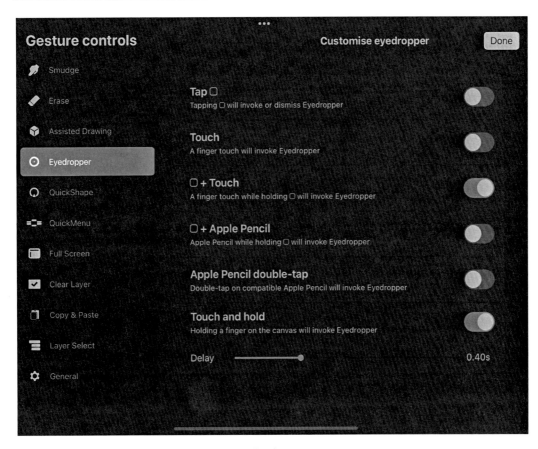

Figure 6.24: Eyedropper gestures

For **Touch and hold**, the slider labeled **Delay** lets you configure how long you must hold before the eyedropper is invoked.

- **QuickShape**: The following screenshot shows the gestures that are available for invoking the QuickShape tool:

178 Using Gestures and Shortcuts

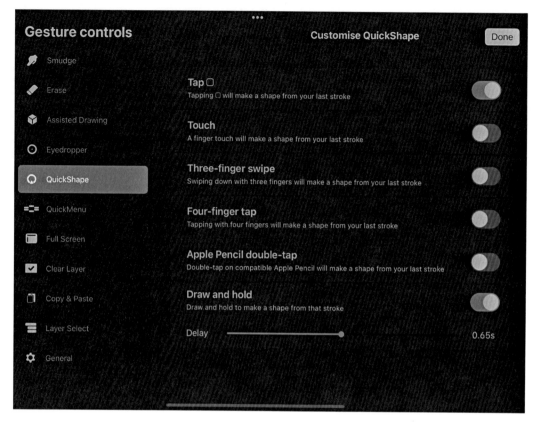

Figure 6.25: QuickShape gestures

Similar to the last option, you can toggle on as many as you like, as long as the same gestures are not assigned to any other feature. For **Draw and hold**, the slider labeled **Delay** lets you configure how long you must hold before QuickShape is invoked.

- **QuickMenu**: **QuickMenu** is an extremely convenient feature that lets you access commonly used actions in the form of a floating menu, as shown here:

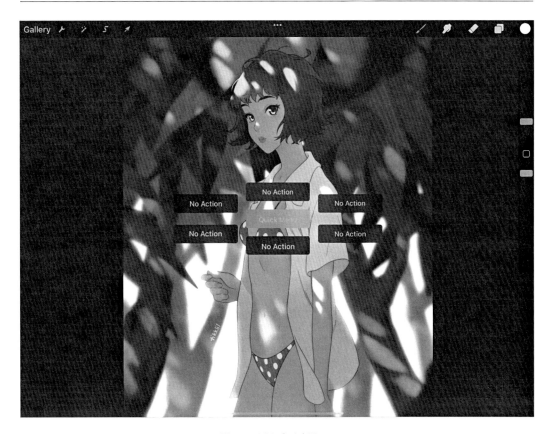

Figure 6.26: QuickMenu

It doesn't have a gesture allotted to it by default, so you have to turn it on yourself. The following gesture options are available for you to choose from, which can invoke **QuickMenu**:

Using Gestures and Shortcuts

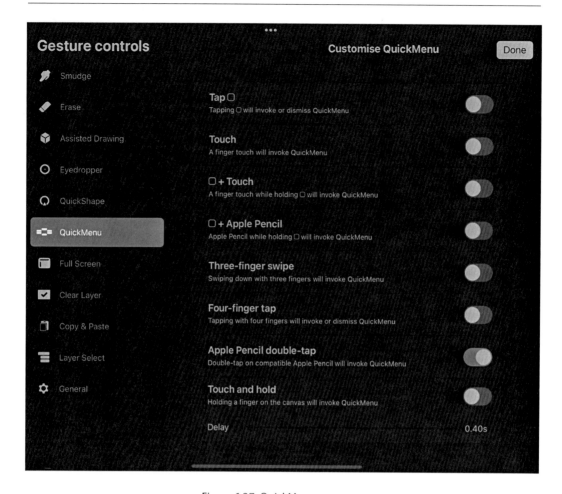

Figure 6.27: QuickMenu gestures

For **Touch and hold**, the slider labeled **Delay** lets you configure how long you must hold before **QuickMenu** appears.

Once you have activated it, you will need to personalize the options available on the menu to suit your needs. Here's how to do so:

1. Invoke **QuickMenu**.
2. Press and hold on the option you want to edit until a popup appears with a list of possible alternatives, as shown:

Figure 6.28: Edit QuickMenu

3. Select the option you want to replace the current one with.

Full Screen gestures

Full Screen is a feature that makes the interface of the software disappear to put complete focus on the canvas. By default, it is done by the four-finger tap gesture. The following gestures are also available to perform this action:

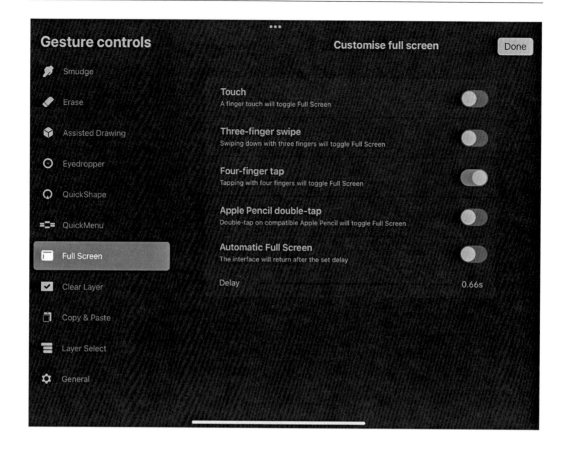

Figure 6.29: Full Screen gestures

If **Automatic Full Screen** is toggled on, then the interface automatically disappears once you start drawing. The slider labeled **Delay** lets you configure how long the interface takes to re-appear after you stop drawing.

Layer content gestures

The next set of features pertains to actions using the contents of layers. These are **Clear Layer**, **Copy & Paste**, and **Layer Select**:

- **Clear Layer**: The following screenshot shows the gestures available for deleting all the contents of the layer:

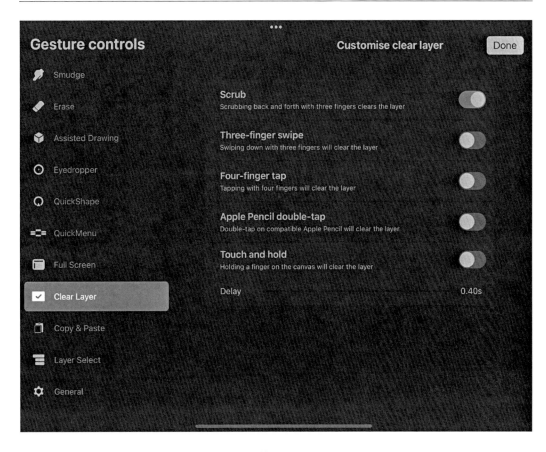

Figure 6.30: Clear Layer gestures

By default, it is done by the three-finger scrub gesture.

- **Copy & Paste**: The following screenshot shows the gestures that are available for invoking the menu with **Copy**, **Paste**, and other clipboard tools:

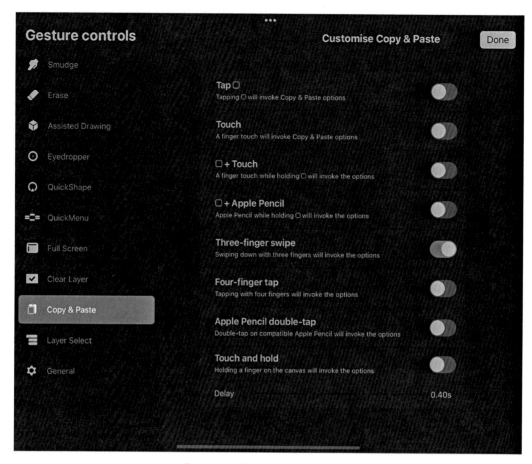

Figure 6.31: Copy & Paste gestures

Refer to *Chapter 5*, *Selecting and Transforming*, to learn more about this menu.

- **Layer Select**: This is different from **Select Layer Contents**. **Layer Select** lets you switch between layers without opening the **Layers** panel, just by touching their contents. It doesn't have a gesture allotted to it by default, so you have to turn it on yourself. The following gesture options are available for you to choose from, which can invoke **Layer Select**:

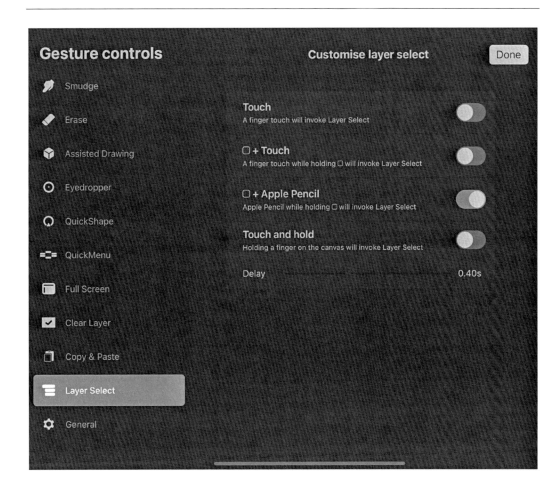

Figure 6.32: Layer Select gestures

Once you have activated this feature, follow these steps to use it:

1. Invoke **Layer Select**.
2. Hold and drag on the canvas, until you're touching the element you want to focus on.
3. Wait for a moment until a layer menu pops up, as shown in the following screenshot, containing the possible layers the element could be on:

Figure 6.33: Layer Select

4. Select the layer of your choice to jump to it.

General gesture options

The last item in the left column is labeled **General**. It has options to configure the overall way your gestures function, as shown here:

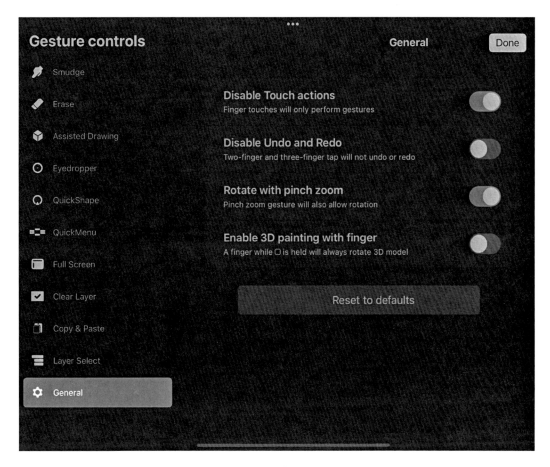

Figure 6.34: General gesture options

The following general options are available:

- **Disable Touch actions**: Enabling this will ensure that touches can only perform gestures. Drawing and using other painting tools such as **Smudge** and **Erase** will no longer work with finger touches.
- **Disable Undo and Redo**: This option disables two-finger tap **Undo** and three-finger tap **Redo**.
- **Rotate with pinch zoom**: This option lets you choose whether pinching can also rotate the canvas, along with zooming.
- **Enable 3D painting with finger**: By default, the Apple Pencil is used to paint on 3D models, while the finger touch is used to rotate the models. This option allows you to use your finger to paint 3D models. Rotating would then require you to hold the **Modify** button while rotating with your finger.
- **Reset to defaults**: Tap this button to revert all gestures to the default.

Once you are happy with the edits, tap on **Done** to finalize the changes. We have now covered the entirety of gestures in Procreate, so let's summarize.

Summary

Procreate has a robust and intricate system of gestures to enhance its functionality and accessibility. In this chapter, we covered the most commonly used default gestures, single touch gestures for accessibility, and basic gestures associated with layers. Finally, we discussed how you can customize these gestures for yourself, using Gesture Controls.

By now, you should have a general understanding of what gestures are, the different combinations of gestures available on the app, and how they can be used to complement your workflow. Gestures take a bit of practice to get used to, so it would help to tinker around with the software at your own pace.

In the next chapter, we will delve into the framework holding all artwork together—layers.

7
Organizing Your Layers

One of the major differences between digital painting applications such as Procreate and traditional paper or canvas-based art is the concept of layers. If you are familiar with other software, you already know this. However, for beginners or artists who are transitioning from traditional to digital art, layers can be hard to get used to. So, what are layers?

Unlike traditional art, which usually happens on a single surface, digital art often uses multiple layers stacked on top of each other to create the final image. You can visualize them as layered transparent plastic sheets, where each sheet contains a different part of the artwork, as shown in the following figure:

Figure 7.1: The artwork (left) and the separated layers (right)

Working with multiple layers instead of a single one is advantageous. It allows you to work on different elements without affecting the others. But, there's much more to layers than just convenience. They can actively augment and improve your workflow. In this chapter, we will look at all the different functions of layers and how to use them.

We're going to cover the following broad topics in this chapter:

- The Layers interface
- Organizing layers
- Exploring Layer Options
- Understanding blend modes
- Sharing layers

The Layers interface

The **Layers** panel can be opened using the overlapping squares icon at the top right-hand corner of the Procreate interface, as shown in the following screenshot:

Figure 7.2: The Layers panel

To be able to effectively work with layers, let's first get familiar with the different elements of the interface in the following sections.

Create a new layer

In the top right-hand corner of the **Layers** panel, you will spot a + icon. This button lets you create a new layer on top of your current layer.

Any image you import into the canvas automatically gets inserted as a new layer. This is done using the **Add** menu, shown in the following screenshot:

Figure 7.3: The Add menu

If you want to import an image or file but don't want it to appear on your time-lapse video, you can swipe left on **Insert a file** or **Insert a photo** to reveal a button that says **Insert a private file/photo**. If you tap this button, any image file you insert will not show up on the time-lapse video.

Layer thumbnail

On each layer, you can see a small box with a preview of the contents of that layer. This is the layer thumbnail:

Figure 7.4: Layer thumbnail

Layer name

Every layer, by default, is named "Layer x", where "x" is the order in which it was created. Layer names are customizable, as we will learn later in this chapter.

Primary layer

The primary layer is the one that is currently selected. When you draw, erase, or smudge, it will affect this layer. In the **Layers** panel, the primary layer is indicated with light blue. Tap on any layer to select it:

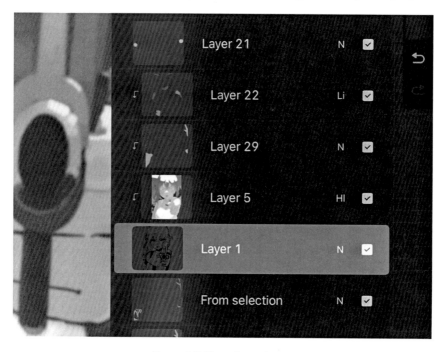

Figure 7.5: The primary layer

Blend mode

Procreate lets you use the contents of one layer and blend them with others using different modes. The blend mode of a layer is indicated by the small letter/s next to the layer name.

Tapping on the blend mode opens a drop-down menu below the layer, which has an opacity slider as well as a list of all the possible blend modes. This slider can be used to adjust the opacity of the layer.

Blend modes are discussed in further detail later in this chapter.

Layer visibility

The checkbox to the right of the blend mode can toggle layer visibility on and off. Check it to make a layer visible, and uncheck it to hide it.

Background color

Every Procreate document comes preloaded with a white canvas background. It appears at the very bottom of the **Layers** panel. The background can't be deleted like regular layers, only made invisible. Tap it to bring up the color slider and select a new background color, as shown in the following screenshot. If you disable it, it becomes possible to export PNG images with a transparent background.

Figure 7.6: Background color

Layer Options menu

When you tap on a layer, it brings up a menu, as shown in the following screenshot:

Figure 7.7: The Layer Options menu

This is the Layer Options menu. This offers you a wide variety of functions that you can perform using layers. We will learn more about Layer Options further ahead in this chapter. Now that we know the basic interface of the **Layers** panel, let's move on to the next section where we will be learning how to organize layers.

Organizing layers

There are several ways you can work with layers to take advantage of the numerous features they offer, such as selecting, grouping, moving, and transferring them. You will also learn about actions such as locking, duplicating, and deleting layers in the following sections.

Selecting layers

When selecting layers to work with, there are several ways you can do it:

- **Primary layer**: Also called the active layer, this is the layer that your drawing will apply to. Tap on a layer to select it as your primary layer. In the **Layers** panel, it will be highlighted with light blue.

- **Secondary layers**: To select more than one layer, select any one of them as the primary layer, then swipe right on all the other layers you wish to select, as shown in the following screenshot:

Figure 7.8: Primary and secondary layers

The primary layer is indicated in light blue and the secondary layers in dark blue. When multiple layers are selected, it makes it easier for you to transform, reposition, group, or delete them all at once.

All drawing, erasing, smudging, and adjustments, however, will only apply to the primary layer. For instance, you cannot apply **Hue**, **Saturation**, and **Value** adjustments to multiple layers at once.

Moreover, clipboard actions such as **Cut** and **Copy** also apply only to the primary layer.

- **Select Layer Contents**: You can select the layer as a whole or only the pixels used by its contents. This is done by a two-finger hold on the layer in question. Doing so will activate the **Selections** tool around those pixels and keep it active irrespective of which layer is currently the primary one. This is especially useful when you want to work on the area occupied by the contents of one layer, while being on a different layer. To learn more about the **Selections** tool, refer to *Chapter 5, Selecting and Transforming*.

- **Layer Select**: Though it sounds similar to the previous point, **Layer Select** refers to a completely different function. It's useful when you want to locate an element but can't find the layer it's sitting on. **Layer Select** can be invoked by a gesture of your choice. You can do so using the pathway **Actions | Prefs | Gesture Controls**, which will bring up the following screen, where you can assign a gesture to **Layer Select**:

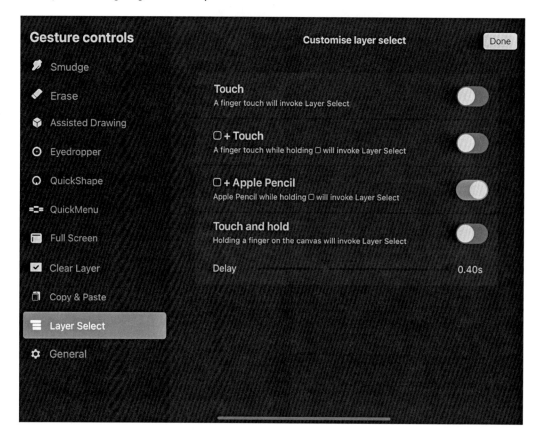

Figure 7.9: Layer Select gesture controls

To learn more about gestures, refer to *Chapter 6, Using Gestures and Shortcuts*.

Once you have activated this feature, follow these steps to use it:

1. Invoke **Layer Select** using your assigned gesture.
2. Hold and drag on the canvas until you're touching the element you want to focus on.

3. Wait for a moment until a layer menu pops up containing the possible layers the element could be on, as shown in the following screenshot:

Figure 7.10: Layer Select

4. Select the layer of your choice to jump to it.

Grouping layers

Layer groups are like collapsible folders that contain multiple layers. They are a great way to arrange and compartmentalize your layers to avoid confusion. There are three main ways to group layers:

- **Selecting multiple layers**: When you select more than one layer using the right-swipe gesture, a button called **Group** appears at the top of your **Layers** panel, as shown here:

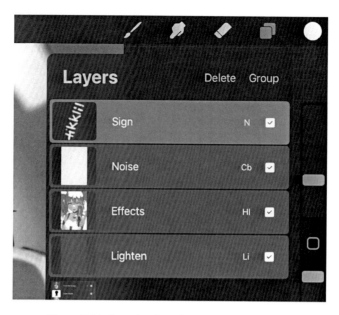

Figure 7.11: Grouping by selecting multiple layers

Tap this to group all selected layers into a single layer group.

- **Using Layer Options**: Tap on your primary layer to bring up the Layer Options menu.

  Tap on the **Combine Down** option to create a group with the layer immediately below. This works on layer groups as well, in which case the bottom layer gets shifted into the primary group. Moreover, you can also use this feature to combine two groups sitting back-to-back in the **Layers** panel.

- **Using gestures**: In the **Layers** panel, drag any layer or group over to another layer or group and hold until a blue box appears around the thumbnail of the latter, as shown in the following screenshot:

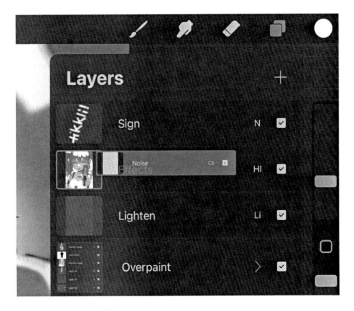

Figure 7.12: Grouping by dragging

At this point, release it to instantly group the elements together. Similarly, you can select multiple layers to drag and group.

> **Important Note**
> It's not possible to draw on a single layer when a group is selected. If this situation arises, **Layer Select** will be invoked and you'll have the option to hop to any layer in that group.
>
> Similarly, no effects and adjustments (such as **Gaussian Blur**) can be applied to a group as a whole.

Moving layers

It's very easy to re-order or move layers in the **Layers** panel. You might want to move a single layer, multiple selected layers, or a group of layers. To do so, simply press and hold the selected layers or groups. Then, drag them along the list of layers and release them at your preferred position, as shown in the following screenshot:

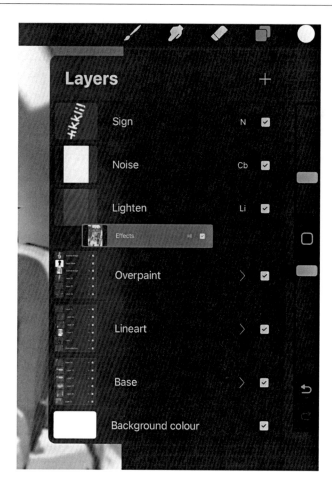

Figure 7.13: Moving layers

Transferring layers between canvases

It's possible to transfer layers from one canvas to another. This is useful when you want to reuse elements of one canvas in another. This action is performed by a series of simple gestures, as follows:

1. From the **Layers** panel, hold and pop out a layer, as shown in the following screenshot:

Organizing layers 201

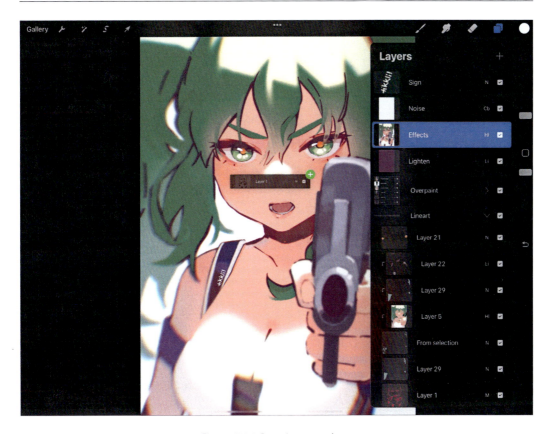

Figure 7.14: Popping out a layer

2. While holding the floating layer, use another finger to tap on **Gallery** at the top-left corner of the screen, and exit the canvas.

   At this point, you could directly release the layers into the Gallery. It will create a new canvas from each layer. This canvas will have the same dimensions as the parent canvas. If you had selected multiple layers in the first place, each layer will create a separate new canvas.

Figure 7.15: New canvas from transferred layer

3. Alternatively, keep holding the floating layer and use a free finger to tap on the canvas into which you want to transfer it.
4. Once the destination canvas loads, release the layer. Doing so will import the transferred layer into the current canvas right above its active layer.

These steps work with single as well as multiple layers.

Lock, duplicate, and delete layers

The last set of actions we're going to learn about are **Lock**, **Duplicate**, and **Delete**. In the **Layers** panel, swipe left on any layer to reveal these three buttons, as shown here:

Figure 7.16: The Lock, Duplicate, and Delete buttons

These actions work in the following ways:

- **Lock**: A locked layer shows a little lock icon next to its name. Turning on this option prevents any edits to the layer in question. This includes drawing, transforming, performing adjustments, or even deleting the layer. The **Lock** feature is useful when you want to preserve a layer and make sure you don't make any accidental edits to it.
- **Duplicate**: This option creates a copy of the layer on top of it.
- **Delete**: This option removes the layer from your canvas. This deletion can be reversed using **Undo**, but once you've closed the canvas or run out of **Undo** chances, it can't be undone.

Now that we have covered all the different ways to organize your layers, let's move on to the Layer Options menu, an essential feature associated with layers.

Exploring Layer Options

Each layer has an associated menu called Layer Options, which has an array of actions you can perform on that layer. Select any layer and tap on it again to bring up the Layer Options menu, as shown in the following screenshot:

Figure 7.17: The Layer Options menu

In this section, we'll look at this menu, one item at a time, to understand how to access the full functionality of your layers.

Rename

The first option is **Rename**. Use this to give your layer a custom name, as shown here:

Exploring Layer Options 205

Figure 7.18: Renaming a layer

Simply select any other tool or minimize the keyboard to save the new layer name.

Select

The **Select** option allows you to select layer contents. This will invoke the **Selections** tool around the pixels taken up by the contents of the layer. The selection will remain active until you turn it off, irrespective of which layer you're working on.

An easier way to select layer contents is by using two fingers to press and hold on a layer until the selection is activated.

Copy

Use the **Copy** option to copy the contents of the layer and make it available on your clipboard. You can paste these contents into the same canvas, a different canvas, or even create a fresh canvas from the Gallery. You can also paste it onto the text editor of most apps, messaging platforms, and emails.

Fill Layer

Tapping on **Fill Layer** fills the whole layer with the currently selected color. If the layer is alpha locked, only the non-transparent pixels will be filled.

Clear

The **Clear** option is used to clear the contents of the layer. This can be reversed using **Undo**, but can't if you have run out of the **Undo** option or closed the canvas.

An easier way to clear the layer is by scrubbing the screen with three fingers.

Alpha Lock

The **Alpha Lock** option locks the opacity of the layer. This means that you can no longer paint on the transparent pixels of the layer. To turn off the alpha lock, simply tap on this option again.

Mask

The **Mask** option helps you create a layer mask on top of a layer.

A layer mask is an adjustment layer that is automatically clipped to the primary layer. The mask is white by default. You can only paint in grayscale on a layer mask. Drawing with black will make the parent layer disappear, while the lightness or darkness of gray directly affects its opacity. We'll create a new white layer over the painting to demonstrate the function of layer masks:

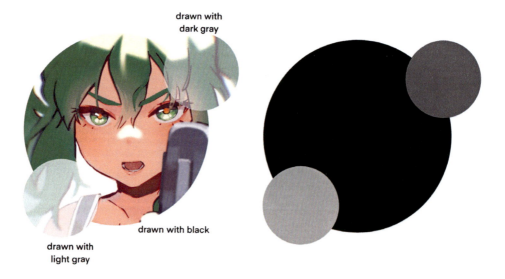

Figure 7.19: Result of a layer mask (left), and how the layer mask looks (right)

As you can see, the portion on the mask drawn in black completely removes the contents of the white layer, like creating a "window" in it. Additionally, the lighter the gray, the more opaque the white appears. A layer mask allows us to make edits to the parent layer non-invasively. This means that you can manipulate how the white fill layer will appear without making any actual edits to it. You can also transform and move the mask layer independently, as shown in the following:

Figure 7.20: Transforming a layer mask

Clipping Mask

The **Clipping Mask** option lets you clip the current layer to the one below it. This means that the layer on top will now follow the opacity rules of the layer on the bottom, and you will only be able to paint on pixels that are opaque on the bottom layer. It's very useful when you don't want your shading or other elements to spill over the edges of the base, as shown here:

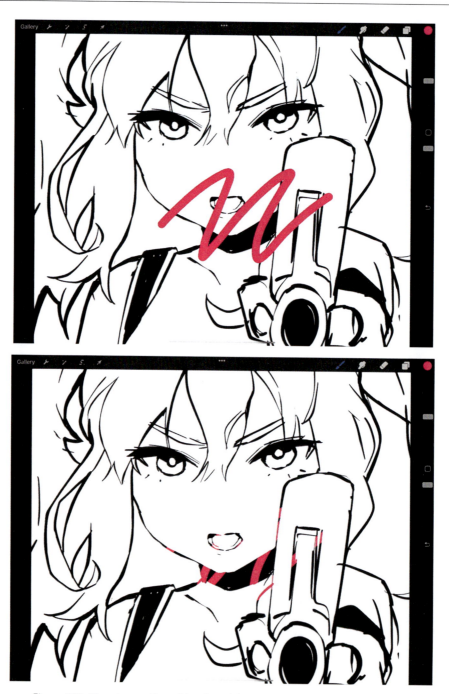

Figure 7.21: Drawing unclipped (top), and drawing clipped to line art (bottom)

Exploring Layer Options | 209

Drawing Assist

Procreate allows you to apply various kinds of assisted drawing tools to your art, such as perspective, symmetry, and grids. The **Drawing Assist** option lets you decide whether these settings will apply to a layer. When turned on, drawing on that layer will adhere to whichever assisted drawing tool is active until turned off again.

Learn more about the app's automated drawing tools in *Chapter 12, Using Assisted Drawing Tools*.

Invert

The **Invert** option changes all colors on the layer to their diametrically opposite color on the color wheel. This gives the layer a "photo negative" look, as demonstrated in the following screenshot:

Figure 7.22: Inverted layer

Reference

Reference is a great feature when you want to fill color easily into line-art. If you set the line layer as the reference, all other layers will respect the line-art while color dropping.

Merge Down

Tap on **Merge Down** to merge the current layer with the one below into a single layer.

Combine Down

Tap on **Combine Down** to group the current layer with the layer below into a layer group. When there is a group below the primary layer, it adds the layer to this group. Inversely, when this option is applied to a group, the layer underneath is added to it.

Now that we have gone through all the Layer Options, we are going to look into different blend modes in the next section, which are essential for making layers interact with each other.

Understanding blend modes

Usually, while drawing on a layer, you will notice that your strokes are appearing as opaque areas of digital "paint" obscuring the contents of any underlying layers. However, there are several ways to make layers "blend" and create different visual effects with each other. Blend modes allow you to choose how your layers interact. The layer on top that affects the layer below with its blend mode is called the blend layer. The layer below the blend layer is called the base layer.

The default blend mode is called **Normal** and is indicated by the letter **N** next to the layer name.

When you tap on **N**, you will see a menu open up under the layer. Aside from the layer opacity slider, it also lists all the blend modes available on Procreate. We will learn more about those in the following sections. They will be demonstrated by placing a block of magenta over the same illustration and applying different blend modes to it.

Multiply

The **Multiply** mode darkens the luminosity of the base layer by multiplying it with the blend layer. The resulting color depends on both the base and blend colors. It's a great option to use for shading:

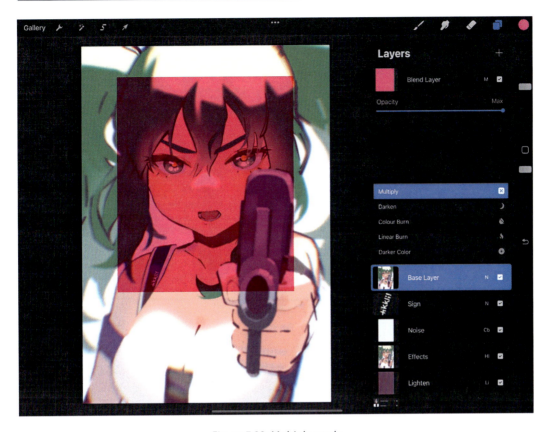

Figure 7.23: Multiply mode

Darken

Darken compares the color of the blend layer and the base layer and selects the darker of the two. As a result, all the pixels on the base layer that are lighter than the blend layer will appear to be the color of the blend layer:

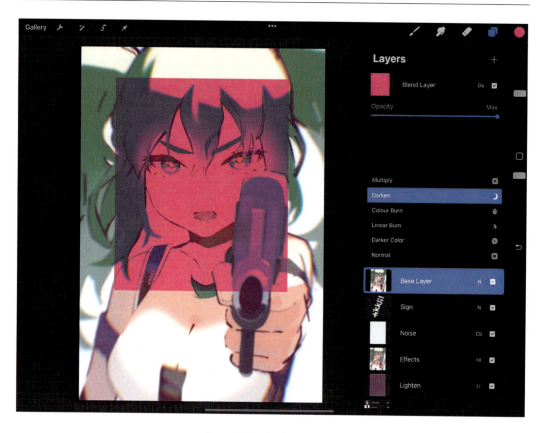

Figure 7.24: Darken mode

Color Burn

Color Burn also darkens the base layer like **Multiply**, but its effects are designed to produce a more traditional burn effect used in photography. Usually, the results are darker than **Multiply**:

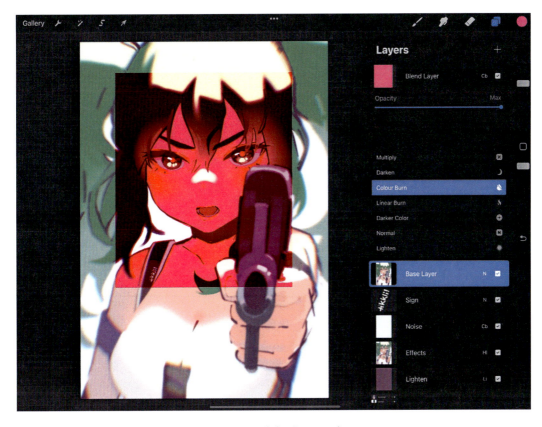

Figure 7.25: Color Burn mode

Linear Burn

Linear Burn burns the base layer according to the value of the blend layer. It produces lower saturation results than **Color Burn**, but generally darker results than **Multiply**:

Figure 7.26: Linear Burn mode

Darker Color

Darker Color functions in a way similar to **Darken**. However, instead of considering each RGB channel individually, it considers a composite of all channels, so it produces a more "averaged" result overall:

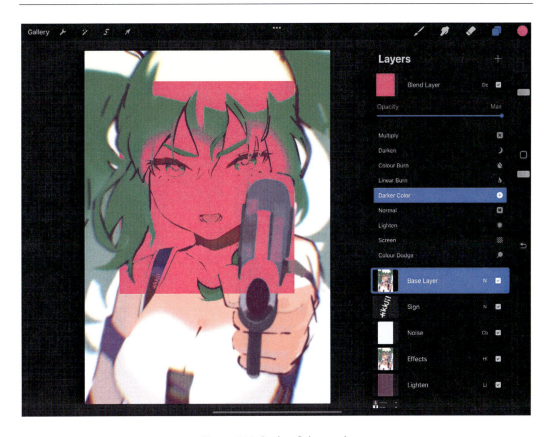

Figure 7.27: Darker Color mode

Lighten

Lighten is the opposite of **Darken**. It compares the color of the blend and base layers and selects the lighter of the two. As a result, all the pixels on the base layer that are darker than the blend layer will appear to be the color of the blend layer:

216　Organizing Your Layers

Figure 7.28: Lighten mode

Screen

The **Screen** mode lightens the luminosity of the base depending on both the base and blend colors. It's a great option to use for lightening and drawing highlights:

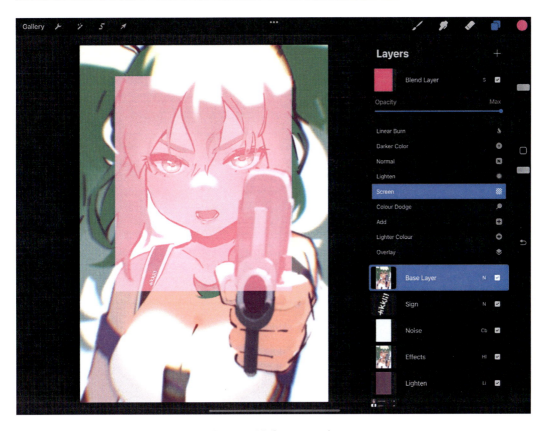

Figure 7.29: Screen mode

Color Dodge

Color Dodge also lightens the base layer like **Screen**, but its effects are designed to produce a more traditional dodge effect used in photography. Usually, the results are brighter than **Screen**:

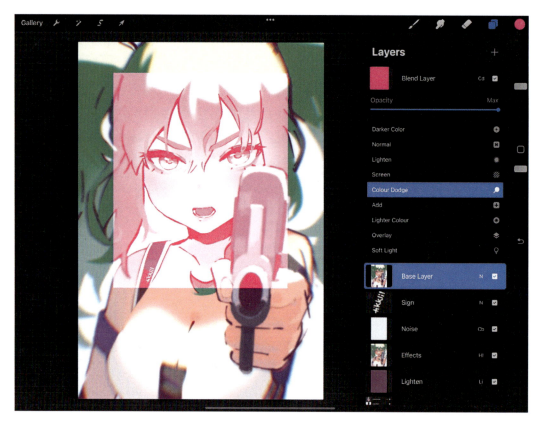

Figure 7.30: Color Dodge mode

Add

Add produces the strongest brightening effect out of all lightening blend modes:

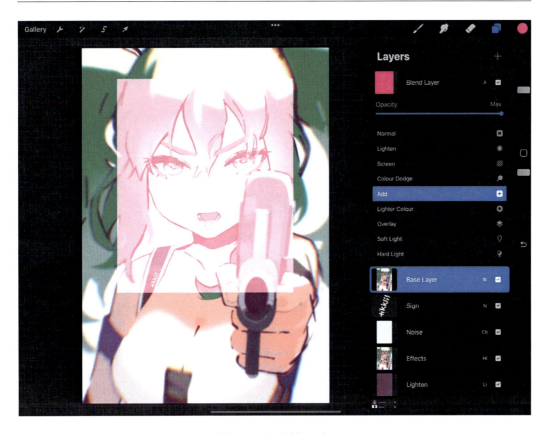

Figure 7.31: Add mode

Lighter Color

Lighter Color functions in a way similar to **Lighten**. However, instead of considering each RGB channel individually, it considers a composite of all channels, so it produces a more "averaged" result overall:

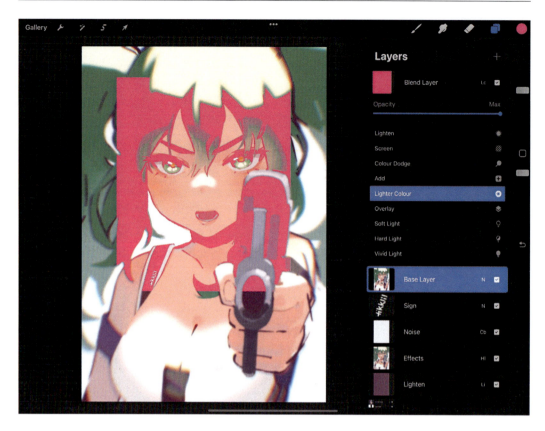

Figure 7.32: Lighter Color mode

Overlay

Overlay performs both lightening and darkening depending on the base layer. Lighter base colors are pushed to be lighter, while darker base colors are darkened further. In a way, it works like **Multiply** and **Screen** combined:

Understanding blend modes

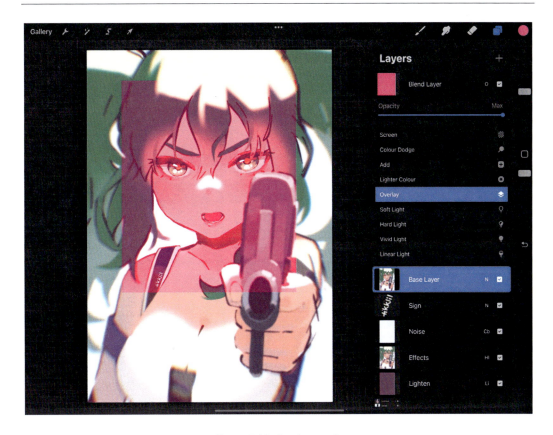

Figure 7.33: Overlay mode

Soft Light

Soft Light works like **Overlay**, but it applies subtler effects without pushing the contrast as much:

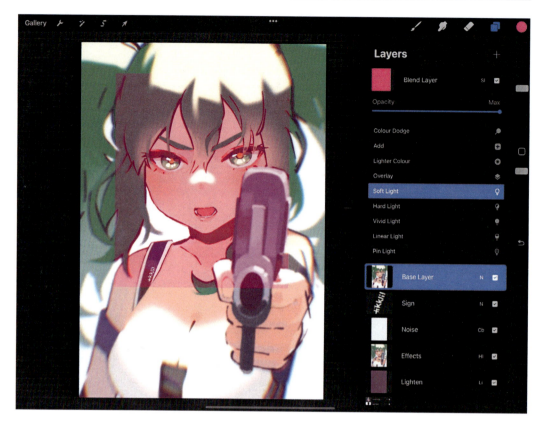

Figure 7.34: Soft Light mode

Hard Light

Hard Light produces similar effects as **Overlay**. It applies **Multiply** and **Screen** together, depending on the brightness of the blend layer, and has an intense effect:

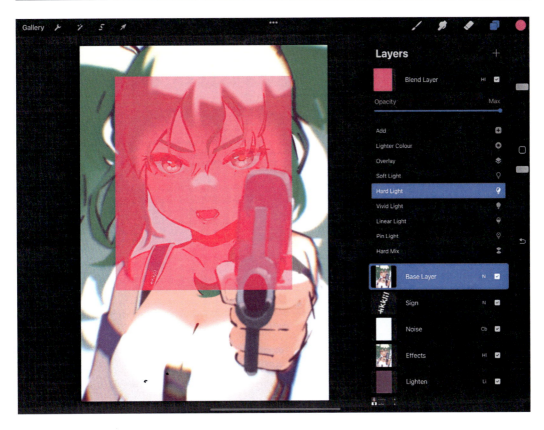

Figure 7.35: Hard Light mode

Vivid Light

Vivid Light works by darkening any color that is darker than 50% gray and lightening any color lighter than 50% gray. It may produce intense results at 100% opacity:

Figure 7.36: Vivid Light mode

Linear Light

Linear Light combines the **Dodge** and **Burn** effects. It applies **Dodge** to lighter colors and **Burn** to darker colors:

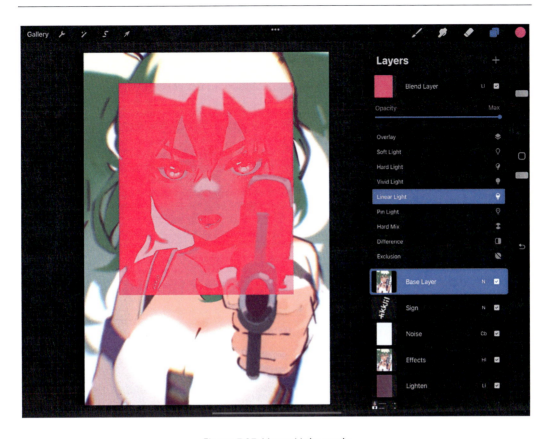

Figure 7.37: Linear Light mode

Pin Light

Pin Light performs **Lighten** and **Darken** together. This results in subdued mid-tones and an overall flattening effect:

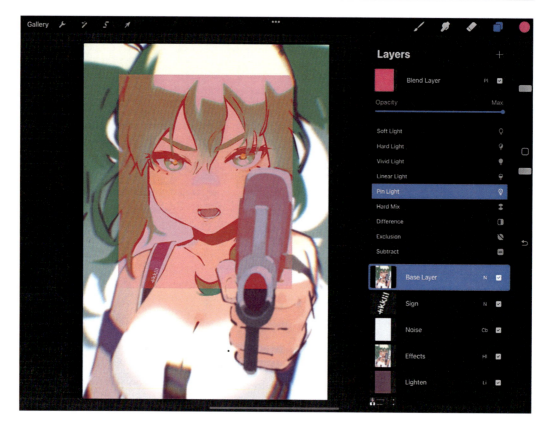

Figure 7.38: Pin Light mode

Hard Mix

Hard Mix has an extreme flattening effect. The image looks "posterized" since the result consists of only black, white, and the six primary colors (red, green, blue, cyan, magenta, and yellow). Which of these primary colors will be produced depends on the hue of the blend layer:

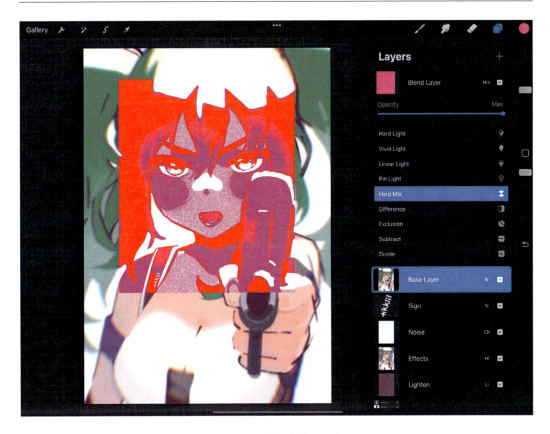

Figure 7.39: Hard Mix mode

Difference

Difference works based on the difference between the base and blend layers to create the resulting effect. White on the base layer inverts the blend color, while black produces no change. Dark grays on the base layer produce slight darkening:

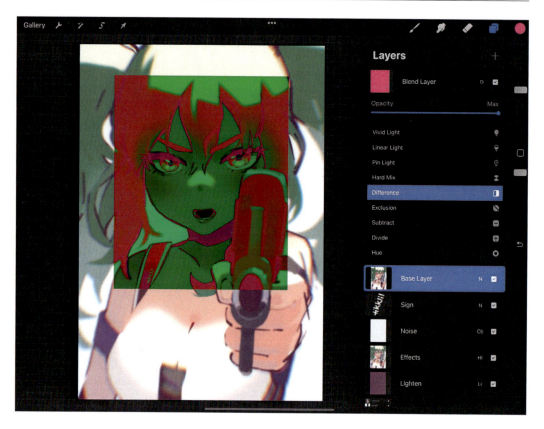

Figure 7.40: Difference mode

Exclusion

Exclusion works the same way as **Difference** when it comes to white and black, but it produces no change with dark grays:

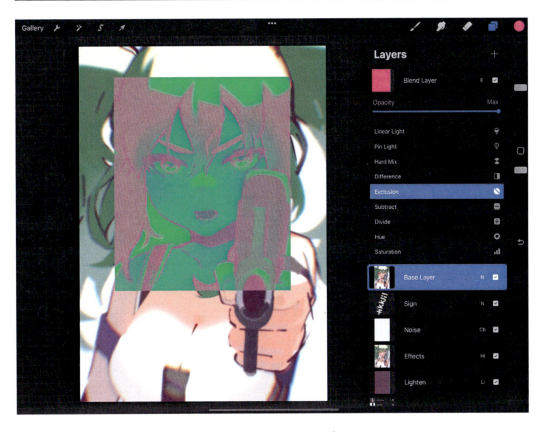

Figure 7.41: Exclusion mode

Subtract

Subtract produces a strong darkening effect by subtracting brightness. While this makes little difference to already dark areas, light areas show significant darkening:

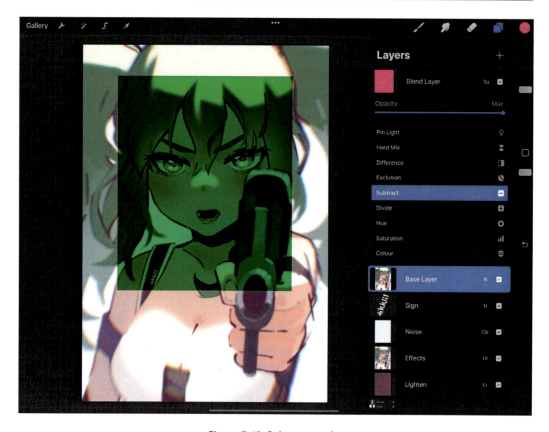

Figure 7.42: Subtract mode

Divide

Divide is the opposite of **Subtract**. Darker colors show significant lightening, while there's not much effect on already light areas:

Figure 7.43: Divide mode

Hue

Hue preserves the saturation and lightness of the base layer while imparting the hue of the blend layer to it. This produces a "monochrome" effect:

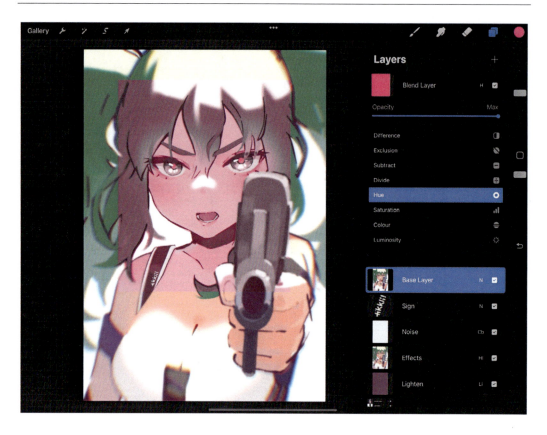

Figure 7.44: Hue mode

Saturation

Saturation preserves the hue and lightness of the base layer while imparting the saturation of the blend layer to it. When the blend layer is black, white, or gray, it gives rise to a grayscale image:

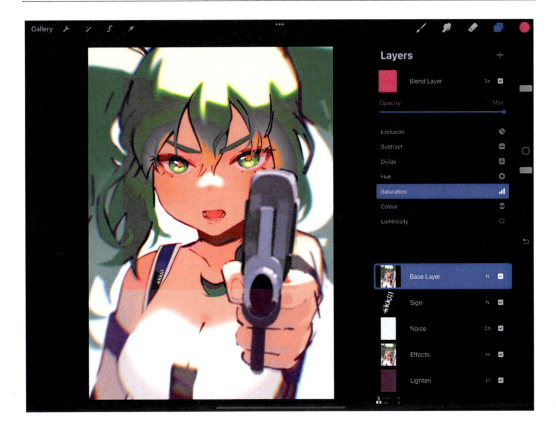

Figure 7.45: Saturation mode

Notice how this particular magenta doesn't produce a noticeable change when applied over this particular painting. This is because the painting is already at a similar saturation level as the magenta.

Color

Color preserves the lightness of the base layer while imparting the hue and saturation of the blend layer to it. This usually produces a more vivid monochrome effect than **Hue**, which doesn't take saturation into account:

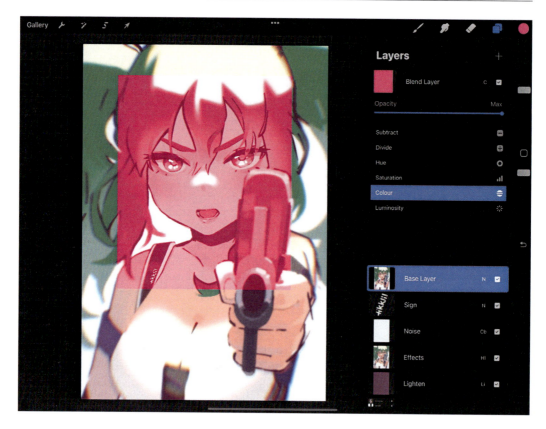

Figure 7.46: Color mode

Luminosity

Luminosity preserves the hue and saturation of the base layer while imparting the lightness of the blend layer to it. This produces an image that is uniformly light or dark but only with color variation:

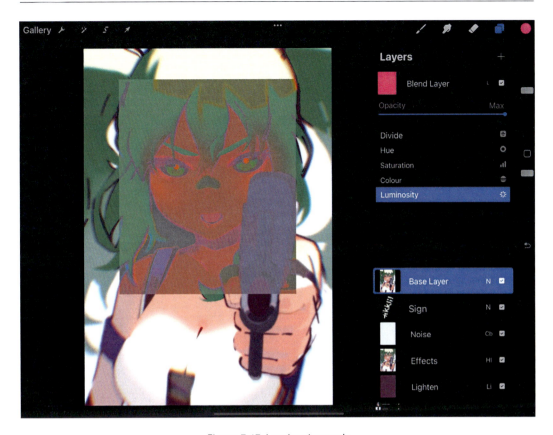

Figure 7.47: Luminosity mode

Blend modes require practice and experience to get used to, so reading their descriptions alone may not be enough to master them. Several of these blend modes produce drastically different results depending on the attributes of the image you're working with, such as lightness and color. Experiment in your own time to become more comfortable using them. Refer to *Chapter 16, Rendering Objects Using Blend Modes,* for a more hands-on explanation of this topic.

Next, we will learn how to share or export individual layers conveniently.

Sharing layers

When we talk about exporting artwork, we usually think of the composite image consisting of all the visible layers. However, there are many ways to export individual layers, a few selected layers, or take separate layers into account while exporting. There are two ways to do this, as we will discuss in the following sections.

Drag and drop export

This feature allows you to drag and drop a selected layer(s) directly into any compatible destination without having to close your canvas. This method works while exporting to another Procreate canvas, Files, Photos, iCloud, and so forth.

This can be done using the following steps:

1. Activate Split View. To learn about how Split View works, refer to *Chapter 1, The Gallery: Organizing Your Files*. Make sure you have both Procreate and your export location open in the two windows.
2. From the **Layers** panel, press and hold a layer to pick it up, and then drag it over to the destination screen.
3. Release the layer to instantly export it as an image of the same dimensions as your parent canvas, as shown here:

Figure 7.48: Drag and drop to export a layer

4. To export multiple layers, pick up one layer, then select the rest with your other hand, and then drag and drop the stack as usual.

Share Layers menu

Share Layers treats the visible layers of your canvas as separate images while exporting. The following are the options available under it:

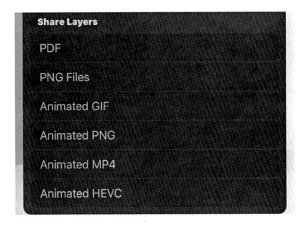

Figure 7.49: The Share Layers menu

Each of these options handles layers differently. Let's look at them one by one:

- **PDF**: The **PDF** option exports every visible layer as a separate page of a multi-page PDF file.
- **PNG Files**: This option exports all your visible layers as separate transparent PNG files.
- **Animated GIF/PNG/MP4/HEVC**: These last four options (**Animated GIF**, **Animated PNG**, **Animated MP4**, and **Animated HEVC**) are used to export animations from Procreate. These export types treat each ungrouped layer and layer group as a separate frame of animation and then export the animated result in the chosen format. Learn more about animation in *Chapter 12, Animating on Procreate*.

We have now covered all the features of layers in detail. Let's summarize our knowledge.

Summary

Layers form the framework of any Procreate document. In this chapter, we learned about the **Layers** panel and the interface associated with layers. We covered the different ways in which layers are organized, including how to select, group, move, and transfer layers, as well as the **Lock**, **Duplicate**, and **Delete** functions.

Next, we explained how two layers can be blended to produce different results using the diverse range of blend modes. Finally, we learned how to export individual layers or layer information in a single export as a multi-page PDF, PNG files, or animation.

In the next chapter, we will look into another robust and essential feature of Procreate—the **Brush Studio**.

8
Painting Tools and the Brush Library – Using and Organizing Brushes

Brushes form an essential part of any digital painting application. As the name suggests, they allow you to *draw and paint* in a digital sense. The term *brush* when used in the context of digital art has a wider scope of meaning than when used for traditional art. The term often refer to all the tools that can possibly be used for drawing, including but not limited to sketching, inking, coloring, and even erasing. All of these actions have types of brushes dedicated to them.

This chapter will take you through the basics of working with them. We will cover how brushes are organized in Procreate and how digital brushes work.

We're going to cover the following broad topics in this chapter:

- Paint, Smudge, and Erase Tools
- The Brush Library
- The Basics of Brush Studio

By the end of the chapter, you will have a working understanding of how digital brushes work on Procreate, how to organize them, and an overview of how to edit their properties.

The Paint, Smudge, and Erase tools

There are broadly three types of brushes that you can use on Procreate—**Paint**, **Smudge**, and **Erase**. As their names suggest, they vary in their usage. All three of these tools are available in the **Painting Tools** section in the top right-hand corner of the interface, as shown in the following screenshot:

Figure 8.1: Painting Tools

In the following sub-sections, we will learn about the **Paint**, **Smudge**, and **Erase** tools in more detail. We will also look at a new feature called Brush Size Memory, which has been recently added to Procreate.

Paint

The brush-shaped icon in the **Painting Tools** section invokes the **Paint** tool. This is the tool you will use to draw on the canvas. Tap on the brush icon again to bring up the **Brush Library** and select any brush to start drawing. The **Brush Library** for **Paint** is shown in the following screenshot:

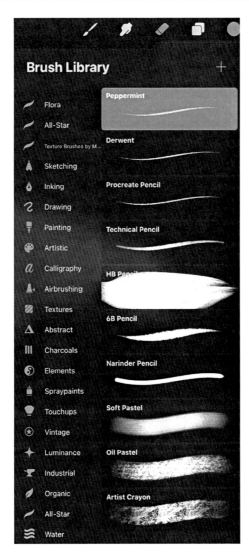

Figure. 8.2: The Brush Library

Smudge

The finger-shaped tool right next to **Paint** is called **Smudge**. It is used for distorting pixels on your artwork to give the "smudged" effect that is traditionally achieved by rubbing on paper with your finger. This effect is shown in the following screenshots:

Figure. 8.3: Original stroke (left), Blended using Smudge (right)

Similar to **Paint**, you can use any brush to smudge with, and the results will vary depending on the type of brush used.

> **Important Note**
> **Smudge** can have drastic effects if used with high pen pressure. It's recommended to use a softer touch while smudging to have subtler results.

Erase

The **Erase** tool is third from the left in the **Painting Tools** section, to the right of **Smudge**. It works as an eraser. It's used in the same way as **Paint** or **Smudge**, that is, by drawing with your finger or Apple Pencil.

The properties of the **Erase** tool depend on which brush you select. Many artists choose to work with the same brush for **Paint** as for **Erase**, for consistency.

Brush Size Memory

In the newest update of the application, Procreate 5.2, it's now possible to save up to four brush sizes on the brush size slider, for each separate brush. This feature is useful when you want to work with consistent brush sizes, without having to memorize the values on the slider.

Follow these steps to use Brush Size Memory:

1. Choose your preferred brush and adjust the size slider to get the brush size you want to save.

    You will see a window pop up next to the slider, which shows the current brush size. In the top-right corner of this window, you'll see a + sign, as shown in this screenshot:

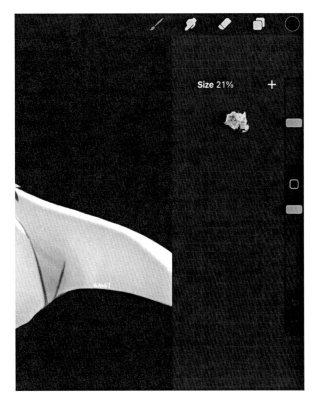

Figure 8.4: Adding brush size

2. Tap on the + sign. You'll notice a marker appear on the current position of the slider. This means that your selected brush size has been saved.

3. Similarly, you can add more sizes to the Brush Size Memory, up to a maximum of four per brush. In the future, you can simply tap on a marker to jump to any of the saved sizes.

4. To remove a saved brush size from the slider, tap on it to show the brush size pop up, as you did earlier. You'll notice that the + sign is now a - sign. Tap on the - sign to remove the saved size.

> Important Note
> Saved brush sizes are available across canvases. However, sizes saved to a painting brush will not apply to erasing and smudging brushes of the same type.

Now that we have covered the **Paint**, **Smudge**, and **Erase** tools, the next section will introduce the **Brush Library**, where the brushes are stored.

The Brush Library

Brushes on Procreate are stored in a carefully arranged list called the **Brush Library**. You can view this library by tapping twice on any one of the **Paint**, **Smudge**, or **Erase** tools, as shown in the following screenshot:

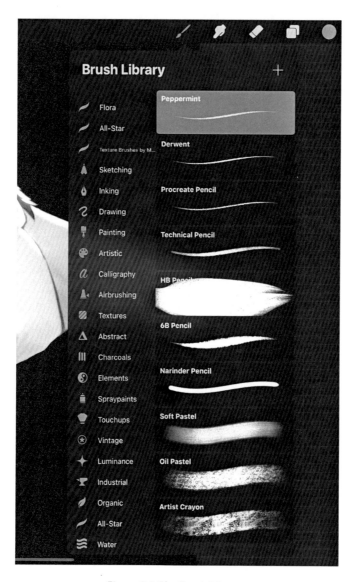

Figure 8.5: The Brush Library

The **Brush Library** offers a simple way to access and organize your brushes. In the following sub-sections, we will delve into the different features of the **Brush Library** and learn how to use these features.

Brush sets and brushes

When you open the **Brush Library**, you'll see that it's divided into two vertical panels. The one on the left contains brush sets. By default, the brushes are organized into sets or categories, such as **Inking**, **Sketching**, **Calligraphy**, and several more, as shown in the following screenshot:

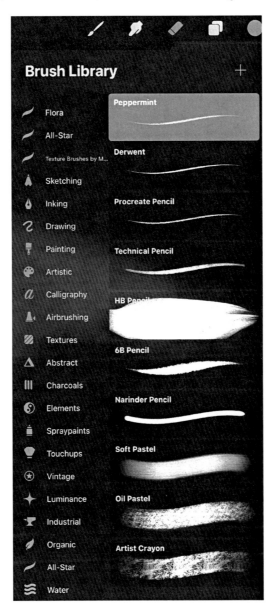

Figure 8.6: Brushes and brush sets

The second vertical panel lists all the brushes contained in the selected brush set. Each brush has a name along with a preview of the kind of stroke it can make.

Brush Library basics

The **Brush Library** provides an interface that allows you to edit, create, and organize brushes in a variety of different ways, as introduced in the following points. These actions apply separately to brushes and brush sets:

- **Add**:

    You can add your own new brushes or brush sets to your library.

    To add a new brush, tap on the + icon in the top-right corner of the **Brush Library** popover, as shown in the following screenshot:

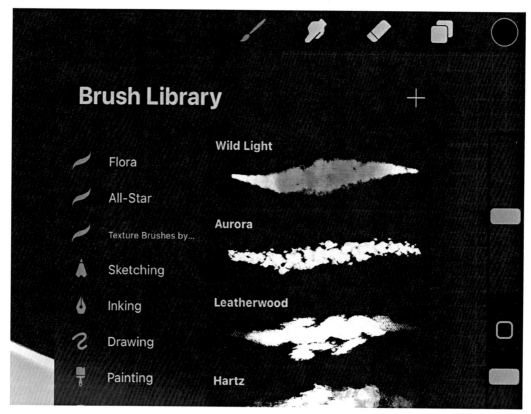

Figure 8.7: Add brush

This will open up the **Brush Studio**, as shown in the following screenshot:

Figure 8.8: The Brush Studio

Here, you can customize the properties of your new brush. We'll discuss the **Brush Studio** in further detail later, in *Chapter 9, Brush Studio Settings – Editing and Combining Brushes*.

To add a new brush set, scroll to the top of the **Brush Library** and tap on the + icon, as shown in the following screenshot:

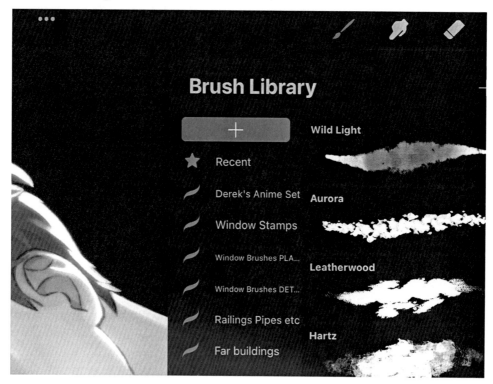

Figure 8.9: Adding a brush set

Doing so will instantly create a new brush set labeled `Untitled Set` at the very top of the column. The keyboard is also invoked automatically, as shown in the following screenshot:

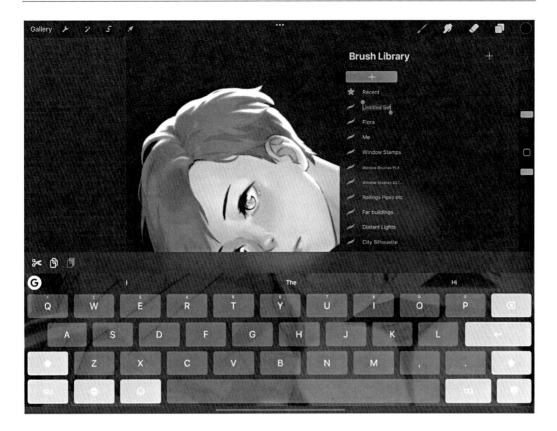

Figure 8.10: New brush set

This lets you name the new set whatever you want.

- **Edit**:

    You can open the **Brush Studio** directly from the **Brush Library**, to make edits to any existing brush.

    Simply select the brush you'd like to edit and tap on it again to bring up the **Brush Studio**.

- **Organize**:

    There are several ways to organize your brushes and sets. Most of them are done by dragging and dropping.

To organize brushes, simply touch and hold a brush until it *pops out* as shown:

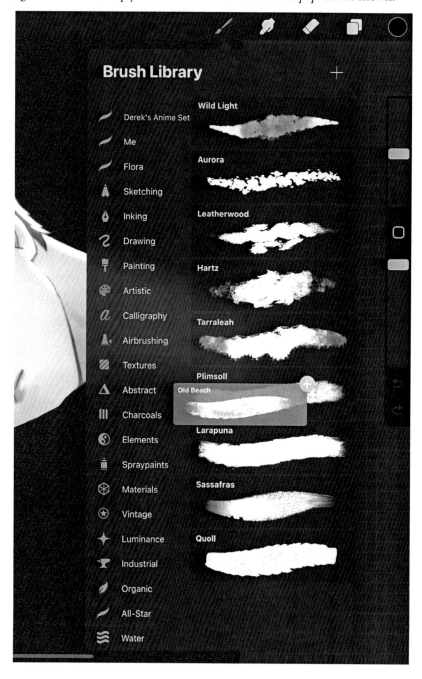

Figure 8.11: Popping out a brush

Then drag it over to your preferred brush set and lift your finger. The brush will be moved to that set.

Another way to do this is by popping out a brush and tapping the destination brush set with another finger. This will open the brush set, and you can directly release your preferred brush into it.

To organize brush sets, touch and hold a brush set until it pops out, then drag it to a desired position on the list.

You can also move several brush sets at once. When you pop out one set, a green + symbol appears on it, as shown in the following screenshot:

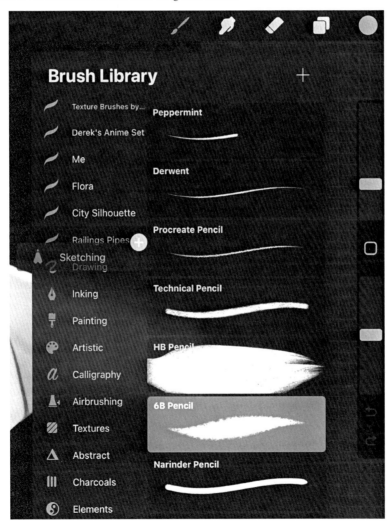

Figure 8.12: Popping out a brush set

Using another finger, tap on any other brush sets you want to reposition. They will be added to the floating stack, which you can drag and release at any position on the list.

> **Important Note**
> Moving a default brush from its parent brush set to another set will not remove it from the original set but will just create a copy of that brush in the destination set.

- **Duplicate**:

    Duplicating a brush is useful when you want to edit it without losing the original settings. Swipe left on a brush to reveal the following three options, as shown:

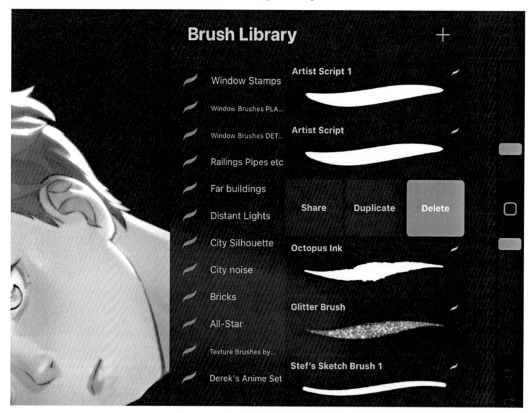

Figure 8.13: Brush menu

Tap on **Duplicate** to create a copy of the brush.

Similarly, you can also duplicate a brush set. Tap on a set you want to edit to reveal the menu as shown in the following screenshot:

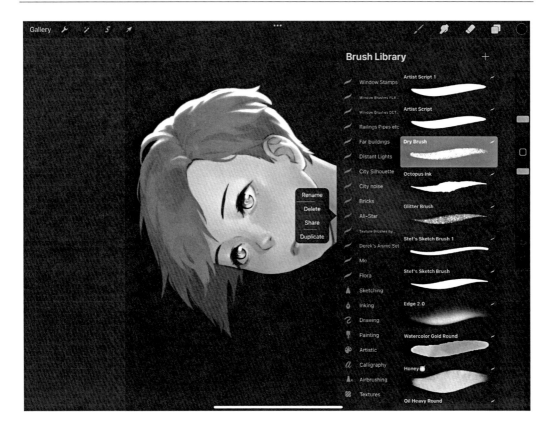

Figure 8.14: Brush set menu

Tap **Duplicate** to create an exact copy of the set just below the original. Since you can't delete or rename any default Procreate brushes or brush sets, this is a convenient way of making a completely editable copy of a core brush set. You can rename, delete, and share all the brushes in this duplicated default brush set.

- **Rename**:

Renaming a brush must be done through the Brush Studio, which will be explained later in the chapter, that is, in the *Brush Studio basics* section.

You can rename any non-default brush set or copies of the default sets. Tap on the brush set to bring up a menu as shown here:

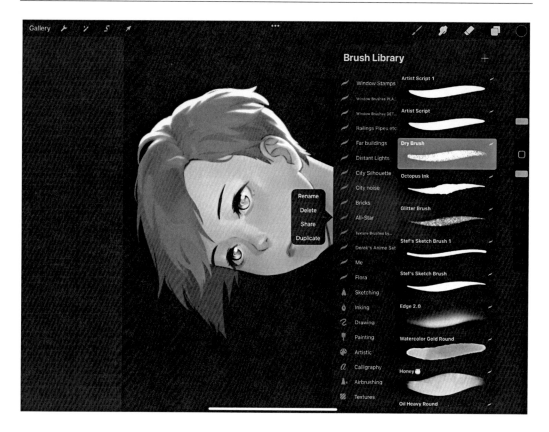

Figure 8.15: Brush set menu

Tap **Rename** to invoke the keyboard, type in the new name of the brush set, and minimize the keyboard to commit.

- **Delete**:

To delete a brush, swipe left on it to reveal the three buttons.

Tap on **Delete** to remove it from your library. Be careful while doing this, since this is a permanent action that can't be undone.

To delete a brush set, tap on said set to select it, and then tap on it again to bring up the menu. On this menu, select **Delete** to remove the brush set.

Default brushes and brush sets can't be deleted.

- **Share**:

Brushes and brush sets can be exported as `.brush` and `.brushset` files, which you can share with other users, who can then import them into Procreate.

To share a brush, swipe left on it and tap **Share**. This will create a `.brush` file that you can export to any location you'd like.

To share a brush set, tap on said set to select it, and then tap on it again to bring up the menu. On this menu, select **Share**. This will create a `.brushset` file, which you can then export to any location.

- **Import**:

    This function allows you to import external brushes and brush sets into the **Brush Library**. Follow these steps to import external brushes and brush sets into your library:

    I. Tap the + sign in the top-right corner of the **Brush Library** to create a new brush.

    II. When the **Brush Studio** opens, tap on **Import**, as shown in this screenshot:

Figure 8.16: Import a brush

III. Choose any .brush or .brushset file from **Files**, to add it to your library.

IV. To import a brush or brush set from outside Procreate, simply tap the file to open it. It'll either automatically open in Procreate or a prompt to open it in the app will appear.

Imported individual brushes appear at the bottom of the **Brush Library** in a set called **Imported**. Imported brush sets appear at the top of the library.

In the next subsection, we'll introduce how to organize your frequently used brushes.

Recent and pinned brushes

In the latest update, Procreate 5.2, two new features of the **Brush Library** were introduced, namely **recent** and **pinned** brushes. Let's get into the details of these two features:

- **Recent brushes**:

    At the very top of the **Brush Library**, you will notice a brush set named **Recent**. This set stores a list of your last used brushes, with the most recently used one at the top, as shown in the following screenshot:

The Brush Library

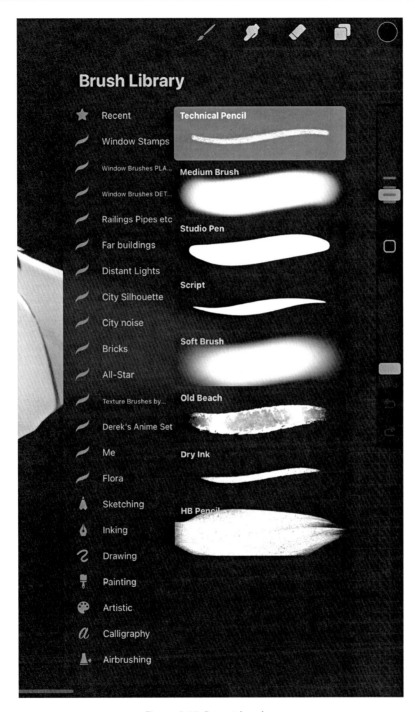

Figure 8.17: Recent brushes

It's useful when you want easy access to your recent brushes without having to jump between brush sets.

- **Pinned brushes**:

The **Pin** feature allows you to pin brushes to the top of the **Recent** list. These brushes have a little star symbol on them, as shown in this screenshot:

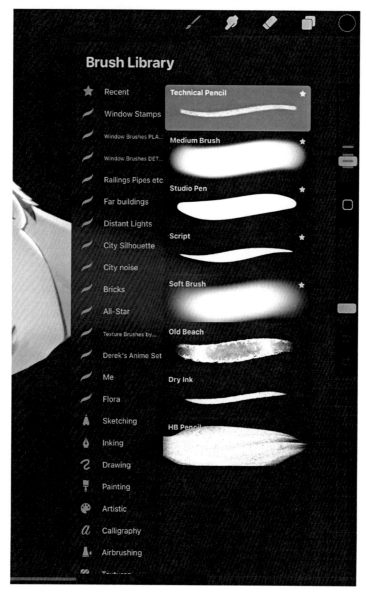

Figure 8.18: Pinned brushes

To pin a brush, swipe left on it and tap on **Pin**, as shown in the following screenshot:

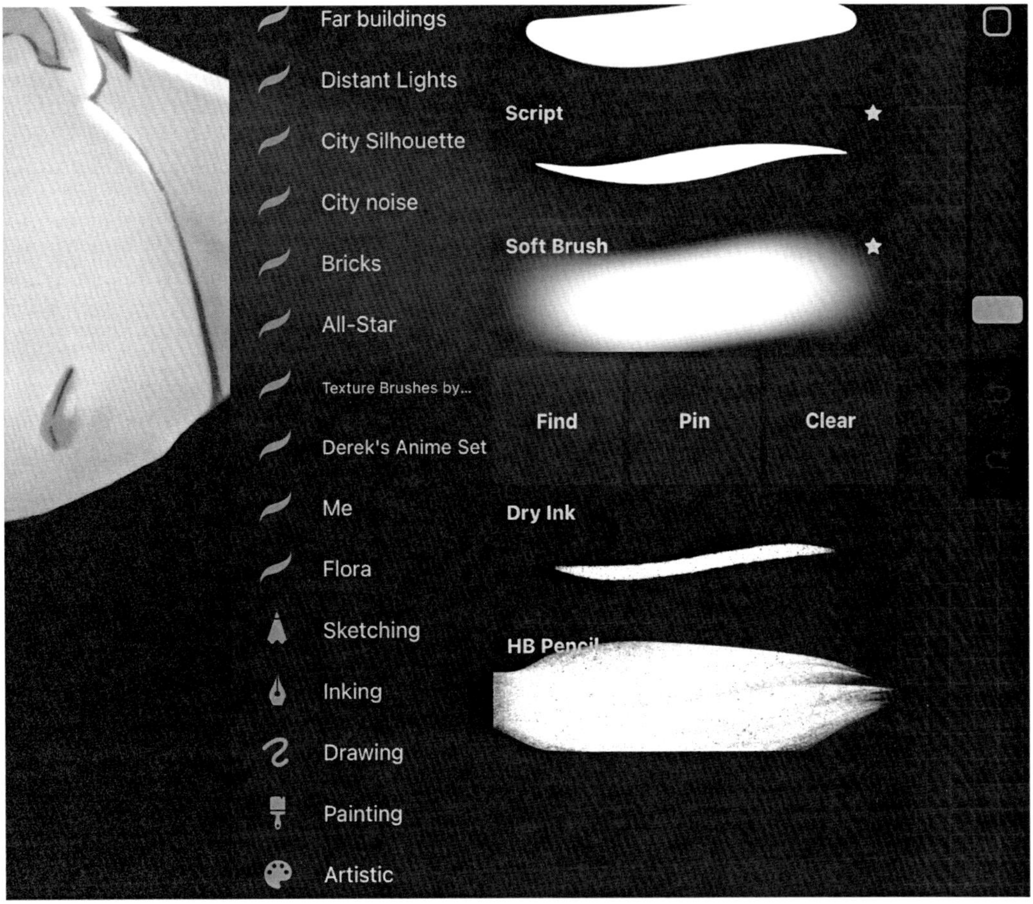

Figure 8.19: Pin a brush

Pinned brushes permanently stay at the top of the **Recent** brush set until you unpin them. It's useful if you frequently work with specific brushes and want to access them easily.

In this section, we covered the basics of the **Brush Library**. Here, you learned how to create, organize, import, and share brushes, as well as brush sets. Now that we know everything about the **Brush Library**, let's dive right into the next section, where you will learn about the basics of **Brush Studio**.

The basics of Brush Studio

Brush Studio is where you can create and edit brushes. It's a robust, feature-packed tool that allows you to have fine control of every aspect of your brushes, be it pre-existing brushes or your own creation. In this section, we'll look at an overview of the **Brush Studio** and some of its features.

There are two ways to open the **Brush Studio**. Tap on any existing brush to select it, and then tap on it again to open it in the **Brush Studio**, as shown in the following screenshot:

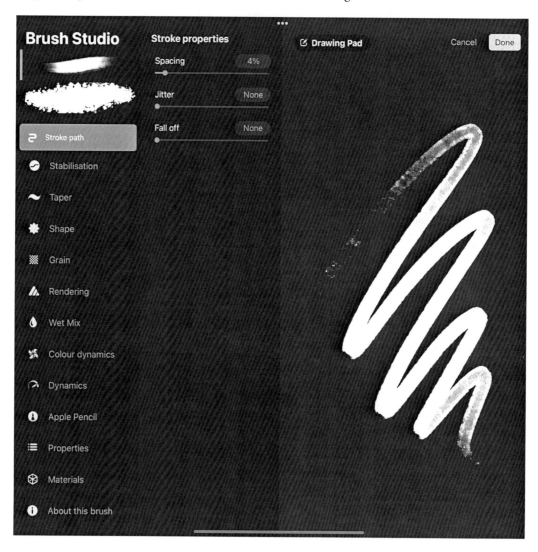

Figure 8.20: The Brush Studio

This is where you'll be able to make any edits to the selected brush.

The other way to open the **Brush Studio** is by creating a new brush. Open the **Brush Library**, and tap on the + symbol in its top-right corner. This will take you to the **Brush Studio** interface, where you can create a brush from scratch, as shown in the following screenshot:

Figure 8.21: Creating a new brush

There's one difference between these two pathways. If you try to create a new brush, the **Brush Studio** will sport an **Import** button in the top-right corner, which you won't find otherwise.

Interface

The **Brush Studio** interface is divided into three broad sections, as vertical panels:

- **Attributes**:

    The panel to the left lists the various attributes that a brush can have. You can make edits to these attributes separately to customize a brush according to your needs. Each attribute applies to specific features of a brush, and they are explained in detail in the *Brush attributes* section later in the chapter.

- **Settings**:

    The second panel is where the tweaking happens. The contents of this panel change with the currently selected attribute. The **Settings** panel consists of sliders, toggles, and buttons, to make it easier to adjust brush attributes. These controls are discussed in more detail in *Chapter 9, Brush Studio Settings – Editing and Combining Brushes*.

- **Drawing Pad**:

    The last section is the **Drawing Pad**, which serves as a scribbling area for you. It lets you test the edits you make to a brush without leaving **Brush Studio**. The strokes you make in the **Drawing Pad** are responsive to the changes you make to the brushes and update in real time to match with the current settings.

    Tap on **Drawing Pad** to bring up a panel that has more controls, as shown in the following screenshot:

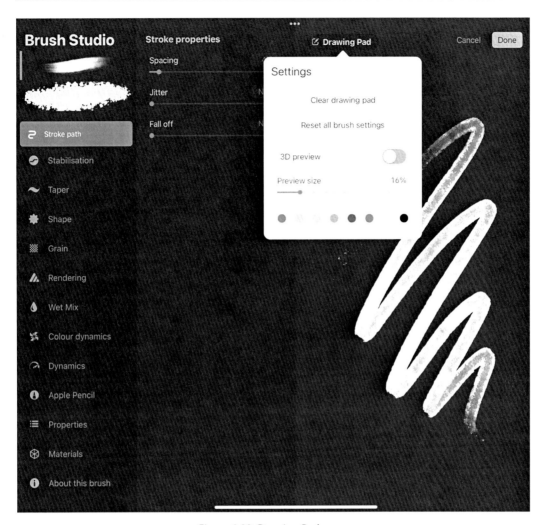

Figure 8.22: Drawing Pad menu

Clear drawing pad will clear all the scribbles you have made.

Tap on **Reset all brush settings** to revert the brush to its default settings and undo all your changes.

The slider labeled **Preview size** allows you to choose the preferred brush size for the preview.

Finally, the eight colored circles at the bottom of this panel let you choose a color to preview the brush in.

There is much more to the sliders, which offer finer control. The next subsection will introduce them.

Advanced brush settings

Each slider in the **Settings** panel has more advanced and precise controls, which will be introduced in this section. The number showing the value of a slider can be tapped like a button to bring up a number pad, which has finer settings to control it. There are three types of settings that can be applied to a slider:

- **Numeric**:

    This is the most basic type of setting, which is available on every slider. You can use this number pad to manually enter the value you'd like to assign to the setting, as shown in the following screenshot:

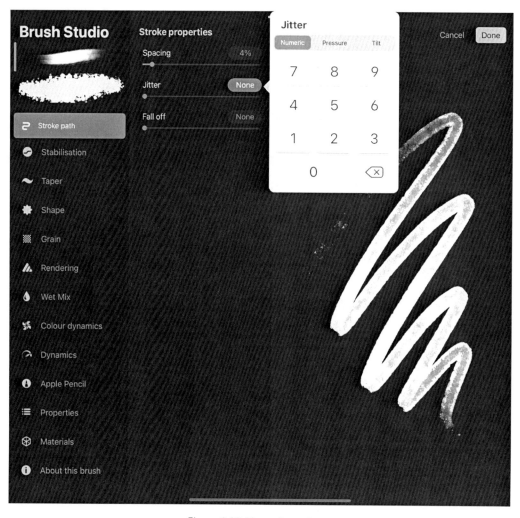

Figure 8.23: Numeric settings

It allows you more precise control rather than using the slider alone.

- **Pressure**:

    This is a special type of control that is only available in selected settings. It's toggled off by default. It lets you assign a pressure curve to the setting in question. The curve is a straight diagonal line by default, with two blue control points at either end, as shown in the following screenshot:

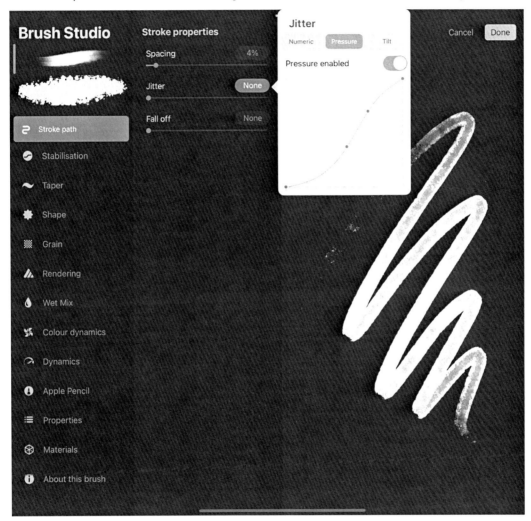

Figure 8.24: Pressure settings

Tap anywhere on the line to create a new control point and drag to change the shape of the curve. It can be edited using up to six control points in total.

To learn more about how pressure curves work, refer to *Chapter 4, Using the Actions Menu*.

- **Tilt**:

    This is another special control only available to select settings. It's toggled off by default. When activated, **Tilt** lets you choose the tilt angle of your Apple Pencil, beyond which the setting will be applied. Tilt is controlled by an interface with a quarter circle with a line intersecting it. Where these two meet is a blue control point, which lets you edit the angle, as shown in the following screenshot:

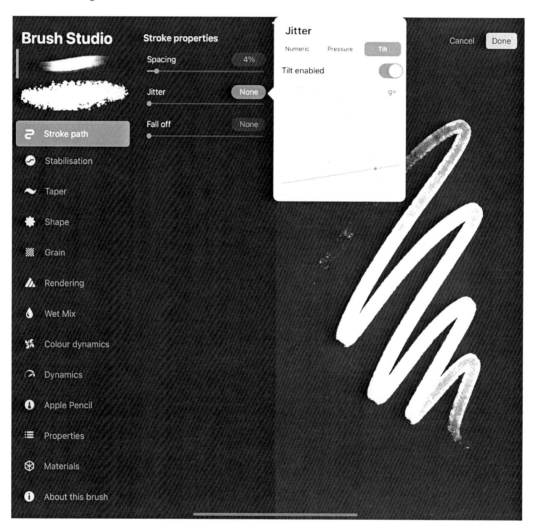

Figure 8.25: Tilt settings

By default, this angle rests at 9°. It can be adjusted to anywhere between 0° and 90°.

In the next subsection, we'll learn about what features of a brush are under our control.

Brush attributes

Brushes work on several attributes in Procreate. Each of them contributes to specific behaviors of the brush. This section will briefly introduce these attributes to make it easier for you to understand how to better use the Brush Studio. These attributes are as follows:

- **Stroke Path**:

  A brush works by placing a shape multiple times along a path created by the pencil while drawing. This attribute consists of settings to adjust how the shapes will behave with respect to the stroke.

- **Stabilization**:

  This attribute decides how "stable" a stroke is, by allowing you to reduce or increase its sensitivity to shakiness.

- **Taper**:

  This attribute makes your strokes thin at the beginning and at the end where the pencil lifts off, to mimic the way traditional drawing instruments work.

- **Shape**:

  Each brush has a basic shape that is repeated along a stroke. This attribute allows you to edit this shape. You may import your own shapes, or choose from the vast library that Procreate has to offer.

- **Grain**:

  Similar to **Shape**, some brushes have a texture overlaid onto their shape. This texture is also applied to the stroke. This attribute helps you edit the source grain, as well as to decide how the grain will behave while drawing.

- **Rendering**:

  This attribute helps you edit how "blended" your strokes will appear.

- **Wet Mix**:

  This attribute consists of a group of settings that help you mimic the way traditional wet paints work, such as saturating your brush with paint or mixing colors.

- **Color Dynamics**:

  This attribute contains a set of controls specific to how colors work in digital art, such as a brush changing colors in the middle of a single stroke, or precise variations in hue, saturation, and brightness in response to different pressures or tilts of your Apple Pencil.

- **Dynamics**:

  Controls how your brush responds to speed and tilt using this attribute.

- **Apple Pencil**:

    Use this attribute to explore how the Apple Pencil translates pressure and tilt to a stroke.

- **Properties**:

    This attribute lets you control certain aspects of the brush such as its behavior with respect to the screen orientation and size limits.

- **Materials**:

    This attribute lets you adjust what properties the current brush will have when it's used to paint on 3D models.

- **About this Brush**:

    This section contains important information about the brush, such as its name, creator, and creation date. You can rename the brush under this section. When creating an original brush, this is where you can sign your name, which will be associated with your brush.

Now that you have a working knowledge of how brushes work on Procreate, we can summarize this chapter.

Summary

Brushes are one of the most extensive, information-packed tools of Procreate. In this chapter, we covered the types of brushes and how to organize them. With **Paint**, **Smudge**, and **Erase**, you have learned about the three different roles a brush can take on. With the **Brush Library**, we discussed how brushes are sorted and organized, as well as how you can create, import, and share brushes and brush sets.

The chapter also briefly touched upon the **Brush Studio** and introduced the basics of editing a brush. In the next chapter, we will take a detailed look at features of the **Brush Studio** for a more complete understanding of brushes.

9
Brush Studio Settings – Editing and Combining Brushes

Every Procreate brushis, at it's core, is editable. In the last chapter, we learned how brushes have 11 attributes that can be tweaked to achieve desired effects. The **Brush Studio** is the tool that is used to do so. In this chapter, we will delve deeper into the myriad of settings it has to offer.

While the **Brush Studio** can be used to create and edit a wide variety of brushes, it also lets you configure how two brushes can be combined. This feature is called **Dual Brushes**, which you will also learn about.

We're going to cover the following broad topics in this chapter:

- Exploring the **Brush Studio** settings
- Dual Brushes

Exploring Brush Studio settings

In this section, you'll be introduced to the settings available under each attribute in detail. It's highly recommended that you apply these edits to your own brushes as you read, to see the changes in action. Some settings are more visible when observed in person.

Stroke path

To understand this attribute, you need to understand how digital brushes work. Each brush has a shape associated with it, just like traditional paintbrushes can be round, flat, or pointy. Digital brushes create the effect of a **stroke** by placing their shape multiple times in quick succession along a specific path. This path is the stroke made by your finger or pencil.

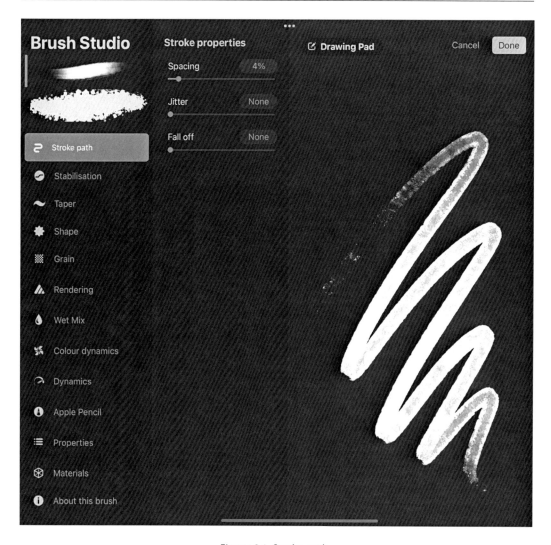

Figure 9.1: Stroke path

For convenience, let's call each instance of the brush shape a **stamp**, and the line on which stamps rest the **stroke path**. There are three adjustable settings under **Stroke path**:

- **Spacing**: This is the first slider. It lets you adjust the spacing between each stamp. The more you increase it, the more you'll see the brush stroke separate into its component shapes, as shown in the following screenshot:

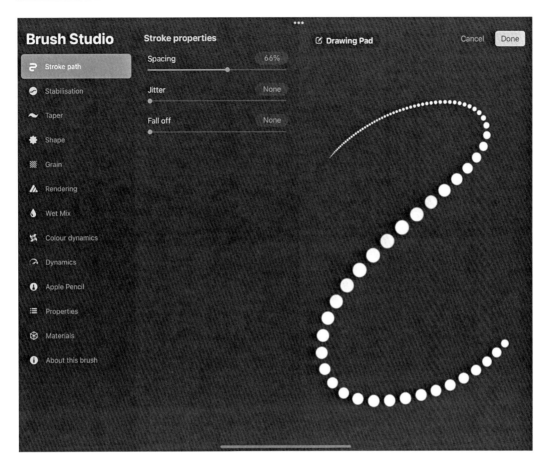

Figure 9.2: Spacing

Similarly, as you reduce spacing, the shapes will gradually merge to give rise to a single solid stroke.

- **Jitter**: This is a setting that offsets each stamp from the stroke path by a random amount. This gives the edges of your stroke a jagged look, as shown in the following screenshot:

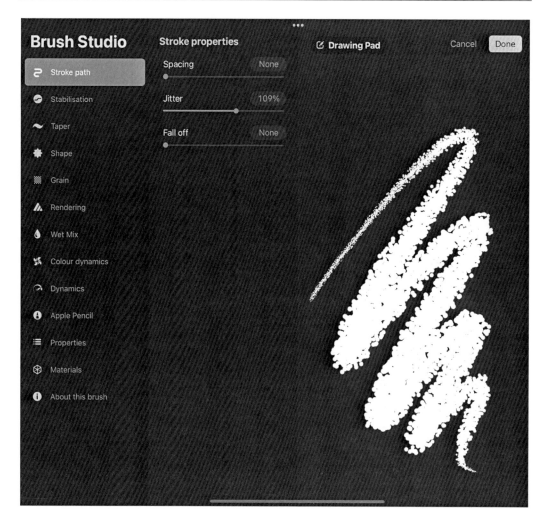

Figure 9.3: Jitter

As you increase the jitter, your stroke will go from slightly jagged to scattered around the stroke path. A high-jitter brush is great for making brushes with random features, such as particle effects, scattered leaves, and so on.

- **Fall off**: This setting gradually lowers the opacity of a stroke toward its end, until it completely disappears. With a high **Fall off** value, a stroke will start fading out sooner, and vice versa. The effects of **Fall off** are demonstrated in the following screenshot:

Figure 9.4: Fall off

Stabilisation

Stabilisation imparts a smoothing effect on your stroke by omitting the extremities of a shaky stroke, to give rise to a fluid, averaged-out stroke. The settings panel for this attribute looks like this:

Figure 9.5: Stabilisation settings

To understand the difference between a non-stabilised and a stabilised stroke, refer to the following screenshots:

Exploring Brush Studio settings 275

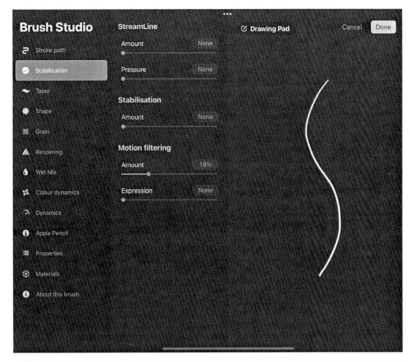

Figure 9.6: Non-stabilized stroke (top); stabilized stroke (bottom)

There are three settings under **Stabilisation**:

- **StreamLine**: **StreamLine** helps smooth out any wobbliness in your lines. This is especially useful in getting smooth strokes while inking and lettering. There are two sliders under this setting:

  - **Amount**: This controls the degree of stabilization applied to the strokes.
  - **Pressure**: This can be used to adjust how fast pressure sets in while drawing with the brush. When increased, pressure is applied to a stroke gradually and smoothly. If the slider is set lower, changes in pressure are registered quickly.

- **Stabilisation**: This setting also smoothes out your strokes. It does so by considering the average between the start and end points of the stroke and bringing the entire stroke closer to it. This results in overall straighter lines. **Stabilisation** is speed-sensitive, meaning the faster a stroke is drawn, the more stabilized it will be. Use the slider to determine how much stabilization to apply to your strokes.

- **Motion filtering**: This is Procreate's own way of interpreting stroke stabilization. While traditional stabilization squashes the extremities of a stroke toward the stroke path, **Motion filtering** gets rid of those extremities entirely, without any squashing. Unlike **Stabilisation**, **Motion filtering** works irrespective of the speed at which a stroke is drawn. There are two sliders used to adjust this setting:

  - Use **Amount** to control how much motion filtering is applied. Take note of how the strokes on the Drawing Pad change with the slider.
  - **Expression** is used to cancel out some of the effects of motion filtering, which can result in lines that are too smooth and lacking in character. **Expression** brings back some of the stroke's flavor. This slider is only active if **Motion filtering** is active and produces less noticeable effects the higher the filtering amount.

Taper

The next attribute on the list is **Taper**. It determines whether the start and end points of a stroke taper off to a pointy end like traditional paintbrushes. There are separate controls for adjusting the taper for the Apple Pencil and for touch. That means you will see two groups of similar settings titled **Pressure taper** (for Apple Pencil) and **Touch taper** (for dumb styluses and finger touch). The settings under this attribute are shown in the following screenshot:

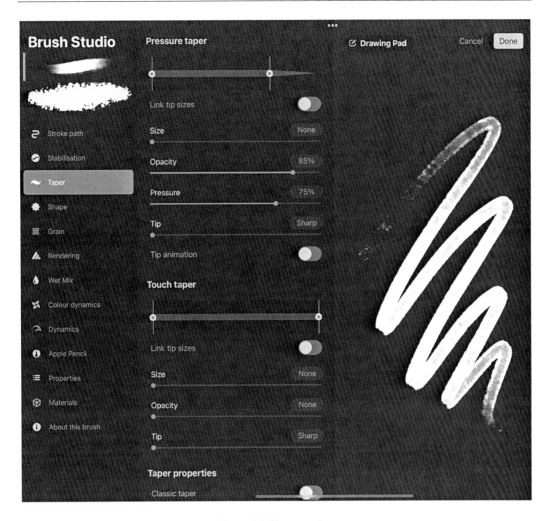

Figure 9.7: Taper settings

There are two main types of taper available on Procreate:

- **Pressure taper**: The Apple Pencil and other pressure-sensitive styluses apply taper by registering drawing pressure. These settings help you adjust how your strokes will be tapered when drawing with any such smart stylus.

  The **Pressure taper** slider gives you a visual representation of how strokes are tapered at both ends. The following are the settings under **Pressure taper**:

    - Toggle on **Link tip sizes** to make sure both sliders move together, ensuring equal taper at both ends of a stroke.

- The **Size** slider helps adjust how much the brush size is affected by the taper. A higher value results in more variation in size during tapering.
- The **Opacity** slider controls the transparency of the taper at the end of the stroke.
- The **Pressure** slider uses the pressure sensitivity of the Apple Pencil to apply a further tapering effect for a smoother, natural-looking transition.
- **Tip** lets you mimic painting with a brush whose own thickness affects the stroke. At low values, strokes appear as though they've been drawn using a fine-tipped brush. At higher values, strokes appear to have been drawn by a thick-tipped brush.
- **Tip animation** can be toggled on if you want to see taper effects applied to your strokes in real time as you draw. This purely depends on your preference.

- **Touch taper**: The second group of settings titled **Touch taper** affects strokes drawn with an instrument that is not pressure-sensitive, such as a finger or a regular stylus.

    The **Touch taper** slider works the same way as the **Pressure taper** slider. It gives you a visual representation of how strokes are tapered at both ends. The following are the settings under this option:

    - Toggle on **Link tip sizes** to make sure both sliders move together, ensuring equal taper at both ends of a stroke.
    - The **Size** slider helps adjust how much the brush size is affected by the taper. A higher value results in more variation in size during tapering.
    - The **Opacity** slider controls the transparency of the taper at the end of the stroke.
    - **Tip** lets you mimic painting with a brush whose own thickness affects the stroke. At low values, strokes appear as though they've been drawn using a fine-tipped brush. At higher values, strokes appear to have been drawn by a thick-tipped brush.

- **Classic taper**: The **Classic taper** toggle is the last heading under this attribute. It lets you switch back to Procreate's older style of taper.

> **Important Note**
> There's no **Pressure** slider under **Touch taper** since these settings are meant for styluses with no pressure sensitivity, and hence no pressure feedback.

Shape

The next attribute we will discuss is **Shape**. As mentioned earlier, every brush has a shape associated with it, which is stamped along a path to create a stroke. These settings, as shown in the following screenshot, help you control how this shape behaves for each brush:

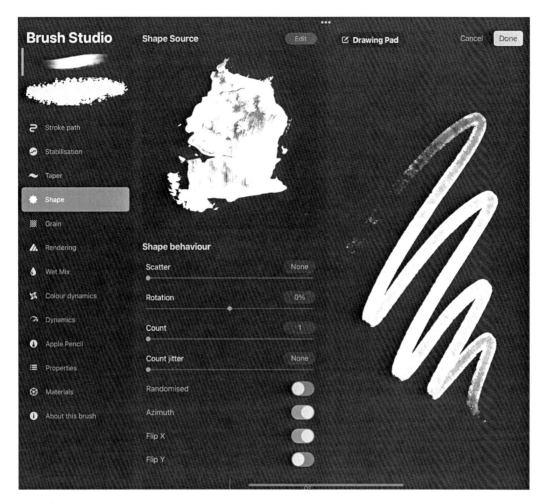

Figure 9.8: Shape settings

The settings under **Shape** are divided into the following subcategories:

- **Shape Source**: This is the original shape of your brush when stamped just once. It's displayed at the very top. You can, however, edit **Shape Source** by tapping on **Edit**, at the top-right corner of the settings panel. This will take you to **Shape Editor**, as shown in the following screenshot:

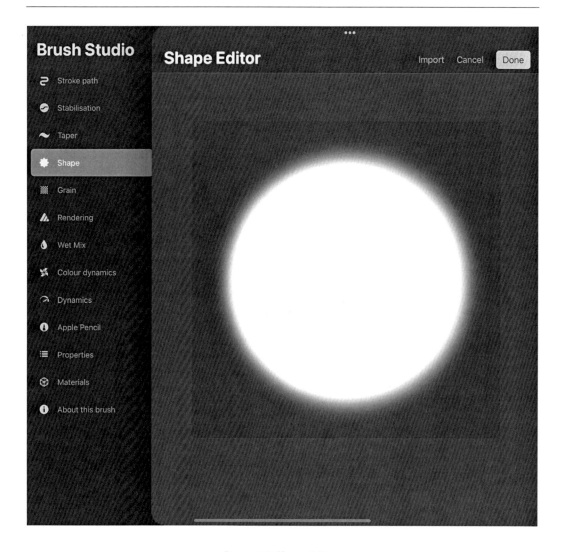

Figure 9.9: Shape Editor

Tap on **Import** in the top-right corner of the screen to bring up the menu shown in the following screenshot:

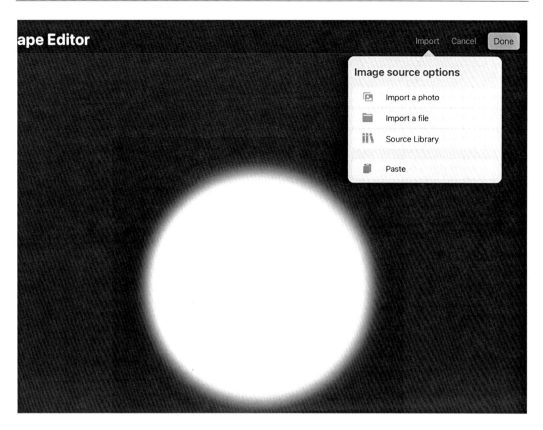

Figure 9.10: Import shape

As you can see, there are four options under **Import**:

- **Import a photo** lets you choose a new shape source from the **Photos** app.
- **Import a file** lets you choose a shape from the **Files** app.
- **Source Library** lets you access Procreate's own collection of shapes, shown in the following screenshot:

Brush Studio Settings – Editing and Combining Brushes

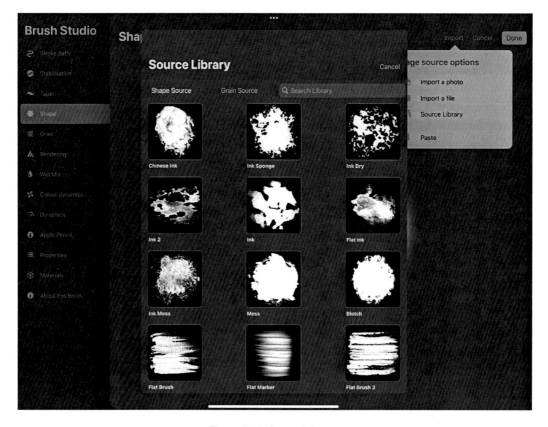

Figure 9.11: Source Library

- Tap on **Paste** if you have the new shape source already copied to your clipboard.

> **Important Note**
>
> Any image can be a shape source, which means you can draw custom shapes for your own brushes on Procreate itself. Remember that the luminosity information of the image will translate to transparency in the brush. The black parts of the image source will give rise to transparent areas and the white parts will result in opaque areas. So, if you prefer to draw the shape in black, import it into **Shape Editor** and double-finger tap it to invert its colors.

- **Shape behaviour**: The next set of controls is used to adjust specific behaviors of the shape, which we'll look into here:

    - The first slider in this section is titled **Scatter**. It makes each stamp rotate by a random amount, as shown in the following screenshots:

Figure 9.12: (Top) no scatter; (bottom) with scatter

The direction of rotation is independent of the stroke direction.

- **Rotation** lets you control the shape's rotation with respect to stroke direction. When turned up to **100**, it makes the stamp follow the direction of the stroke, as shown in the following screenshots:

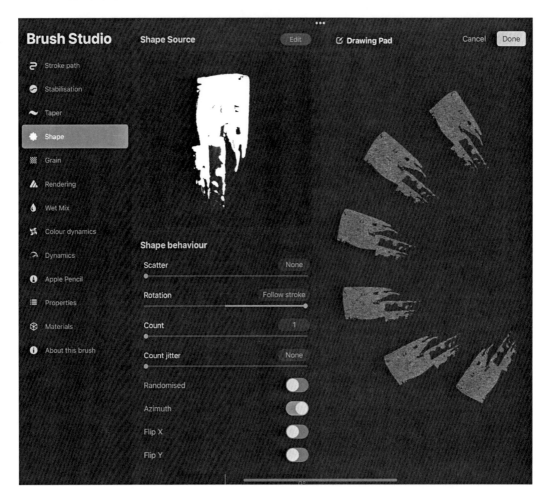

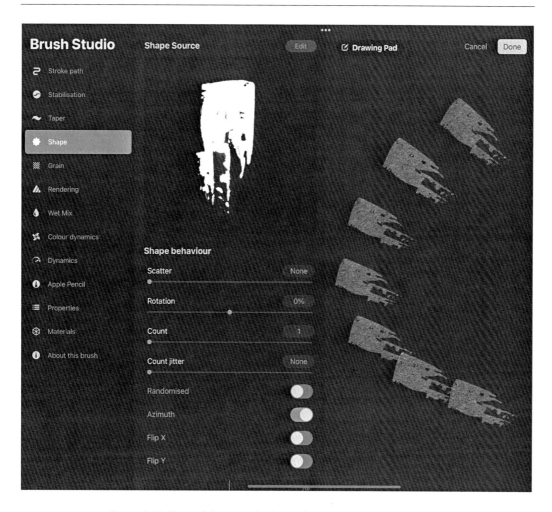

Figure 9.13: Shape follows stroke (top); shape doesn't rotate (bottom)

At **0**, the stamp doesn't rotate in relation to the stroke. When the slider is set to **-100** at the extreme left of the slider, it makes the stamp rotate in the direction opposite to the stroke.

- **Count** lets you decide how many times a shape stamps at once. You can adjust the count to lie between 1 and 16 times. It's useful when you want a brush to have a more solid stroke or vice versa. Note that functions such as **Scatter** will still treat each individual stamp as a separate unit, even if they occur at the same point. This can give rise to some interesting effects.

- **Count jitter** randomly varies the count of the stamps at each point. Set the slider to the highest count you want to allow, say **10**. You will now get anywhere between 1 and 10 stamps in any instance.

- **Randomised** is used to randomly rotate the shape for each stroke. This gives an organic feel to your brush.
- **Azimuth** works with tilt feedback from your Apple Pencil to affect the rotation of the stamps. It overrides the **Rotation** setting, but only while using the Apple Pencil.
- **Flip X/Y** can be used when you want to flip the base shape horizontally or vertically.
- The **Brush Roundness Graph** is a handy tool to transform your base shape easily. It's shown in the following screenshot:

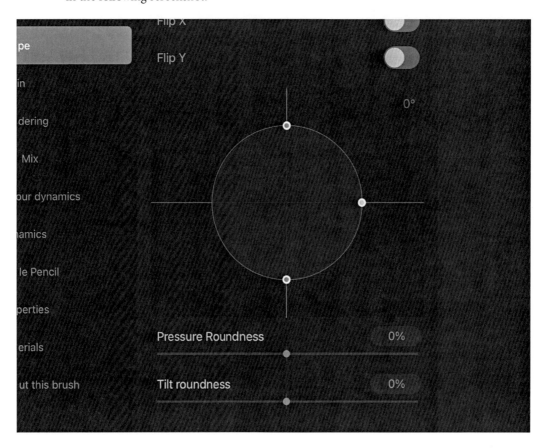

Figure 9.14: Brush Roundness Graph

The green node rotates the shape and the blue nodes squash it.

- **Pressure Roundness** correlates the Apple Pencil pressure with how squashed the shape will be. The higher the value, the more squashed stamps become when drawn with low pressure, as shown in the following screenshots:

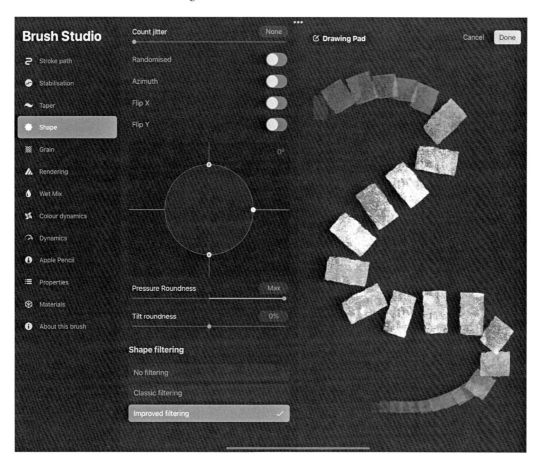

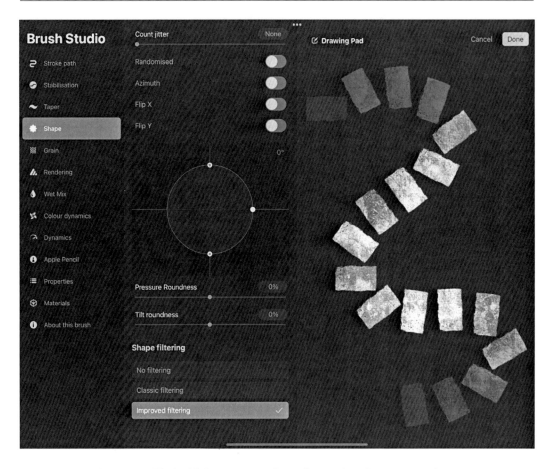

Figure 9.15: (Top) with Pressure roundness; (bottom) no Pressure roundness

- **Tilt roundness** correlates the Apple Pencil tilt with how squashed the shape will be. The higher the value, the more squashed stamps become when drawn with a low tilt angle, as shown in the following screenshots:

Exploring Brush Studio settings 289

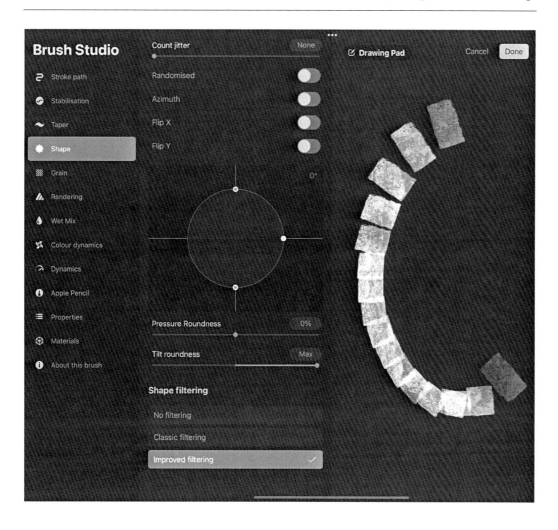

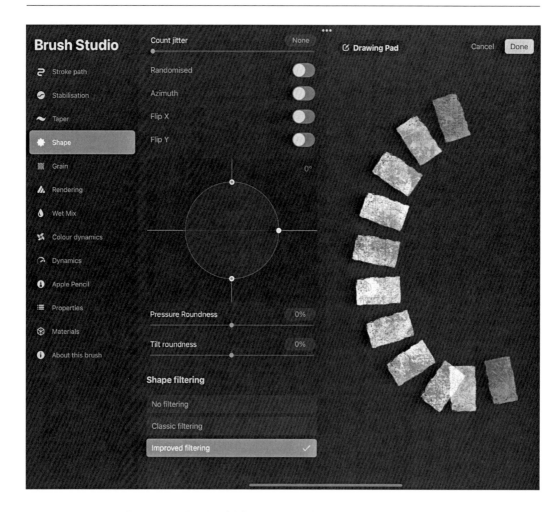

Figure 9.16: (Top) with Tilt roundness; (bottom) no Tilt roundness

- **Shape filtering**: Filtering controls how sharp the edges of a shape will appear. This is also known as **anti-aliasing**. The following are the settings under this option:

  - **No filtering** makes the brush retain the sharpness of the shape without any loss of information.

  - **Classic filtering** uses Procreate's older filtering method. This makes the edges of the brush appear less jagged.

  - **Improved filtering** uses a more advanced form of filtering, compatible with recent versions of Procreate.

Grain

Every brush consists of a shape, as we have learned in the previous sections. A brush has another associated attribute called **Grain**. This is the texture that is overlaid onto the shape. The grain, just like Shape, is one of the building blocks of a brush. The **Grain** settings allow us to control how the grain behaves. The settings panel is shown in the following screenshot:

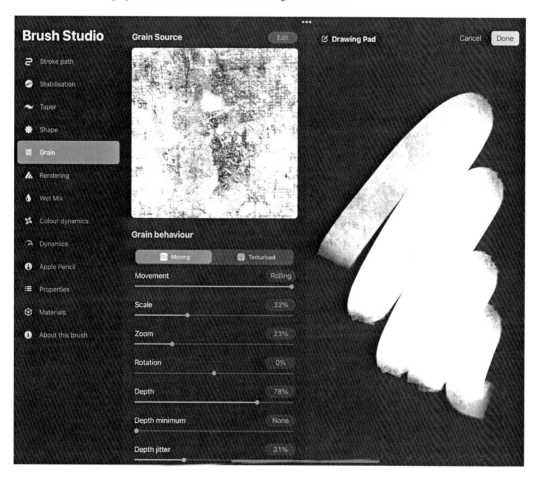

Figure 9.17: Grain settings

The settings under **Grain** are divided into the following subcategories:

- **Grain Source**: Just like **Shape Source**, **Grain Source** is an image containing the texture that is overlaid onto the brush. It is displayed at the top of the settings panel. For textureless brushes, the grain is a plain white image.

Edit the grain source by tapping on **Edit**, in the top-right corner of the settings panel. This will take you to **Grain Editor**, shown in the following screenshot:

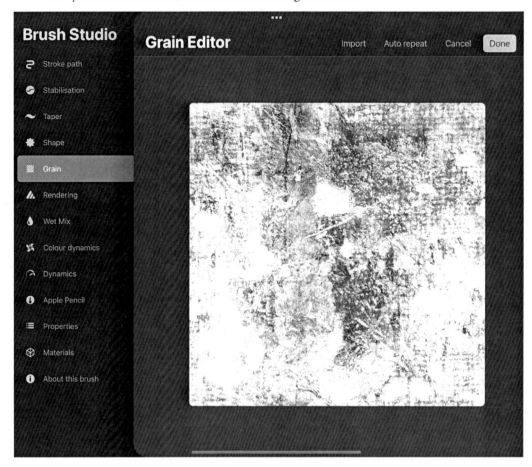

Figure 9.18: Grain Editor

Tap on **Import** in the top-right corner of the screen to bring up the menu shown in the following screenshot:

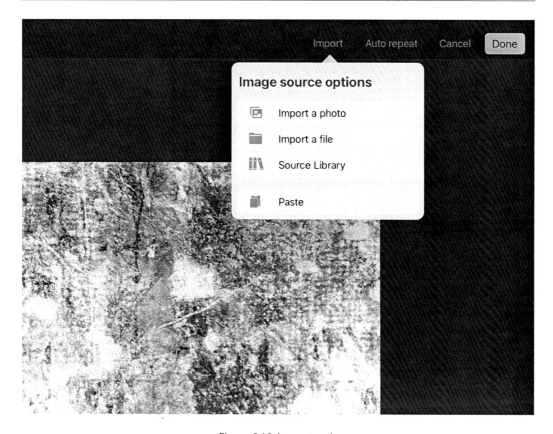

Figure 9.19: Import grain

It has the same four options that we saw in the *Shape* section previously:

- **Import a photo** lets you choose a new grain source from the **Photos** app.
- **Import a file** lets you choose a grain from the **Files** app.
- **Source Library** lets you access Procreate's own collection of grains, shown in the following screenshot:

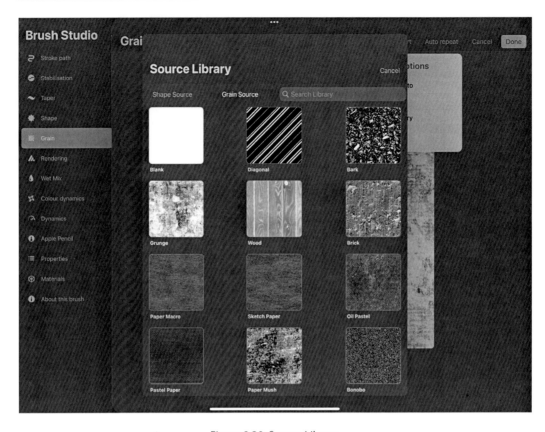

Figure 9.20: Source Library

- Tap on **Paste** if you have the new grain source already copied to your clipboard.

  Right next to **Import**, there's an option named **Auto repeat** that allows you to tweak how the grain image will be tiled to seamlessly cover larger areas. **Grain Editor** is explained in more detail later in this chapter.

- **Grain behaviour**: As the name suggests, this group of settings controls how the grain behaves. There are two ways a grain is applied to a brush—**Moving** and **Texturised**:

  - **Moving** and the settings under it make the grain drag along the brush stroke. Imagine this to be like painting by rubbing with a crumpled paper. It results in a streaky effect that is more organic.

  - **Texturised** and the settings under it apply the grain "under" the painted strokes as a continuous rolling texture. The results are similar to applying textured paper using a stencil. Use this for a uniform look.

We will go through the settings under these options in the following points:

- The **Movement** slider is only available when the grain is set to **Moving**. It's used to adjust how much the grain will drag along the stroke. At high values, it has an effect similar to texturized grain, while at low values the streaky dragging effect becomes more pronounced.
- The **Scale** slider adjusts the size of the texture.
- **Zoom** lets you decide whether the scale of the grain will change with brush size. At the highest value, labeled **Cropped**, the grain size stays constant at all brush sizes. At the lowest value, labeled **Follow Size**, the grain size scales proportionally with the brush size.
- The **Rotation** slider is available only under **Moving**. It's used to adjust the rotation of the grain in relation to the stroke direction. At the maximum value, the grain follows the stroke direction; at 0, the grain doesn't rotate at all, while at -100 the grain rotates in the opposite direction to the stroke to the stroke.
- **Depth** controls how strongly the grain is applied. You might want to make it completely disappear by setting the slider to the minimum or to increase its definition by upping the value. When the grain is set to **Moving**, the depth can vary with pressure.
- **Depth minimum** can be used to set the minimum depth of the grain, below which you can't go, even at the lowest pressure. This setting only works when **Depth jitter** is set to more than zero.
- **Depth jitter** randomly varies the depth of the grain at each individual stamp, ranging between the maximum and minimum depth values.
- **Offset jitter**, when toggled on, will offset the position of the grain itself with every individual stroke.
- **Blend mode** decides how the grain will blend with the underlying color of the brush.
- The **Brightness** and **Contrast** sliders are used to adjust the lightness and sharpness of the grain image. These sliders are available for both **Moving** and **Texturised** grains.

- **Grain Filtering**: Like **Shape Filtering**, this controls the anti-aliasing of the grain. The following are the settings under this option:

  - **No Filtering** makes the texture retain its sharpness without any loss of information.
  - **Classic Filtering** uses Procreate's older filtering method.
  - **Improved Filtering** uses a more advanced form of filtering, compatible with recent versions of Procreate.

- **3D Grain Behavior**: This setting consists of a toggle labeled **Grain follows camera**. This controls how the grain behaves on a 3D model.

  When toggled off, the grain remains static no matter which direction the camera is pointing.

  When toggled on, the grain shifts to face the direction of the camera.

Before we move on to the next attribute, we should learn more about **Grain Editor**, which has a slew of useful functions. The interface of the editor is shown in the following screenshot:

Figure 9.21: Grain Editor

To use **Grain Editor**, follow these steps:

1. The first step is to use the **Import** button, and import a source image from **Photos**, **Files**, Procreate's **Source Library**, or your clipboard. Ideally, it should be a square image, otherwise, it can appear squashed. This image will act as the grain texture, as shown in the following screenshot:

Figure 9.22: Grain Source

2. Use two fingers to rotate it at right angles to suit your preferred orientation. A two-finger tap will invert the colors in the image, if you want dark and light colors to be switched.

3. Tap on the **Auto repeat** button in the top-right corner. This will take you to the interface shown in the following screenshot:

Figure 9.23: Auto repeat

These controls help you adjust how the grain source will be tiled over a continuous surface and provide a real-time visual of how seamlessly one tile blends into another. Here's what each control does:

- **Grain scale** is used to resize the scale of each tile.
- **Rotate** applies rotation to the grain.
- **Border overlap** dictates how much of a tile's edge overlaps with the next.
- **Mask hardness** is used to adjust how sharp the mask of the overlapping tiles should be.
- **Mirror overlap**, when toggled on, symmetrically mirrors the grain at the overlap, so the transition between tiles is seamless.
- **Pyramid blending** is used for extra refinement, especially while dealing with irregular textures. It doesn't work as well with defined geometric patterns.

4. Once you are happy with the changes, tap on **Done** in the top-right corner. If you'd like to discard all your changes instead, tap on **Cancel**. This will take you back to the **Brush Studio**.

Rendering

This attribute is responsible for how your brush strokes interact with the canvas, and how individual brush strokes behave with each other. The settings panel for this attribute is shown in the following screenshot:

Figure 9.24: Rendering settings

The settings for **Rendering** are grouped into two sets:

- **Rendering mode**: The first section consists of options that let you choose the rendering style of each individual brush stroke. This is similar to working with diluted paint, all the way up to thickly applied paint. There are six types of rendering modes available:
    - **Light Glaze** is the lightest rendering mode. It's akin to using diluted paint.

- **Uniformed Glaze** is stronger, made to imitate the rendering used in Adobe® Photoshop® software.
- **Intense Glaze** is a heavier type of rendering that is like laying down slightly thicker paint.
- **Heavy Glaze** has a deeper rendering style. It preserves the opacity of the paint while mixing.
- **Uniform Blending** combines **Uniformed Glaze** with sharper rendering to create a thick, intense effect.
- **Intense Blending** is the heaviest rendering mode. This makes brush strokes and colors blend together while painting.

- **Blending**: The next set of sliders controls how brush strokes behave. The following are the various options available under this option:
  - **Flow** controls how much *paint* is laid down by the brush.
  - **Wet edges** blurs and dissolves the ends of a stroke to give the impression of wet paint bleeding into the canvas.
  - **Burnt edges** applies a fringe-like *burn* effect to the edges of a stroke, especially when strokes overlap, as shown in the following screenshot:

Figure 9.25: Burnt edges

  - **Burnt edges mode** decides the blend mode of the burnt edge effect.
  - **Blend mode** pertains to the mode individual strokes will use to blend with each other.
  - **Luminance blending** can be toggled on if you want the brush to consider only lightness and not color when applying blend modes.

Wet mix

This attribute is used to configure how and whether a brush will behave like it's using wet paint. This includes dilution effects, blending colors, as well as wet paint-specific behaviors, such as how much "paint" is loaded onto a brush and how quickly it runs out. The interface for the **Wet mix** settings is shown in the following screenshot:

Figure 9.26: Wet mix settings

These are the settings available under this attribute:

- **Dilution**: As the name suggests, this slider controls how diluted your strokes will look. Increasing the value adds more "water" to the paint.

- **Charge**: **Charge** refers to how much paint your brush is charged with at the beginning of each stroke. As a stroke gets longer, paint begins to run out and gradually disappears. Lift your pencil to recharge your brush with fresh paint. This gives you the experience of dipping your brush into paint before each stroke. The more the dilution, the more visible the effects of Charge are.
- **Attack**: Adjust how much paint the canvas catches from your brush. The more Attack, the thicker, more evenly applied the paint will be.
- **Pull**: This setting lets you control how much one stroke will be able to drag around the color from its surroundings. Visualize this like drawing on wet oil paint, so that your brush can still pull the previously applied paint with its current stroke.
- **Grade**: Every brush has a grade, which is how thickly it applies its own texture. Adjust the grade of your brush using this slider.
- **Blur**: This setting allows you to blur your brush strokes as much as you'd like.
- **Blur jitter**: Randomly vary the blurriness of the brush.
- **Wetness jitter**: Randomize the water content of your stroke. This works well when the dilution is set to high.

Color dynamics

This attribute affects how color behaves on your brush. One of the many advantages of digital paint is that you don't have to stick to one color in one stroke or even between strokes. **Color dynamics** is responsible for applying variations to the color of your brush while you draw. The settings under this attribute are shown in the following screenshot:

Figure 9.27: Color dynamics settings

These settings are divided into four sections:

- **Stamp color jitter**: This introduces variation in a stroke by randomly varying the color of each individual stamp. It'll result in every stroke having color differences within it. This jitter acts on any of the five properties of a color. Under this, we have the following settings:

    - **Hue** lets you adjust the degree of variation in hue that can happen between stamps. A low value makes the brush jitter between a small spectrum of colors, while a high value makes the colors swing through a large range.

- **Saturation** works the same way as **Hue**, except it makes the saturation of each stamp jitter randomly within the specified range.
- **Lightness** is used if you want your stamps to randomly jump to lighter colors, and **Darkness** makes them jump to darker colors.
- **Secondary color** lets you adjust how frequently stamps will jitter between the current color and the secondary color. You can set the secondary color from the **Colors** panel.

- **Stroke color jitter**: This set of sliders introduces variation in color by changing the color of each stroke randomly within the specified settings. This will result in strokes that have the same color individually, but where each stroke is of a different color. This setting has the same five sliders under it as **Stamp color jitter**, and they function identically. The only difference is that they affect strokes as a whole, instead of each individual stamp.
- **Color pressure**: Use these settings to make brush color vary with pen pressure. It contains four sliders labeled **Hue**, **Saturation**, **Brightness**, and **Secondary color**. These sliders control how widely the respective color properties will vary with pressure.
- **Color tilt**: Use these settings to make brush color vary with pen tilt. This section, too, contains four sliders labeled **Hue**, **Saturation**, **Brightness**, and **Secondary color**. These sliders control how widely the respective color properties will vary with tilt.

Dynamics

Brush dynamics add flavor and character to your brush by making it respond to speed and supplying jitter settings. The settings panel for this attribute is shown in the following screenshot:

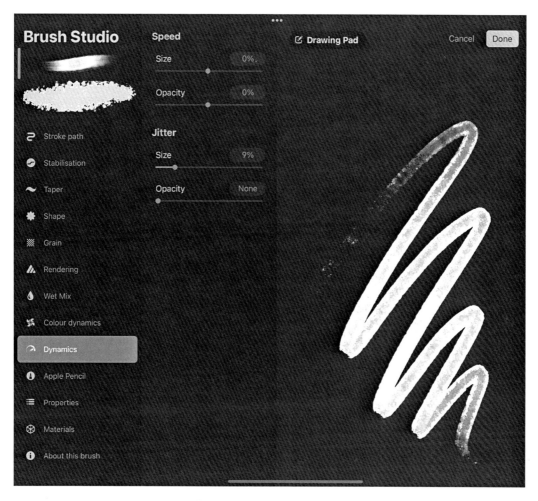

Figure 9.28: Dynamics settings

The controls are divided into two sections:

- **Speed**: Make your brush sensitive to the speed at which a stroke is made. We have the following two options under this:
  - **Size** lets you control how much the brush size will be affected by speed.
  - **Opacity** helps you adjust how much the brush opacity will be affected by speed.
- **Jitter**: Add jitter to brush properties using these settings. We have the following two options under this:
  - **Size** is used to make the brush size randomly change while making a stroke, within the limit on the slider.

- **Opacity** works the same way, by randomly changing the brush opacity between the set limit.

Neither of these settings is affected by stroke speed, so they are a good way to introduce dynamism while drawing with your finger or other styluses that can't register speed.

Apple Pencil

This attribute pertains to how different aspects of your brush change in response to feedback from your Apple Pencil. This feedback comes in two types, **Pressure** and **Tilt**. The settings for the Apple Pencil are shown in the following screenshot:

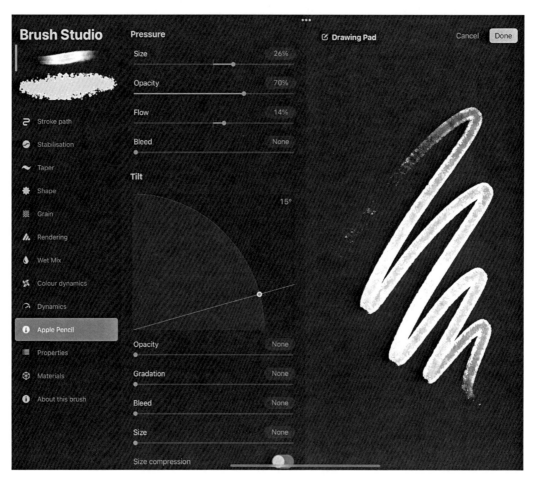

Figure 9.29: Apple Pencil settings

The sections under this attribute are separated for **Pressure** and **Tilt**, as follows:

- **Pressure**: Controls how the brush responds to changes in pencil pressure. Pressure can affect these four brush properties:
  - **Size** lets you adjust how much variation in brush size will occur with a change in pressure.
  - **Opacity** works similarly, helping you control how and whether pencil pressure will affect brush opacity.
  - **Flow** controls how much paint flows through your brush, in relation to pressure.
  - **Bleed** lets you adjust how much paint will spill around the edges of the brush with changes in pencil pressure.
- **Tilt**: This next section works similarly to the previous but in relation to the tilt of your Apple Pencil. You have the following settings under this:
  - The tilt graph used for adjusting the tilt angle is displayed first. It's a quarter circle with a straight line intersecting it, and a blue node where they intersect. Use this node to change the tilt angle. By default, it rests at **9°**.
  - **Opacity** helps you control how and whether tilt will affect brush opacity.
  - **Gradation** lets you recreate the effect of tilting a graphite pencil while shading.
  - **Bleed** lets you adjust how much paint will spill around the edges of the brush with a change in pencil tilt.
  - **Size** lets you adjust how much variation in brush size will occur with tilt.
- **Size compression**: Toggle this button on if you want to prevent the texture inside your brush from stretching out along with the brush size.

Properties

This section contains a bunch of properties that affect how a brush is displayed in the preview and how it behaves with respect to the canvas. The following screenshot shows the settings under this attribute:

Brush Studio Settings – Editing and Combining Brushes

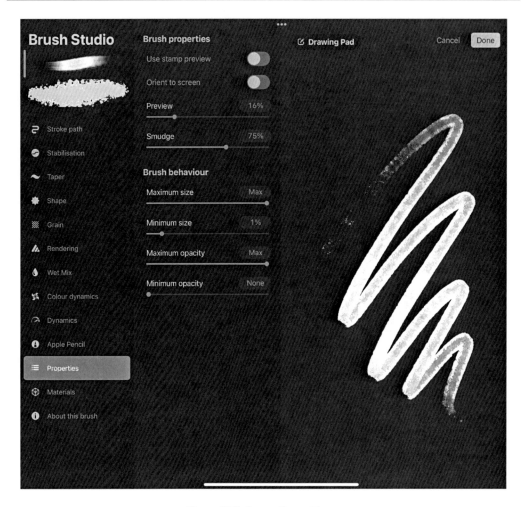

Figure 9.30: Properties settings

The controls are split into two sub-headings:

- **Brush properties**: The following are the settings under this option:

  - **Use stamp preview** decides how the brush preview will appear in the **Brush Library**. Usually, the preview is a stroke, but this toggle can be turned on to show the stamp instead.

  - **Orient to screen**: This setting produces the most noticeable change when the brush has an asymmetrical shape, which has different results depending on its orientation to the canvas. When it's toggled off, the orientation of the brush is locked to the canvas. When toggled on, it's locked to the orientation of the device.

  - **Preview** is a slider that can adjust the size of the stroke or stamp in the preview of the brush in **Brush Library**.

- **Smudge** allows you to set a base value for how much the brush smudges when used as the **Smudge** tool.

- **Brush behaviour**: The settings under this section allow you to set some bounding limits for brush size and opacity:

    - **Maximum size** lets you set the largest size your brush can be. After you exit the **Brush Studio**, this will be the size you get when you turn up the brush size slider all the way to the top. Similarly, **Minimum size** pertains to the smallest a brush can get. If both these sliders are set to the same value, you will have a brush that has a fixed size.

    - **Maximum opacity** and **Minimum opacity** work the same way, by letting you set the highest and lowest opacity value for the brush.

Materials

By using this attribute, you can decide what kind of material texture your brush will have when painting on a 3D model. The settings panel for it looks like this:

Figure 9.31: Materials settings

In Procreate, every material has two aspects – **Metallic** and **Roughness**, which we will talk about here:

- **Metallic**: This property of a material brush determines how metallic the brush will look when painting in 3D. We have the following options under this:
  - Use the **Amount** slider to set the degree of metallic appearance from 0 (non-metallic) to 100 (metallic).
  - **Metallic source** acts almost the same way as **Grain Source**, mentioned in the previous sections. You can import a grayscale image into this editor. The white parts of the source will show the metallic properties of the brush, while the black areas will block it out.
  - **Scale** is used to size the metallic source image up or down.
- **Roughness**: This setting controls how matte or shiny your brush will appear on 3D models. We have the following options under this:
  - Use the **Amount** slider to set the degree of roughness from 0 (smooth) to 100 (rough).
  - **Roughness source** acts the same as **Metallic source**, mentioned in the previous point. You can import a grayscale image into this editor. The white parts of the source will show the roughness of the brush, while the black areas will block it out.

About this brush

The last section in the **Brush Studio** contains information about the brush, which is shown in the following screenshot:

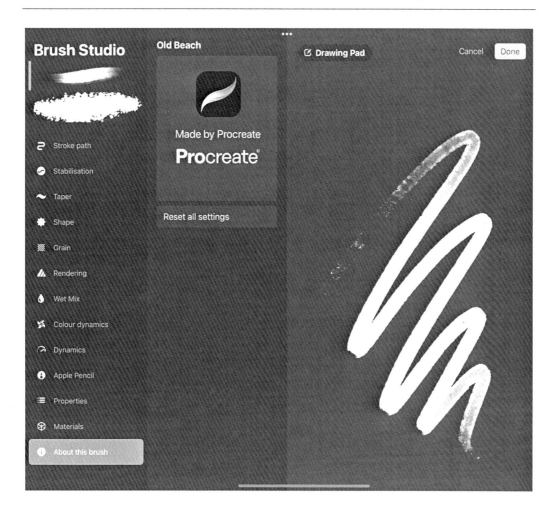

Figure 9.32: About this brush

The first section shows details about the brush such as the name of the brush, who it's created by, and its date of creation. When a brush is the default in Procreate, this section says **Made by Procreate**. For custom brushes, you can easily edit the details.

Tap on the name of the brush to bring up the keyboard, to edit its name.

You can also add your own name, photo, and signature to your original brushes by following these steps:

1. Tap on the gray human icon to add an image representing the creator of the brush:

Figure 9.33: Creator image

2. Tap on the faded gray text that says **Name** to bring up the keyboard, which will allow you to input your own name:

Figure 9.34: Edit brush name

3. Next, using your Apple Pencil or finger, draw your signature on the dotted line:

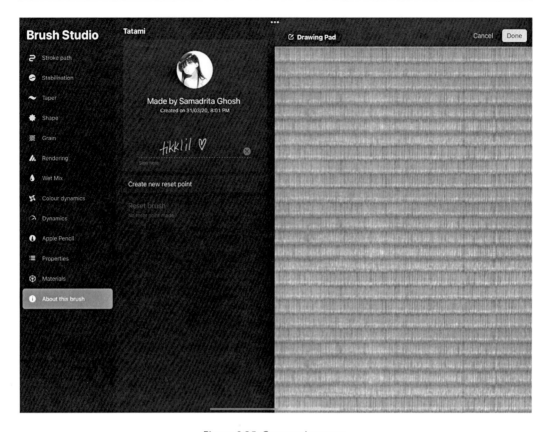

Figure 9.35: Creator signature

The next option lets you reset the brush to its original settings. For a default Procreate brush, there is a single button that says **Reset all settings**. This will reverse any changes you made to the brush and restore its original settings.

For an imported/original brush, you will see a button called **Create new reset point**. This will add a button underneath with the date and time when this reset point was created, as shown in this screenshot:

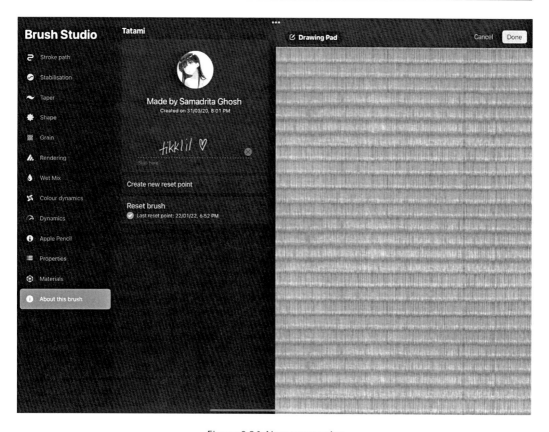

Figure 9.36: New reset point

Save a reset point to continue editing your brushes freely. If you're not happy with the edits you make, you can always jump back to a preferred reset point. You can create multiple reset points like this.

We have now covered the **Brush Studio** settings in detail. The **Brush Studio** is packed with features, all of which require practice to get used to. It's recommended that you spend time testing out these settings on different brushes, since their effects may vary depending on the brush. In the next section, we will look at the last important feature of brushes in Procreate – Dual Brushes.

Dual Brushes

Procreate brushes have a unique feature, where it's possible to combine the properties of two brushes into one composite brush. In this section, you will be introduced to dual brushes. We will learn how to create and edit dual brushes, as well as combining and uncombining brushes.

Creating a Dual Brush

To create a new Dual Brush, you need to select two brushes and combine them. To do so, follow these steps:

1. Select a brush by tapping it. This is your primary brush. Select another brush you want to combine it with, by swiping right on it. This is your secondary brush.//
2. As soon as you have two brushes selected, you will see a button called **Combine** appear in the top-right corner of the **Brush Library** popover, as shown in the following screenshot:

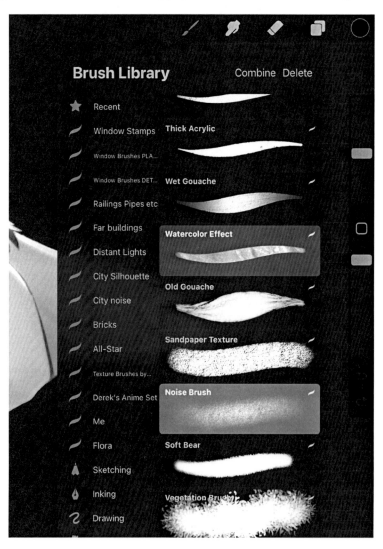

Figure 9.37: Combine button

3. Tap this button to create a new Dual Brush with these brushes.

> **Important Note**
> Procreate's default brushes can't be combined with other brushes. However, you may duplicate a default brush and combine the copy. Additionally, more than two brushes can't be combined.

4. Tap on this new Dual Brush to open it in the **Brush Studio**. The Dual Brush, by default, takes on the name of the primary brush. To change the name, go to the **About this** brush section.
5. Tap on the name of the brush to bring up the keyboard and rename your brush.

Editing a Dual Brush

When a Dual Brush is opened in the **Brush Studio**, it appears in the top-left corner of the screen as two brushes layered on top of each other, as shown in the following screenshot:

Figure 9.38: A Dual Brush

The primary brush lies on top of the secondary brush. Select the brush you want to edit by tapping on it, which makes a blue line appear to its left.

Each brush can be separately edited in **Brush Studio**.

Combine Mode

Dual Brushes use blend modes such as layers to combine with each other and create a composite effect. You can change how the brushes blend to get your desired effect.

Follow these steps to select Combine Mode:

1. Open the Dual Brush in the **Brush Studio**.
2. From the brush preview in the top-left corner, tap on the selected brush to expand the preview and reveal **Combine Mode**, as shown in the following screenshot:

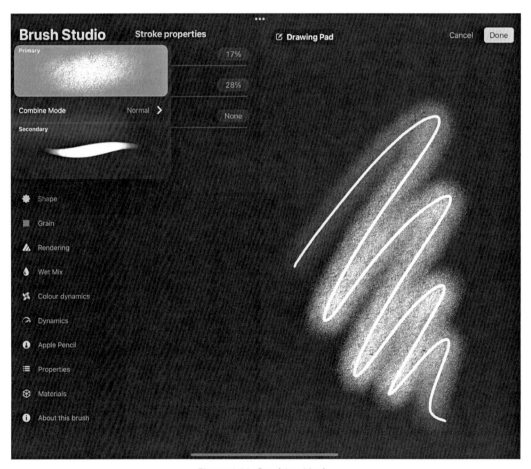

Figure 9.39: Combine Mode

3. Tap on **Combine Mode** to open the blend modes menu, as shown in the following screenshot:

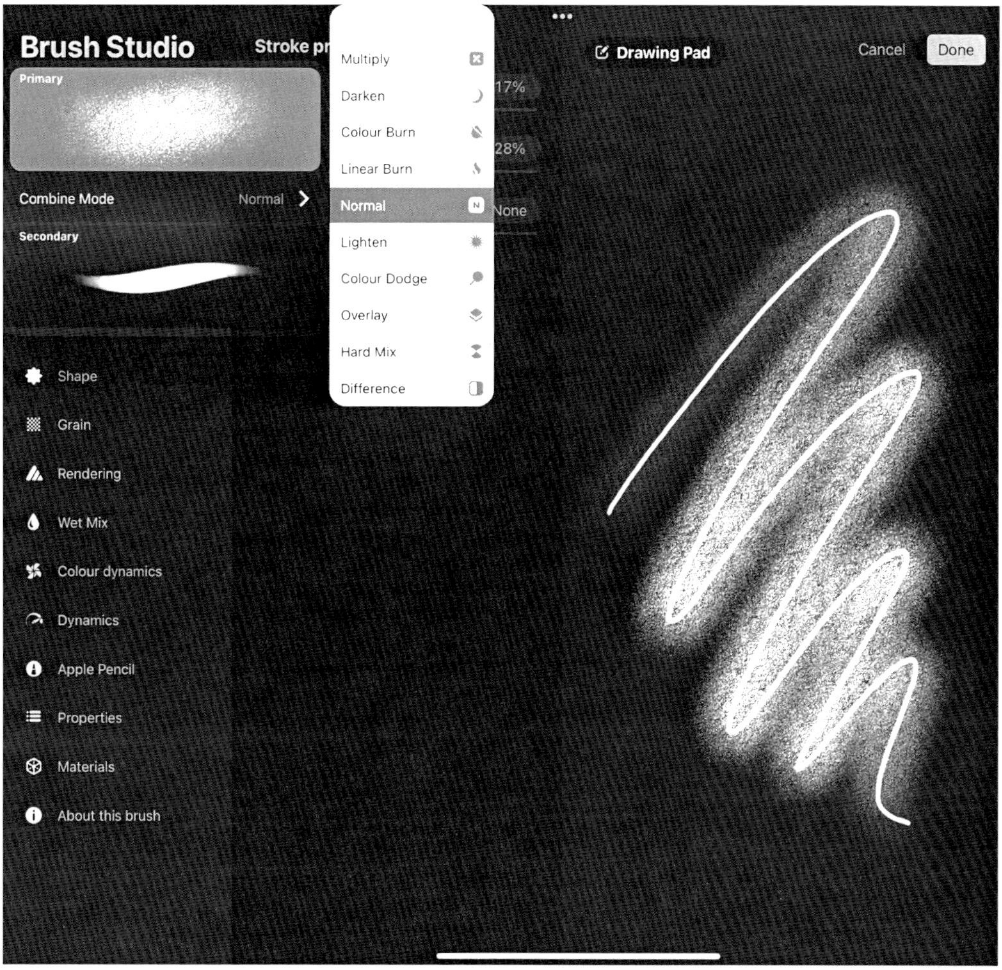

Figure 9.40: Blend modes menu

4. Choose your preferred combine mode, and watch the effects it has on the brush stroke on the **Drawing Pad** in real time.

Uncombine

To re-separate the component brushes of a Dual Brush, follow these steps:

1. Open the Dual Brush in the **Brush Studio**.
2. From the brush preview in the top-left corner, tap on the selected brush to expand the preview.
3. Tap on the secondary brush to select it.

4. Tap on it again to bring up a popup saying **Uncombine**, as shown in the following screenshot:

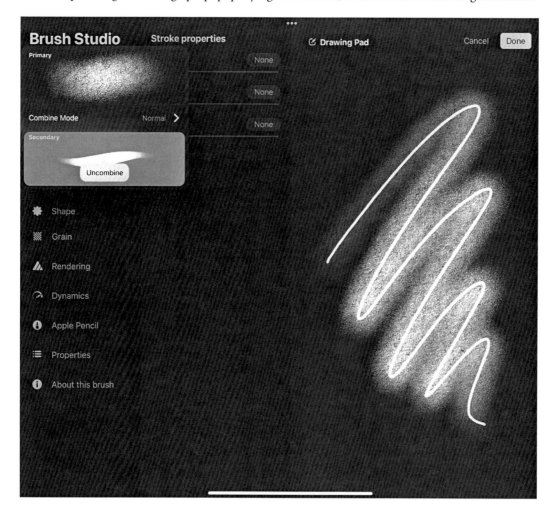

Figure 9.41: Uncombine

5. Tap on **Uncombine** to separate the brushes again.

We have now exhaustively covered the **Brush Studio** and all its features. Let's summarize this chapter.

Summary

The chapter did a deep dive into the **Brush Studio**, where it introduced all the editable attributes of a brush and how to adjust each of them. We now understand how brushes work as shapes stamped along a stroke and how each stamp has its own shape and grain. We covered how the pressure and tilt of the Apple Pencil plays a part in brush behavior. Overall, you have learned how to edit these attributes to create new, interesting brushes or simply reconfigure existing brushes.

Additionally, we discussed Procreate's unique feature, which lets you combine the features of two brushes into one Dual Brush.

The next chapter will introduce you to how colors work in Procreate.

10
Using Colour Tools

Working with colours is an essential part of using any digital painting software. Procreate offers a variety of ways to use and experiment with colours. In this chapter, you will learn how colour tools are organized in the Procreate app. These tools help you choose, edit, and save colours.

There are several types of colour interfaces to aid your unique style of working. Each of them has its own qualities and special functions, which will be introduced as you read further.

We're going to cover the following broad topics in this chapter:

- Colour terms
- The interface
- Disc
- Classic
- Harmony
- Value
- Palettes

Colour terms

Before we dive into the interface, there are a few basic terms you should be familiar with that will help you navigate colour in a digital space. These terms are used to describe certain properties of colour and can be altered to create other colours. If you're already an artist with some experience, you may be familiar with these terms. However, when starting out with digital art or art in general, it's essential that you have a working knowledge of these words. These terms are **hue**, **saturation**, and **value**. Let's look at them one by one.

Hue

Hue refers to the basic pigment making up the colour. For instance, the dark blue and light blue in the following figure both contain the same type of blue, hence their hue is the same:

Figure 10.1: Two colours of the same hue

However, when you look at the new pair of blues shown in the following figure, you'll notice that the pigment differs between the two. In other words, their hues are different:

Figure 10.2: Two colours of different hues

Saturation

Saturation pertains to the intensity of pigment in a colour. In informal terms, this is what we mean when using the terms "bright" or "dull" to describe colours.

The following figure shows two yellow colours of the same hue, but one has high saturation, while the other low:

Figure 10.3: Two colours of the same hue but different saturation

At the lowest saturation, every colour turns into a neutral gray with no associated hue. However, in the real world, there are hardly any colours with zero saturation, which gives rise to "warm" and "cool" grays. Warm hues (such as red, orange, and yellow) at low saturation produce warm grays, as shown in the following figure:

Figure 10.4: Warm grays

Similarly, cool colours (such as blue, violet, and green) produce cool grays, as shown in the following figure:

Figure 10.5: Cool grays

Value

The lightness or darkness of a colour is called its value. The value of a colour can be changed by pushing it towards black or white.

When a hue at maximum saturation is pushed towards black, its value decreases, giving rise to darker colours. This is demonstrated in the following figure:

Figure 10.6: Values moving towards black

When a hue at maximum saturation is pushed towards white, its value increases, creating lighter colours, as shown in the following figure:

Figure 10.7: Values moving towards white

In the next section, we'll jump right into the different tools Procreate offers you for working with colours.

The interface

When working with colours on Procreate, the interface plays a big role. This section will introduce the controls available to you that will allow you to explore the colour tools.

The Colours panel

The **Colours** panel is the window where all colour tools are available. It can be invoked by tapping on the coloured circle in the top-right corner of the screen, called the colour button. It is shown in the following figure

Figure 10.8: The Colours panel

The **Colours** panel has the following tools:

- **Active colour**: The colour displayed on the colour button is called the active colour. It's the currently selected colour and shows you what you're working with.
- **Primary colour**: In the top-right corner of the **Colours** panel, you will notice two coloured rectangles. The one on the left is called the primary colour. Usually, the primary colour is also the active colour.
- **Secondary colour**: The coloured rectangle to the right is the secondary colour. Just like the primary colour, it can be changed to any colour. However, if you close the **Colours** panel with the secondary colour selected, when you open it back up, the secondary colour will have switched positions with the primary colour.

  Primary and secondary colours are useful when working with brushes that switch back and forth between the two. Learn more about using a secondary colour in brushes in *Chapter 9, Brush Studio Settings – Editing and Combining Brushes*.

- **Reticle**: When selecting colours from the **Colours** panel, a transparent circle sits on the colour wheel, highlighting the active colour. This is the reticle. It can be dragged around on the colour wheel to pick another colour. When dragged, it expands and shows a split view of the previous colour and the current one. This helps you see how these colours look in relation to each other.
- **History**: This section shows the last 10 colours used. It's constantly updating, which means with every new colour picked, the oldest one at the end disappears.

  Each new canvas comes with a clear history, but you can use the **Clear** button to get rid of it on your current canvas, too.

  This section is available on iPad and iPad Pro models with a screen larger than 10.2 inches.

- **Default palette**: You can choose any palette from the **Palettes** section to be your default palette, that is, the colour palette that will be displayed in the **Colours** panel by default on every canvas. The default palette allows you to keep a commonly used palette at hand, so you can jump to specific colours easily.
- **Colour selection interface**: Procreate offers you five different ways to select and adjust colours – **Disc**, **Classic**, **Harmony**, **Value**, and **Palettes**. Depending on which of these you select, your colour selection interface will vary. We will talk about each of these tools in detail further in this chapter.

The **Colours** panel can be transformed into a floating window called **Colour Companion**. It is a feature that helps you keep the **Colours** panel within easy reach while you work. To invoke it, use the following steps:

1. Open the **Colours** panel.

2. Place your finger on the light gray bar at the top of the panel and drag.
3. This will make the **Colours** panel pop out as a miniature floating window, called **Colour Companion**, as shown in the following figure:

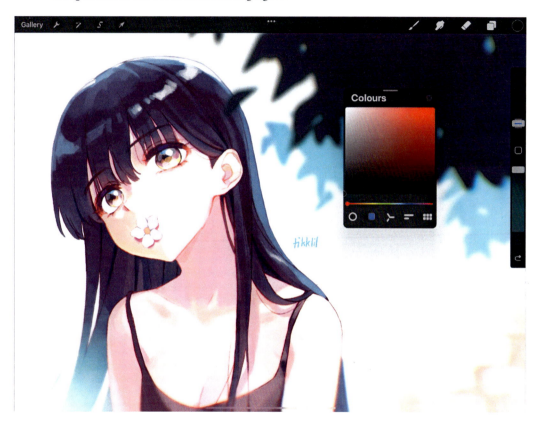

Figure 10.9: Colour Companion

4. To close it, tap the **x** in the top-right corner of the window.

The next element of the **Colours** panel is the active colour.

Active colour

The colour button in the top-right corner of the screen shows the active colour. It primarily has two functions:

- **Previous colour**: Press and hold the active colour to switch to the previously selected colour.

- **ColourDrop**: This is Procreate's version of colour filling. Simply drag the active colour over to any area of the canvas and release it to fill said area with the active colour. This gesture is demonstrated in the following figure:

Figure 10.10: ColourDrop

The next subsection will elaborate more on ColourDrop.

ColourDrop

ColourDrop helps you flood fill areas of the canvas, such as colouring line art, filling in shapes, and creating mono-colour layers. This is done by dragging the active colour over to the desired area and releasing it to fill it in.

An important feature of this tool is **ColourDrop Threshold**. This dictates how much area will be filled by ColourDrop. At low threshold values, the colour fill will stay confined to smaller spaces. At higher values, it will spill over the edges and cover more area by breaking colour or transparency boundaries. To activate the ColourDrop threshold, follow these steps:

1. Drag the active colour to the area you want to fill, but don't release your finger.
2. A blue slider bar will appear at the top of your screen. This shows the threshold.

3. Without lifting your finger, slide it toward the left or right to change the threshold value. At this point, another dropdown will appear above the slider bar, displaying the threshold value, as shown in the following figure:

Figure 10.11: ColourDrop Threshold

4. As you slide your finger to the left, you will see the threshold value decreasing and the colour fill receding to take up less space. Similarly, slide to the right, and the threshold value will increase to make the colour fill expand and break out of the edges.

5. When you're happy with the fill, release your finger. Procreate will remember your chosen threshold value and auto-apply it the next time you use ColourDrop. You can, however, change the threshold every single time.

The next feature of ColourDrop is also especially useful when used in conjunction with the threshold. It's called **Recolour**, and it helps you fill colour multiple times in quick succession, without having to drag and drop the active colour over and over. To use **Recolour**, follow these steps:

1. Use ColourDrop once. As soon as you lift your finger, you will see a drop-down message at the top of the screen that says **Continue Filling with Recolour**, as shown in the following figure:

Figure 10.12: Continue Filling with Recolour

2. Tap it to activate **Recolour**. A crosshair will appear at the center of the screen. Drag it anywhere to instantly fill it with the active colour. The crosshair is shown in the following figure:

Figure 10.13: Recolour in action

3. You can now simply tap on areas to continue filling them.
4. A separate **Flood** slider will also appear at the bottom of the screen as soon as **Recolour** is activated. Use this to configure the fill threshold every time you fill a space:

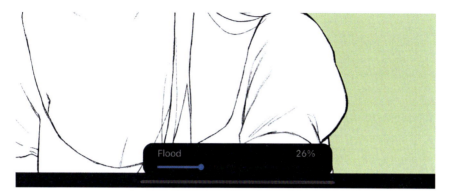

Figure 10.14: Flood slider

5. **Recolour** lets you change the active colour between individual fills, so you can switch between several colours within a single use of **Recolour**.
6. To exit **Recolour** and commit, simply tap any other tool and continue drawing normally.

The next subsection will introduce SwatchDrop, which is a feature similar to ColourDrop.

SwatchDrop

SwatchDrop lets you fill colours directly from a palette into your canvas. It works the same way as ColourDrop. The only difference is that instead of dragging the active colour, you drag a colour from a palette.

To access the palettes, follow these steps:

1. Tap on the active colour to bring up the **Colours** panel.
2. At the bottom, you'll find five options, as shown in the following figure:

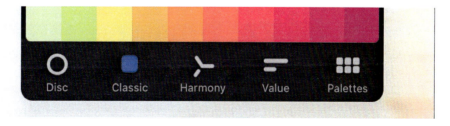

Figure 10.15: Colour interface options

3. Select **Palettes**. This will reveal the colour palettes available, as shown in the following figure:

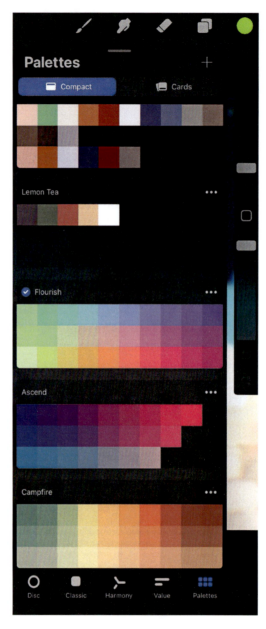

Figure 10.16: Palettes

4. Drag and drop any colour directly from the palettes onto the canvas to colour fill it.

SwatchDrop works exactly like ColourDrop, including Drop Threshold and Recolour, so the previous section has all the information you'll need for this.

In the next subsection, you will learn how to sample colours from your artwork using the Eyedropper.

Eyedropper

Pick a colour from any area of the canvas to make it your active colour, using the **Eyedropper** tool. There are several ways to use this tool.

The first way to invoke the Eyedropper is by tapping and holding. Touch the point on the canvas that you want to sample and hold it until a disc pops up there. The upper half of this disc shows the colour you are currently sampling, and the bottom half shows the last active colour, as in the following figure:

Figure 10.17: Eyedropper

You can sample colour throughout the canvas by just dragging your finger across the screen with **Eyedropper** activated. The disc will show you the picked colours in real time. In the center of the disc, you'll see a zoomed-in section of the artwork from where you're picking the colour.

The second way to use the Eyedropper is by using the **Modify** button. This is the square-shaped button found between the brush size and brush opacity sliders, shown in the following figure:

Figure 10.18: Modify button

The **Modify** button can be used to colour pick in either of these two ways:

- Tap and hold the **Modify** button, and with your other hand, touch the point on the canvas that you want to pick a colour from.
- The second option is a one-handed version of the last one. Tap the **Modify** button to invoke a floating Eyedropper tool, which will stay until you tap on the screen to pick a colour.

You can edit how the **Modify** button behaves using **Gesture Controls**. To learn more about gestures, refer to *Chapter 6, Using Gestures and Shortcuts*.

In the next few sections, we will learn about the five different interfaces that let you pick colours using the **Colours** panel.

Disc

The color disc is a versatile way to choose colours, by giving you control of the hue and saturation separately. Tap on the active colour and choose **Disc** from the options at the bottom, which will show you the disc interface, shown in the following figure:

Figure 10.19: Disc

Let's take a closer look at these controls.

Interface

The color disc allows you separate control over hue and saturation. The outer ring is a colour wheel from which you can choose a hue. The disc in the middle displays the saturation and value range for the chosen hue, from which you can pick your preferred colour.

Saturation disc controls

The saturation disc is quite small, which may make it difficult to make finer adjustments. To remedy this, it can act as a separate unit when certain gestures are used.

These gestures help you use the saturation disc more conveniently:

- **Zoom**: Perform a pinch-out gesture on the saturation disc to temporarily make it larger, as shown in the following figure:

Figure 10.20: Saturation disc

This makes the hue ring disappear and gives you a bigger area to work with. Once you close the **Colours** panel, the disc goes back to normal.

- **Snap**: Double-tap on the reticle to snap to the closest perfect value. These values include pure white/black, half-saturation, full saturation, and 50% gray. Snap can be used on both the default size and the zoomed-in saturation disc.

Classic

For experienced digital illustrators looking for a more traditional approach to colours, the **Classic** interface is ideal. Tap on the active colour and select **Classic** to switch to this style colour selection. It is shown in the following figure:

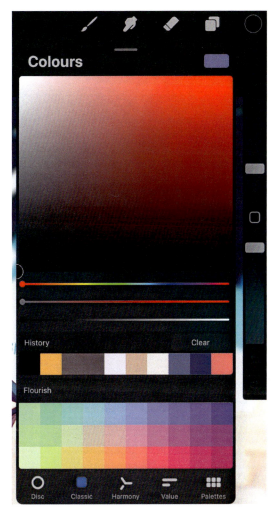

Figure 10.21: Classic

Let's take a closer look at these controls.

Interface

The **Classic** interface has two major elements. The **Classic** colour window displays the saturation and value range of the selected hue, similar to the saturation disc in the previous section. It also has a reticle to let you choose colours.

Below that are three sliders pertaining to hue, saturation, and value. These sliders allow for finer control over all aspects of a chosen colour.

Harmony

The next option is a great way to pick colours that work well with each other to create harmonious combinations. Tap on the active colour and choose **Harmony** to use this tool, as shown in the following figure:

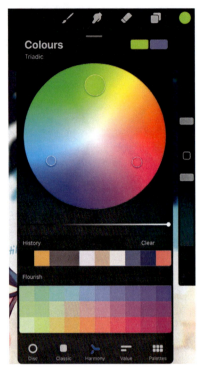

Figure 10.22: Harmony

Let's take a closer look at these controls.

Interface

The interface of **Harmony** consists of a hue and saturation disc, with a separate slider for value. Changing the value slider makes the colour disc uniformly darker and lighter.

Reticles

The hue-saturation disc can have one or more reticles, depending on the harmony mode. These reticles rest on harmonious colour combinations. The larger reticle is called the primary, and the smaller ones are called the secondary reticles. When one is moved, the others move along with it, still maintaining their interrelationships.

Modes

Modes let you choose the type of colour relationships that will be selected by **Harmony**. Modes can be chosen from a menu in the top-left corner of the **Colours** panel, as shown here:

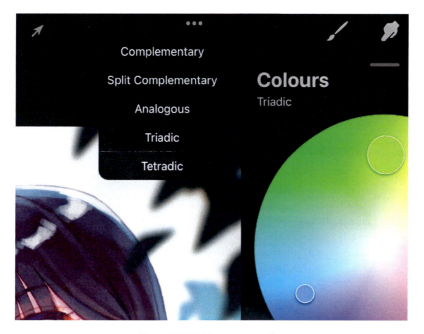

Figure 10.23: Harmony modes

There are the following types of harmony modes:

- **Complementary**: This mode offers two reticles that rest on diametrically opposite sides of the colour disc, that is, on complementary colours. The colours in such combinations produce very high contrast. So, it's advised to be careful while using them together.

- **Split Complementary**: This mode has three reticles arranged in a narrow triangle shape. Aside from the primary reticle colour, it picks two colours on symmetrically opposite sides of its complementary colour. This gives rise to a subtler contrast than the last option. When using split complementary colours, it's recommended to use the colour at the far end of the triangle as a base, with the other two used sparingly as shades and accents.

- **Analogous**: Analogous colours lie in the same area on the hue-saturation disc. This is a low-contrast mode that offers you three reticles to work with; they rest close to one another for subtle hue and saturation variation in colours.

- **Triadic**: This mode places three reticles in an equilateral triangle formation. Doing so creates a powerful combination of colours, each of which is equally impactful.

- **Tetradic**: This mode helps you choose colours using four reticles placed in a square formation. So, you get colours from diagonally opposite ends of the disc. Like the previous mode, this mode also places equal importance on all the colours with no clear hierarchy, so it can get tricky when balancing them together.

Choosing colors

When **Harmony** is activated, you can switch between colours by simply tapping any of the reticles.

You can also save your favorite colour combinations into a blank palette for future use. To do so, select the colour you want to save, and then tap on an empty swatch in your current default palette. This will create a new swatch of that colour in the palette. We'll learn more about palettes in the **Palettes** section later in this chapter.

Value

Sometimes you may be working on a project that needs you to work with precise, accurate colours. **Value** is designed to help you with such requirements. It has precision sliders that help replicate colours and create exact shades. The interface of this tool is shown in the following figure:

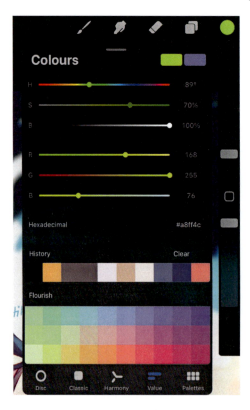

Figure 10.24: Value

Let's take a closer look at these controls.

Interface

The interface of **Value** consists of six sliders and one text input box, as follows:

- **Hue/Saturation/Brightness** sliders: The first three sliders are labelled **H** (hue), **S** (saturation), and **B** (brightness or value). These work the same way as the sliders in **Classic**, affecting the hue, saturation, and value of the colour. Additionally, each slider has an input box next to it, which allows you to set its value manually. This gives you more precise control.

  The **Hue** slider can have values ranging from 0-360° since this slider is essentially the circular colour wheel straightened out into a line. It starts at red, becomes green at 180°, and ends in red again at 360°.

  The **Saturation** slider has values ranging from 0-100%, where 0% means no saturation, and 100% means the highest saturation.

  The **Brightness** slider works the same way, where 0% is black and 100% is the brightest point of the colour.

- **Red/Green/Blue** sliders: Digital colour is made up of varying levels of red, green, and blue light emitted from the screen. These three sliders let you control the amount of each to create the colour you're looking for. Each slider runs from **0** to **255**. Turning all of them up to full value will give you white, and setting all of them to **0** will result in black.

  Turn up **Red** to **255** and the other sliders to **0** to get pure red. This works the same way for pure green and blue. The following table shows some combinations of red, green, and blue:

RGB Values			Result
Red: 255	Green: 255	Blue: 255	White
Red: 255	Green: 0	Blue: 0	Red
Red: 0	Green: 255	Blue: 0	Green
Red: 0	Green: 0	Blue: 255	Blue
Red: 255	Green: 255	Blue: 0	Yellow
Red: 255	Green: 0	Blue: 255	Magenta
Red: 0	Green: 255	Blue: 255	Cyan
Red: 0	Green: 0	Blue: 0	Black

  Hexadecimal: Every digital colour has a unique six-character code that represents it. These codes are written after a # symbol and are called **hexadecimal** (**hex**) codes. Procreate lets you input the hex code of your required colour into this text input box. This will let you maintain consistent colour schemes when working on projects that have such requirements.

Palettes

The last option in the **Colours** panel is **Palettes**. As the name suggests, this mode allows you to create and save colour schemes for ready use. Additionally, it also helps turn images into colour palettes. The interface of **Palettes** is shown in the following figure:

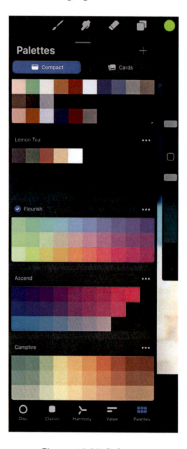

Figure 10.25: Palettes

Let's look into the features of this colour tool in more detail.

Swatches

Swatches are the building blocks of a palette. Each individual colour in a palette, represented as a coloured square, is called a swatch. There are two ways that swatches are represented in Procreate:

- **Compact**: This is the more traditional view of colour palettes, with the swatches represented as small coloured boxes arranged in rows of 10, as shown in the following figure:

Palettes 345

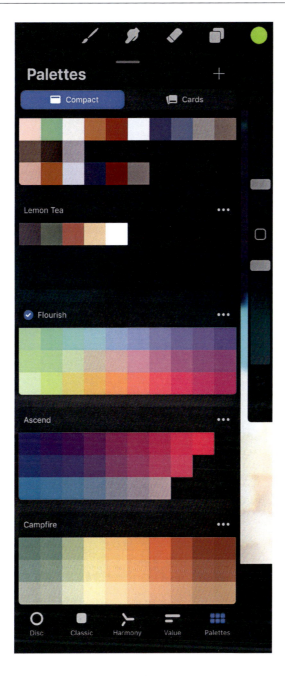

Figure 10.26: Compact view

- **Cards**: This is a new feature rolled out in Procreate 5.2, which displays each swatch as a much larger box in rows of three. Each swatch also has an auto-generated name to describe its colour, making it a great accessibility tool. Colour cards are shown in the following figure:

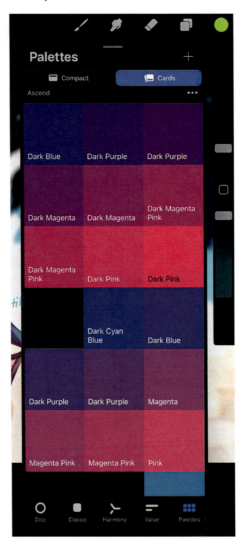

Figure 10.27: Cards view

To rename a card, tap on the name to invoke the keyboard, and minimize it to commit.

Next, let's introduce some actions you can perform with swatches:

- **Create a swatch**: To create a new swatch, tap on any empty spot on a palette and assign it your active colour.

  Alternatively, you could even create a fresh palette to give yourself more space to make your own swatches. Find more information about creating a palette in the *Palette library* section later in this chapter.

- **SwatchDrop**: This feature lets you drag and drop a swatch to fill colour into your canvas.

- **Reorder swatches**: To change the order in which swatches appear on a palette, simply tap and drag it to your desired position.

- **Set swatch to current colour**: Using this feature, you can change the colour of any swatch into your active/current colour. Tap and hold a swatch to make the following menu appear:

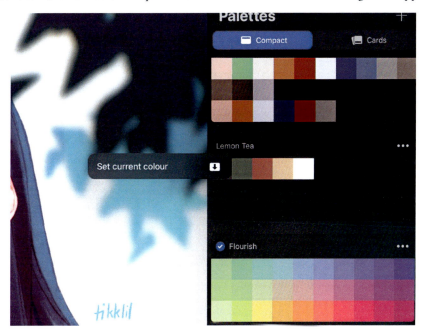

Figure 10.28: Set swatch to current colour

Then, tap **Set current colour**.

- **Delete a swatch**: To delete a swatch, tap and hold it to make the swatch menu appear. Then, tap **Delete swatch**.

In the next subsection, we will discuss the palette library, which is where all your palettes are stored.

Palette library

The palette library houses and displays all your palettes. This is essentially the interface you see when you select **Palettes**. From here, you can create, edit, import, and share palettes.

We will discuss the features of the palette library as follows:

- **Create a palette**: To create a blank palette, follow these steps:

    I. Tap on the + icon in the top-right corner of the library. This will bring up a menu, as shown in the following figure:

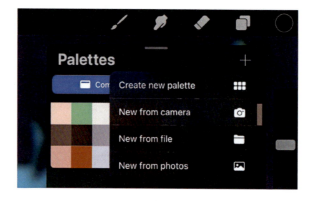

Figure 10.29: New palette menu

   II. From here, select **Create new palette**. This will make a new palette, comprising three rows of 10 swatches each.

   III. By default, a new palette is named **Untitled Palette**. Tap on this name to edit it.

- **Set as default**: A default palette is the one that appears at the bottom of the **Colours** panel when the **Disc**, **Classic**, or **Harmony** modes are active.

    To set a palette as your default, tap on the three dots icon in the top-right corner of the palette. The following menu appears:

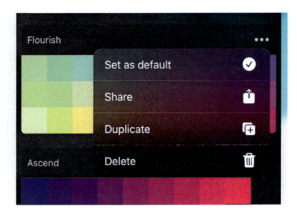

Figure 10.30: Palette menu

Select **Set as default**.

> **Important Note**
> From **Palettes**, simply select a swatch from any palette to automatically set said palette as the default.

- **Share a palette**: The **Palettes** menu also has an option called **Share**, which lets you share a palette to any external location. Alternatively, you can share a palette using drag-and-drop. More information on that can be found later in the *Importing and sharing palettes* section.
- **Duplicate a palette**: Create a copy of any palette using the **Duplicate** option in the **Palettes** menu.
- **Reorder palettes**: Hold and drag a palette to reposition it within the palette library. This method works for both the **Compact** and **Cards** views.
- **Delete a palette**: Bring up the **Palettes** menu using the three dots icon, and tap **Delete** to remove a palette. Be careful since this is a permanent action and can't be undone.

The following subsection will introduce Palette Capture, a handy way to convert images into palettes.

Palette Capture

Palette Capture is an extremely useful feature that allows you to extract colour palettes from images as well as the camera.

There are two types of Palette Capture:

- **Palette Capture from the camera**: This type of Palette Capture uses the camera to create a colour palette with the colours captured by it.

To use it, follow these steps:

I. Open **Palettes** in the **Colours** panel.

II. Tap the + icon in the top right-hand corner of the window.

III. From the menu, tap **New from Camera**. This will open up your iPad's camera, with a palette of swatches in its center. This palette will change depending on what your camera sees at any given moment. The interface is shown in the following figure:

Figure 10.31: Palette Capture using the camera

Visual and **Indexed** are two modes that process the camera's visual information in two different ways.

Visual considers only the section of the image right behind the floating palette in the center while creating a palette. This gives you a more limited set of swatches, as you can point the box at a specific place that you'd like to pick colours from.

Indexed considers the full field of the camera's view and provides palettes sampled from all parts of the visible scene.

- **Palette Capture from Files**: Create a palette from an image stored in **Files** using this option.

To use it, follow these steps:

I. Open **Palettes** in the **Colours** panel.

II. Tap the + icon in the top right-hand corner of the window.

III. From the menu, tap **New from File**. This will take you to the **Files** app.

IV. From here, you can choose any JPG or PNG file, and the resulting palette will be sampled from the colours available on the chosen file.

- **Palette Capture from Photos**: Create a palette from an image stored in **Photos** using this option.

    To use it, follow these steps:

    I. Open **Palettes** in the **Colours** panel.

    II. Tap the + icon in the top right-hand corner of the window.

    III. From the menu, tap **New from Photos**. This will take you to the **Photos** app.

    IV. From here, you can choose any image you have saved on the device, and the resulting palette will be sampled from the colours available on the chosen image.

> Important Note
> For a quicker import, simply drag and drop an image into the **Palettes** window to instantly create a new palette from the image.

In the next subsection, we will look at importing and sharing palettes.

Importing and sharing palettes

Procreate saves palettes with the `.swatches` extension. In this section, we'll learn about the different ways in which you can import pre-existing palettes into your workspaces, as well as how to share your colour schemes to external locations.

To import a palette, follow these steps:

1. Open **Palettes** in the **Colours** panel.
2. Tap the + icon in the top right-hand corner of the window.
3. From the menu, tap **New from File**. This will take you to the **Files** app.
4. From here, choose any `.swatches` file to import the Procreate palette directly into your app.

    Procreate palettes also support file extensions such as `.ASE` (Adobe® Swatch Exchange) and `.ACO` (Adobe® Colour).

    Alternatively, you can also drag and drop a `.swatches` file from **Files** into **Palettes**.

To share a palette as a `.swatches` file, follow these steps:

1. Open **Palettes** in the **Colours** panel.
2. Go to the palette you want to export and tap the three dots icon in its top-right corner. A menu will appear, as shown in the following figure:

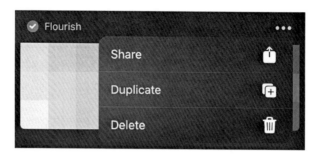

Figure 10.32: Palette menu

3. From here, select **Share**.
4. This will bring up the iOS file sharing interface, where you can pick a destination for this palette file.

Just like importing, you can also share a palette by dragging and dropping it into any compatible location (such as **Files**). Select multiple palettes to export them in bulk.

This chapter has covered all the colour tools available on Procreate. We can now summarize our knowledge.

Summary

Colours play a significant part in digital painting, and Procreate offers a range of useful tools to facilitate working with them. In this chapter, we've learned about the technical terms associated with colours. Then we detailed the app's colour tools interface and gestures such as ColourDrop and SwatchDrop.

We learned about the **Colours** panel, which is the interface essential to working with all the different colour selection tools, namely **Disc**, **Classic**, **Harmony**, **Value**, and **Palettes**. This chapter discussed how each of these interfaces has a unique way of handling colour, and how to use them to suit your needs.

This chapter should help you explore digital colours further, and apply your knowledge to your own workflow.

In the next chapter, we'll learn about the **Adjustments** menu, a handy set of image editing tools on Procreate.

11
Adjustments – Applying Image Effects

The **Adjustments** menu is a collection of image editing tools that let you add an extra touch of polish to your artwork. These effects consist of colour adjustments, blur effects, **Liquify**, and a range of other useful tools. This chapter will take you through the details of each type of adjustment available in Procreate, and how to use them.

We're going to cover the following broad topics here:

- The Adjustments interface
- Colour adjustments
- Blur effects
- Image filters
- The Liquify tool
- The Clone tool

This chapter will take you through a variety of different image adjustment tools. By the end of it, you will have a detailed understanding of how each of these tools works, and how to use them to refine your art with a professional polish.

Exploring the Adjustments interface

Most of the image editing tools found in the **Adjustments** menu share some common features across their interfaces. Once familiarized with these actions, you will be able to apply them across almost the entire list of effects. In this section, we'll look at the commonly used interfaces and gestures of **Adjustments**.

The Adjustments menu

To open the **Adjustments** menu, tap on the **Adjustments** button. This button can be found in the top left-hand corner of the Procreate interface – among a row of four buttons called the **Advanced Features** panel. The second button from the left with a magic wand icon is the **Adjustments** button. Tap this button to bring up the **Adjustments** menu, as shown in the following screenshot:

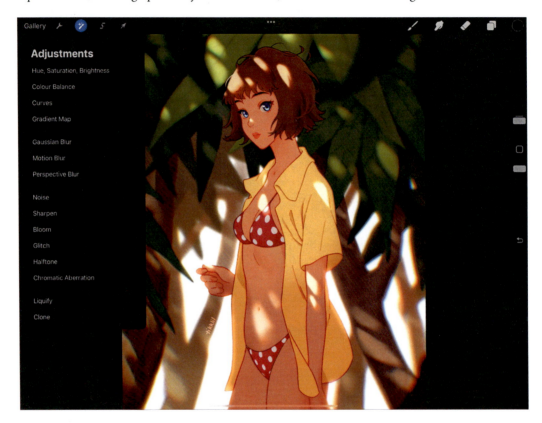

Figure 11.1: The Adjustments menu

There are broadly two types of image effects:

- **Adjustments**: These tools help you tweak the colours in your artwork. They allow fine control over parameters such as hue, saturation, brightness, colour balance, and curves.

  These effects are controlled using a toolbar that appears at the bottom of the screen. This toolbar is different for each kind of colour adjustment, as we'll learn further ahead in the chapter.

- **Filters**: These tools apply special effects over the entire image. They are applied using a slider whose value determines how strong the effects will be. This slider appears as a blue line at the top of the screen, shown in the following screenshot:

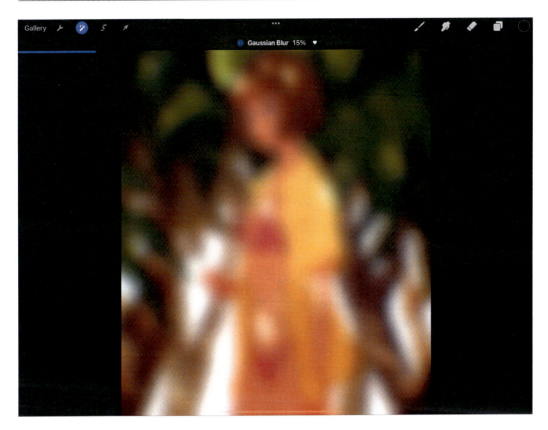

Figure 11.2: Filter slider

The value of the slider is controlled by dragging a finger to the left to decrease or right to increase.

In the next subsection, we'll discuss the two different methods of applying adjustments, which serve different purposes.

The Layer and Pencil modes

You may apply an effect to a layer as a whole or choose specific areas where the effect will be visible. The **Layer** and **Pencil** options allow you to do just that. Some adjustments such as **Liquify** and **Clone** only have **Layer** filters. Other effects have a small downward arrow next to their name when activated. Tap on this arrow to reveal the **Layer** and **Pencil** options, as shown in the following screenshot:

356 Adjustments – Applying Image Effects

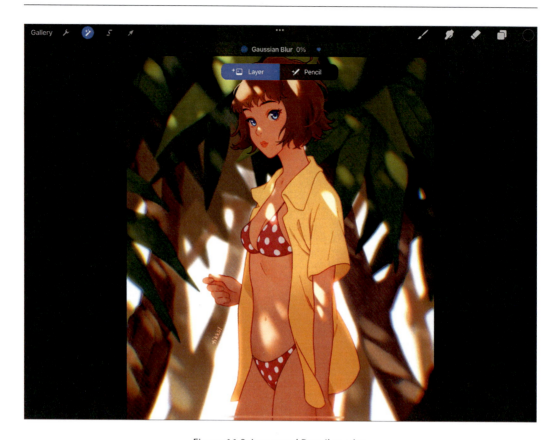

Figure 11.3: Layer and Pencil modes

Let's discuss the functions of these options:

- **Layer**: This is the default option. When selected, the image effect will uniformly apply to the active layer.

- **Pencil**: This option lets you paint an effect onto the image. Only the painted areas will have the adjustment applied, leaving the rest of the layer untouched.

    While applying **Pencil** filters, the **Painting Tools** icons in the top right-hand corner of the screen will sport a sparkle next to the regular graphic. You can choose brushes, erasers, and smudge brushes as you normally would. Your choice of brush will affect the shape of the area where the filter is applied.

The following screenshots show the **Gaussian Blur** filter applied to an image using **Layer** versus using **Pencil**:

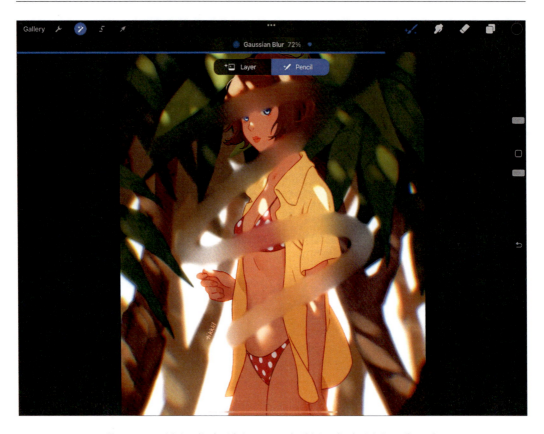

Figure 11.4: (a) Applied with Layer mode (b) Applied with Pencil mode

> **Important Note**
> It's possible to switch between **Layer** and **Pencil** without losing the results of either. You may start off on **Layer** and then switch to **Pencil** for finer adjustments, and so on.

The next subsection introduces the basic menu of actions available for most of the adjustment tools.

Adjustment actions

The term Adjustment actions refers to a floating menu that can be invoked at any time while applying a filter. It's brought up by tapping the screen. The menu is shown in the following screenshot:

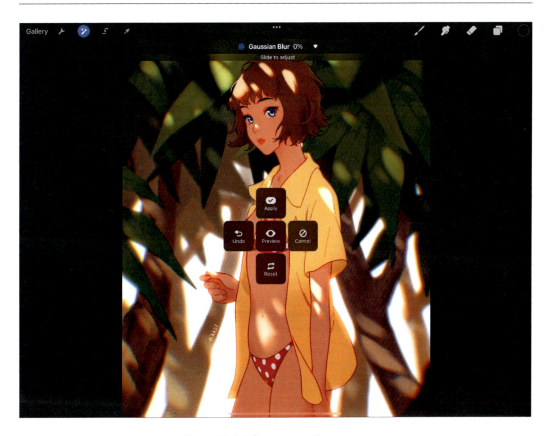

Figure 11.5: Adjustment actions menu

Let's go over each option:

- **Apply**: This option applies the current changes and resets the interface to 0%.
- **Undo**: This option undoes the last adjustment without leaving the interface.
- **Preview**: Touch and hold this button to preview the original image without the applied effects. Release your finger to return to the changes you have made.
- **Cancel**: This option discards all your changes and exits the interface.
- **Reset**: This option discards all your changes and resets the filter to 0% without exiting the interface.

360   Adjustments – Applying Image Effects

> **Important Note**
>
> Before we dive in, keep in mind that all adjustment tools *except* **Liquify** can only be applied to one layer at a time.
>
> **Liquify** may be applied to multiple selected layers or groups, provided none of those layers are alpha locked.

In the following sections, this chapter introduces each type of adjustment in detail.

Tweaking colors with color adjustments

The first set of adjustments has to do with tweaking the colours on your image. There are four colour adjustment tools in Procreate— **HSB**, **Colour Balance**, **Curves**, and **Gradient Map**. We will go through each of these in this section.

Hue, Saturation, and Brightness

This is the first colour adjustment tool, commonly abbreviated to **HSB**. It gives you complete control over the hue, saturation, and brightness of a layer. It consists of three sliders that appear at the bottom of the screen, one for each parameter. The interface is shown in the following screenshot:

Figure 11.6: Hue, Saturation, and Brightness interface

Each slider rests at **50%** and can be moved to either side for observable changes to the active layer. For a better understanding of the terms **Hue**, **Saturation**, and **Brightness**, refer to *Chapter 10, Using Colour Tools*.

Colour Balance

Colour Balance helps you adjust the balance of colours present in the image. This is done with the help of a toolbar at the bottom of the screen, as shown in the following screenshot:

Figure 11.7: Colour Balance interface

This toolbar has three sliders. Each slider is balanced between complementary colours on the colour wheel— **Cyan** and **Red**, **Magenta** and **Green**, and **Yellow** and **Blue**. Pushing the slider toward a colour will increase the concentration of that hue in the image, resulting in a shift in the colour scheme. For example, the following screenshots show the artwork in its original state, followed by showing the scene after its colours were pushed toward red and yellow to give it a warmer tone:

362 Adjustments – Applying Image Effects

Figure 11.8: (a) Original image (b) Red and Yellow enhanced

At the right of the toolbar is a button with a sun icon, called the **Shadows/Midtones/Highlights** button. It lets you decide which range of brightness will be the most affected by **Colour Balance**. When **Shadows** is selected, the darker regions of the image will show maximum effect. **Highlights** affects the lighter parts, and **Midtones** the values in between.

> Important Note
>
> For an even application of **Colour Balance** over the whole image, **Midtones** is recommended.

Curves

Your artwork can be expressed as a graph, with the distribution of red, green, and blue mapped onto it. The **Curves** tool allows you to edit the appearance of the image by tweaking these graphs. Its interface is a toolbar that appears at the bottom of the screen, as shown in the following screenshot:

Figure 11.9: Curves interface

The straight line on the graph represents your image and changing the shape of this line affects its colours. This tweaking is done using control points called **nodes**. When you tap anywhere on the curve, a point appears there. This is a node. You can add a maximum of nine such nodes, not counting the two present at the ends of the curve by default. They can be used to manipulate the shape of the graph, as shown in the following screenshot:

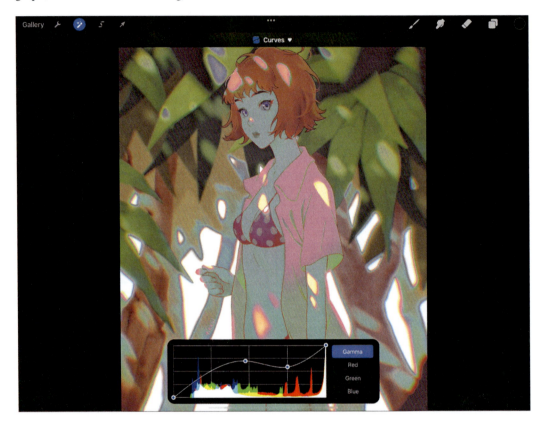

Figure 11.10: Nodes used to manipulate a curve

Moving a node upward increases the brightness of an area and vice versa. Additionally, the right half of the graph controls the brighter portions of the image, while the left controls the darker parts. As an instance of its use, let's assume you want to increase the contrast of a painting. This means making the lights lighter and the darks darker. To do so, you could follow these steps:

1. Place a node at the center of the graph, as shown:

Figure 11.11: Placing a central node

This will act as the anchor for the midtones of the image, which we don't want to change.

2. Create two more nodes on both sides of the center node to divide the graph into four parts, as shown:

366 Adjustments – Applying Image Effects

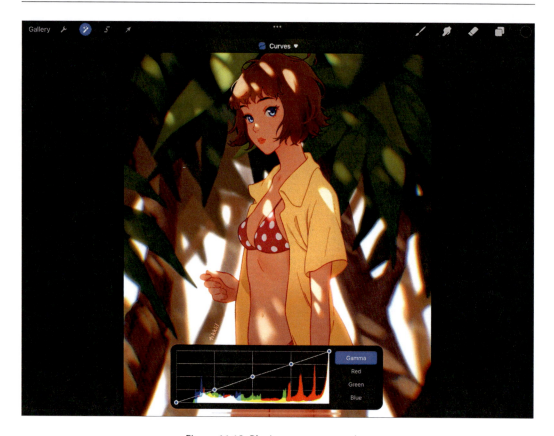

Figure 11.12: Placing accessory nodes

The top node represents the highlights and the one at the bottom controls the shadows.

3. Move the top node further up, and the bottom node further down to create an S shape, as shown:

Tweaking colors with color adjustments 367

Figure 11.13: Nodes creating an S shape

4. This automatically increases the contrast of your artwork by making the light colours lighter (the right node moves up) and the dark colours darker (the left node moves down), without affecting your midtones (the center node doesn't move).

The coloured shapes sitting under the graph show the distribution of the three primary digital colours – red, green, and blue – in the image. These coloured graphs are called **histograms**. Wherever they overlap, they create a different colour. The areas where all three are present are shown in white, true to how digital colour behaves.

On the right side of the **Curves** toolbar, there are four buttons labeled **Gamma**, **Red**, **Green**, and **Blue**. When **Gamma** is selected, moving the graph affects all three histograms together, having a uniform effect on the image. When any of the other three are selected, the graph only affects the histogram linked to the respective colours.

> **Important Note**
>
> **Gamma**, **Red**, **Green**, and **Blue** curves can be tweaked independently of each other. Switching buttons simply switches views; it doesn't reset changes made on individual curves.

Gradient Map

Gradient maps offer a quick and easy way to apply a consistent colour scheme to a painting. To elaborate, each gradient map uses a specific gradient, for instance, the one in the following screenshot:

Figure 11.14: Gradient Map

This is one of Procreate's default gradient maps, called **Blaze**. As you can see, it runs from a dark maroon to a very light yellow. When **Blaze** is applied to an existing image with a different colour scheme, it applies the colours present on its gradient to the source image, by considering the brightness of each pixel of the source image. This means that all the black-coloured pixels on the original image will now be dark maroon, and the white areas will become light yellow. The midtones will all take on colours from the **Blaze** gradient in a similar way. As the source image colours move from dark to light, the final colours will move from dark maroon to red to orange to light yellow. The following images show the artwork before and after applying **Blaze**:

Figure 11.15: (a) Original image (b) Gradient Map Blaze applied

Like **Blaze**, Procreate has several other preset gradient maps in its **Gradient Library**. When **Gradient Map** is activated, the **Gradient Library** appears at the bottom of the library. You can choose which gradient map to apply to a layer by swiping through the library or simply tapping on one. The **Gradient Library** is shown in the following screenshot:

Figure 11.16: Gradient Library

Like most adjustments, gradient maps also come with a slider that can be adjusted to control how strongly they are applied to an image.

To reorder the gradients, simply touch and drag them into a preferred order. Touch and hold a gradient map to make a menu pop up, as shown in the following screenshot:

Figure 11.17: Gradient Map menu

These options let you delete or duplicate a gradient map. To reset your library to its default state, touch and hold the + icon in the top-right corner of the toolbar. Then tap **Restore defaults**.

If none of the preset gradients meet your needs, you can create your own custom gradient. To do so, follow these steps:

1. Tap the + icon in the top-right corner of **Gradient Library**.

    A new default grayscale gradient will appear on the toolbar, which runs from black to white, as shown in the following screenshot:

Figure 11.18: Default grayscale gradient

You will notice two squares on the gradient. These are called Colour Points. They represent the anchor points of the component colours of a gradient, in this case, black and white. The Colour Points can be moved along the gradient, changing how gradually colours shift between one point and another.

2. Tap on a Colour Point to open a miniature colour panel. This will let you assign any colour you want to that point, as shown in the following screenshot:

Tweaking colors with color adjustments | 373

Figure 11.19: Colour Point

3. You can add up to 10 additional Colour Points to the gradient, and adjust their positions to fit your needs, as shown in the following screenshot:

Figure 11.20: Additional Colour Points added and customized

4. To delete a Colour Point, touch and hold it until a popup saying **Delete** appears, as shown:

Figure 11.21: Delete Colour Point

The changes you make will be reflected in your artwork in real time.

5. To name this gradient, tap on the text that says **Gradient** to bring up the keyboard, as shown:

Figure 11.22: Rename Gradient Map

6. Once you are happy with the changes, tap on **Done** to return to **Gradient Library**. You now have a custom gradient in your library, available across all your Procreate documents.

> **Important Note**
> To edit a default gradient map, tap on it to open up the gradient editor. Editing preset gradient maps works the same way as creating one from scratch.

In the next section, we will learn about the different types of blur effects in Procreate.

Working with blur effects

The **Adjustments** menu offers three types of blur effects to add a sense of realism to your art. Blurring softens the details of the image, bringing the effect of a camera going out of focus or objects moving fast, and so on. The following subsections will discuss these effects in more detail.

Gaussian Blur

Gaussian Blur softens an image uniformly. It gives rise to a smooth, out-of-focus effect. It's demonstrated in the following screenshot:

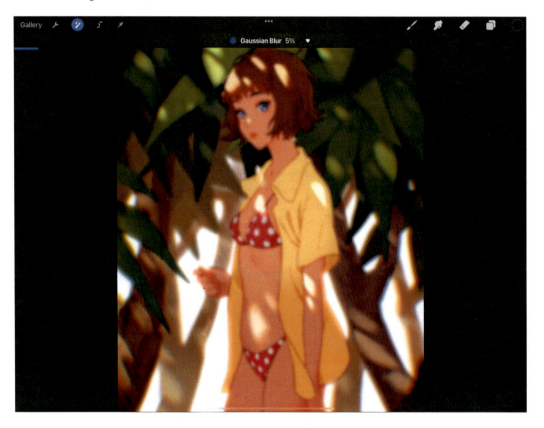

Figure 11.23: Gaussian Blur

To use **Gaussian Blur**, follow these steps:

1. Select the layer you want to blur.
2. Open the **Adjustments** menu and select **Gaussian Blur**.

3. Scrub the screen horizontally with your finger to increase or decrease the blur amount, which will appear as a blue bar and a percentage at the top of your screen.

   If the **Layer** mode is selected, the whole layer will be blurred. If **Pencil** is selected, the blur will only affect the areas you have drawn on.

4. Once you are happy with the changes, tap the **Adjustments** button to commit and go back to drawing.

Motion Blur

Motion Blur captures the essence of a high-speed motion by blurring an image in a single direction. Its effects are shown in the following screenshot:

Figure 11.24: Motion Blur

To use **Motion Blur**, follow these steps:

1. Select the layer you want to blur.
2. Open the **Adjustments** menu and select **Motion Blur**.
3. Scrub the screen with your finger in the direction you want the motion blur to appear. As you move your finger around, the blur direction changes.
4. To increase or decrease the blur amount, simply move your finger farther away from its starting point. The blur amount will appear as a blue bar and a percentage at the top of your screen.

   Note that every time you lift your finger and touch the screen again, the blur resets.
5. If the **Layer** mode is selected, the whole layer will be blurred. If **Pencil** is selected, the blur will only affect the areas you have drawn on.
6. Once you are happy with the changes, tap the **Adjustments** button to commit and go back to drawing.

Perspective Blur

Perspective Blur applies radial blur to an image. This means that the blur radiates from a point, so the farther away from that point you look, the blurrier the image gets.

There are two types of **Perspective Blur** effects:

- **Positional**: This option radially blurs an image in all directions, away from a selected focal point. The blurriness increases with distance from the focus. Positional blur is shown in the following screenshot:

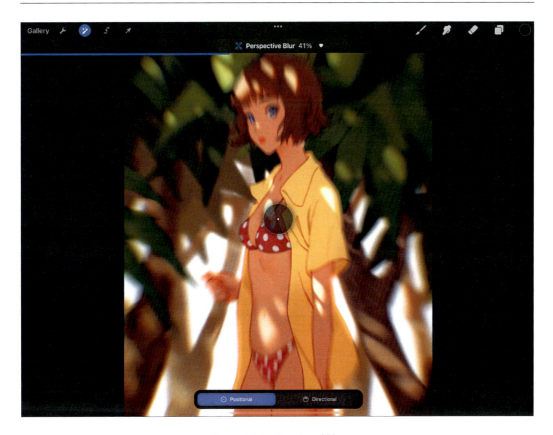

Figure 11.25: Positional Blur

- **Directional**: This option mostly works the same way as **Positional**, with one difference. It lets you choose the direction in which the perspective blur will be applied. The portion of the image on the opposite side remains untouched. **Directional** blur is shown in the following screenshot:

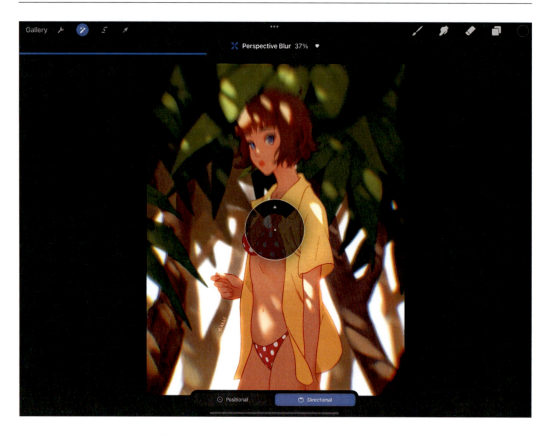

Figure 11.26: Directional blur (applied upward)

To use **Perspective Blur**, follow these steps:

1. Select the layer you want to blur.
2. Open the **Adjustments** menu and select **Perspective Blur**.
3. Choose between **Positional** and **Directional** blur from the bottom of the screen, as shown in the following screenshot:

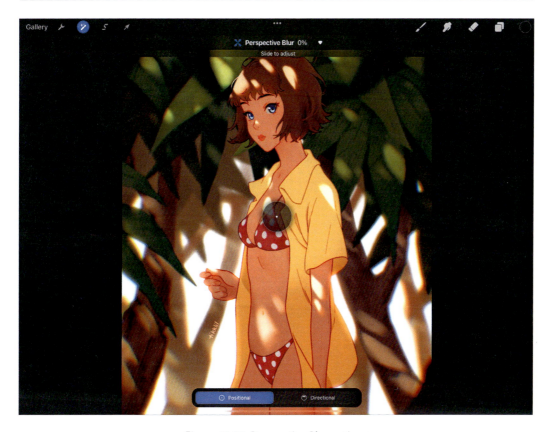

Figure 11.27: Perspective Blur options

4. A disc will appear at the center of the screen. Touch and drag it to the point you want to set as the focal point, as shown in the following screenshot:

Figure 11.28: Positional Blur disc

When working with **Directional** blur, the disc will sport a triangular arrow icon, as shown in the following screenshot:

Figure 11.29: Directional blur disc

5. Touch and rotate the arrow toward the direction you want to apply the blur.
6. Scrub the screen horizontally with your finger to increase or decrease the blur amount, which will appear as a blue bar and a percentage at the top of your screen.

    If the **Layer** mode is selected, the whole layer will be blurred. If **Pencil** is selected, the blur will only affect the areas you have drawn on.

7. Once you are happy with the changes, tap the **Adjustments** button to commit and go back to drawing.

> Important Note
>
> **Positional** and **Directional** blur can't be applied in combination. If you switch between the two modes while applying the blur, the changes made by the first will be undone. When you want both kinds of blur, it's best to apply them one at a time.

In the next section, we'll delve into the range of versatile image effects available in the **Adjustments** menu.

Applying image effects

The next cluster of adjustments is collectively referred to as image effects. These are "filter"-like effects that are applied over an image as a whole and make qualitative or stylistic changes to it. The usage of these effects will get clearer as we proceed into this section.

Noise

As the name suggests, **Noise** works by applying a grainy static-like effect to your image. One such possible result is shown in the following screenshot:

384　Adjustments – Applying Image Effects

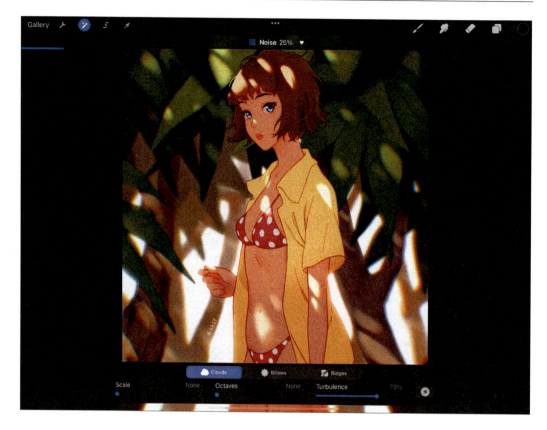

Figure 11.30: Noise

The adjustment interface for **Noise** is shown in the following screenshot:

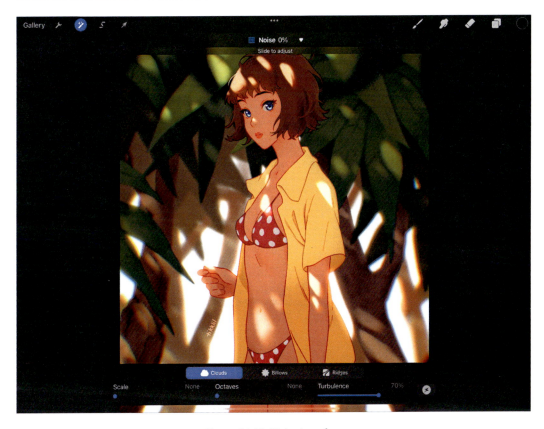

Figure 11.31: Noise interface

The effect is applied by sliding your finger sideways on the screen. Both the **Layer** and the **Pencil** modes are available for it. As you can see in the previous screenshot, there are three distinct types of noise textures in the toolbar:

- **Clouds**: This is the coarsest texture, which looks like clouds when enlarged.
- **Billows**: This texture is finer than **Clouds**, with a billowing effect that gives it more detail.
- **Ridges**: This is the finest, most detailed noise texture.

You may choose to apply any one of these types of noise at a time. Next, let's take a look at the rest of the interface controls of **Noise**.

The toolbar sports three sliders:

- **Scale**: This slider controls the size of the noise texture.
- **Octaves**: This controls the complexity of the noise, thus adjusting its level of detail.
- **Turbulence**: This slider twists and warps the noise texture, adding further complexity to it.

In addition to these sliders, there are also a set of controls on the toolbar called channel buttons. To access them, tap on the button with the lightning bolt icon toward the right of the toolbar. Doing so will bring up a menu, shown in the following screenshot:

Figure 11.32: Channel buttons

Channels have the following controls:

- **Additive**: This is a toggle that determines the transparency of the noise. When toggled on, the noise is overlaid onto the image, allowing it to show through. When toggled off, the noise is applied like a curtain on top of the image, and will completely hide it when set to 100% intensity.
- **Single**: When this option is selected, the noise texture is in a monochromatic grayscale.
- **Multi**: This option makes the noise texture multicoloured.

Sharpen

In many ways, **Sharpen** works in a way that is opposite to blur. It makes the image crisper and creates more contrast at the edges between colours. Sharpened images appear more high-definition. It is demonstrated on a zoomed-in section of a painting in the following screenshots:

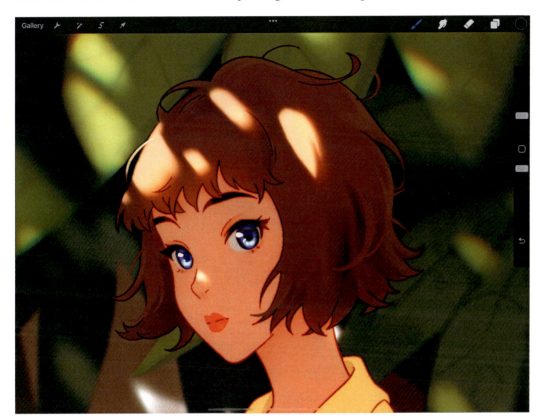

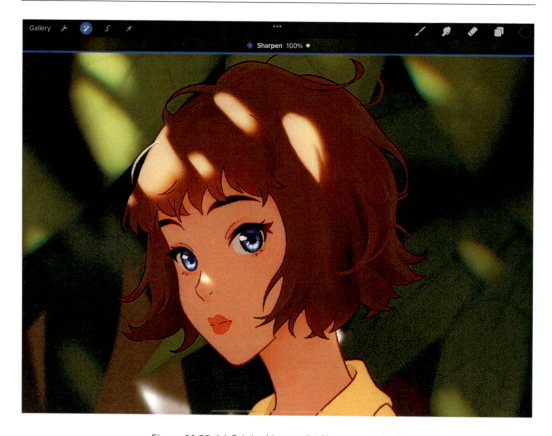

Figure 11.33: (a) Original image (b) Sharpen applied

This adjustment has no exclusive controls. It's applied by sliding your finger sideways on the screen as usual. Both the **Layer** and the **Pencil** modes are available for it.

Bloom

Bloom makes an image appear as if it's glowing. It does so by blowing up most notably the lighter areas of the image to impart a hazy halo-like effect. The following screenshots demonstrate how **Bloom** works:

Applying image effects

Figure 11.34: (a) Original image (b) Bloom applied

It's applied by sliding your finger sideways on the screen as usual. Both the **Layer** and the **Pencil** modes are available for it. The settings for this effect are also controlled by a toolbar at the bottom of the screen, shown in the following screenshot:

Figure 11.35: Bloom interface

This toolbar has the following three sliders that affect the appearance of the filter:

- **Transition**: This slider determines which areas of the image the filter will apply to. At higher values, the glow is applied uniformly throughout the image. At lower values, the bloom is restricted to lighter colours.
- **Size**: This slider controls the size and blur of the bloom edges. The greater the size, the hazier the glow will appear.
- **Burn**: This slider controls the intensity of the bloom.

Glitch

Glitch helps you replicate various types of analog and digital glitch effects that occur when a video is not tuned, experiences interference, or glitches out in general. A possible result of this effect is shown in the following screenshot:

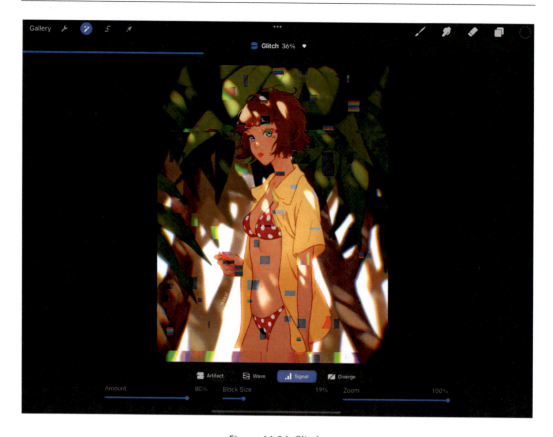

Figure 11.36: Glitch

It's applied by sliding your finger sideways on the screen as usual. Both the **Layer** and the **Pencil** modes are available for it. As you may have noticed, **Glitch** is controlled by a toolbar at the bottom of the screen, shown in the following screenshot:

Figure 11.37: Glitch interface

The top row in the toolbar has four options. In the following points, we will learn more about these four different kinds of glitch effects:

- **Artifact**: This effect consists of scattered horizontal lines and offset blocks, as shown in the following screenshot:

Adjustments – Applying Image Effects

Figure 11.38: Artifact

This effect is controlled by the following settings:

- **Amount**: This controls the amount of offset clocks applied. When increased, your image will be covered in more blocks.
- **Block Size**: This controls the size of the offset blocks.
- **Zoom**: This controls the zoom of all the effects as a whole.
- **Wave**: This effect applies horizontal offset lines, replicating an analog video that is out of tuning, as shown in the following screenshot:

Figure 11.39: Wave

This effect is controlled by the following settings:

- **Amplitude**: This controls the amount of horizontal offset within the offset lines.
- **Frequency**: This controls the amount of vertical offset within the offset lines.
- **Zoom**: This controls the zoom of the effects as a whole.
- **Signal**: At lower levels, this effect applies a light noise and image offset. At higher levels, coloured horizontal scan lines appear on the image, along with both monochrome and coloured blocks, as shown in the following screenshot:

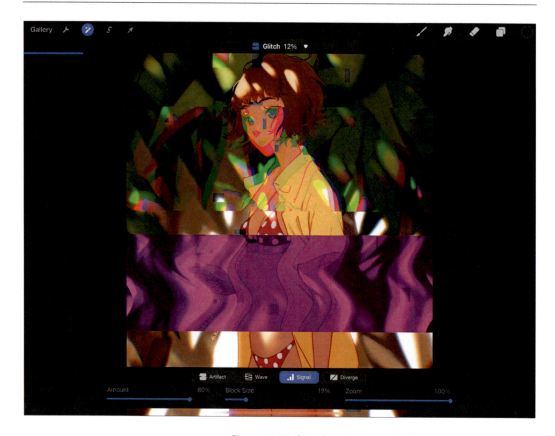

Figure 11.40: Signal

This effect is controlled by the following settings:

- **Amount**: This controls the amount of horizontal scan lines applied to the image.
- **Block Size**: This controls the size of the blocks.
- **Zoom**: This controls the zoom of the effects as a whole.

- **Diverge**: This effect replicates digital glitches. At lower levels, it applies light chromatic aberration and small scan lines. At high levels, the chromatic aberration becomes more pronounced. Large blocks and scan lines also appear, as shown in the following screenshot:

Figure 11.41: Diverge

> **Important Note**
> Chromatic aberration is a type of glitch where the red, green, and blue light planes that make up a digital image split up. We will learn about this effect further in the *Chromatic aberration* section of this chapter.

This effect is controlled by the following settings:

- **Red Shift**: This controls the amount by which the red plane shifts diagonally during chromatic aberration. When the slider has a positive value, the plane shifts down and to the right. At negative values, it shifts up and to the left. Both are shown in the following screenshots:

Adjustments – Applying Image Effects

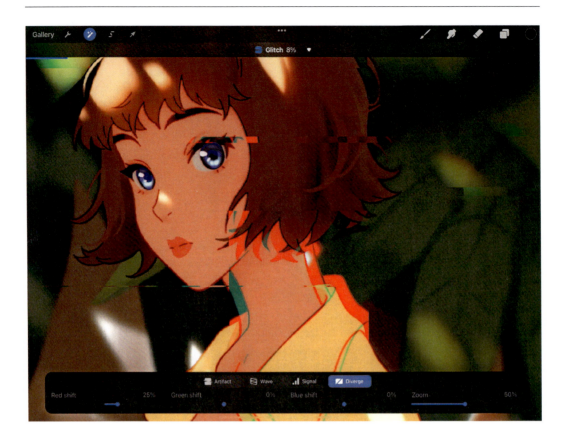

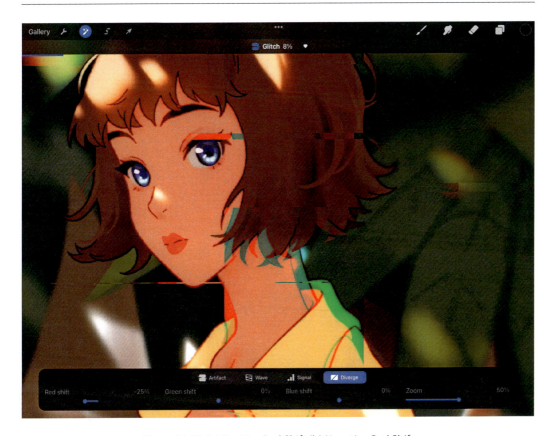

Figure 11.42: (a) Positive Red Shift (b) Negative Red Shift

- **Green Shift**: This works the same way as Red Shift but affects the green plane of the image.
- **Blue Shift**: This too works the same way as the previous two but affects the blue plane of the image.
- **Zoom**: This controls the zoom of the effects as a whole.

Halftone

Halftone is an appealing image effect that lets you replicate the retro style of printing, using evenly spaced ink dots to express a composite image. The results of **Halftone** are shown in the following screenshot:

Figure 11.43: Halftone

It's applied by sliding your finger sideways on the screen as usual. Both the **Layer** and the **Pencil** modes are available for it. **Halftone** has three types of effects under it. These effects are available as buttons at the bottom of the screen, as shown in the following screenshot:

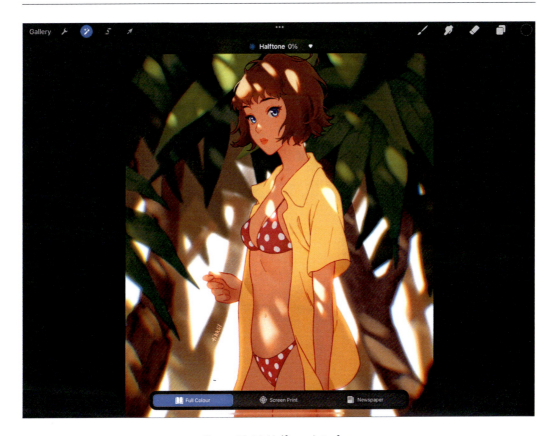

Figure 11.44: Halftone interface

To demonstrate the results of each effect, we will use the following original screenshot:

Figure 11.45: Original image

These are the three types of halftones available:

- **Full Colour**: This is a colour halftone that keeps the colours of the original image in the background of the halftone. Its results are shown in the following screenshot:

Figure 11.46: Full color

- **Screen Print**: This is also a colour halftone, but applied on a white background. Hence, the colours of the original image are only expressed in the dots of the halftone. Its results are shown in the following screenshot:

Figure 11.47: Screen Print

- **Newspaper**: This is a grayscale halftone that replicates the style of newspaper printing. Its effects are shown in the following screenshot:

Figure 11.48: Newspaper

Chromatic Aberration

Every digital image is created by overlapping red, green, and blue light planes, different combinations of RGB colours that give rise to different colours. **Chromatic Aberration** is an image effect that allows you to offset the red and blue planes from their original positions so that the edges of the image appear to have a coloured halo of red or blue. When used properly, it can have aesthetically interesting results. Notice the effects on the background of this image before and after applying **Chromatic Aberration**:

Figure 11.49: (a) Original image (b) Chromatic Aberration applied

It's applied by sliding your finger sideways on the screen as usual. Both the **Layer** and the **Pencil** modes are available for it.

There are two modes of **Chromatic Aberration,** available as buttons at the bottom of the screen:

- **Perspective**: This option applies chromatic aberration radially outward from a focal point. The areas farthest away from the focal point have the most amount of shift. The effects of the **Perspective** mode are shown in the following screenshot:

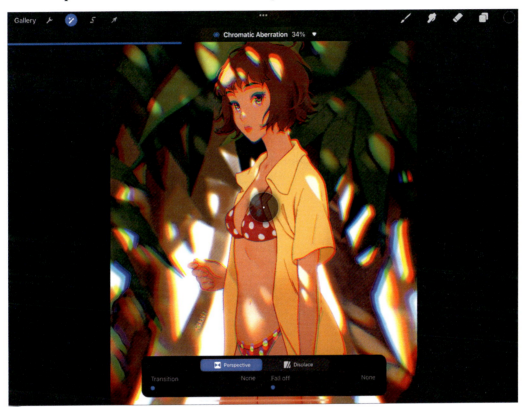

Figure 11.50: Perspective mode

The interface of this mode has the following elements:

- **Focal Point**: When the **Perspective** mode is selected, a gray shaded circle appears at the center of the screen. This will be the point from which the chromatic aberration will radiate outward. It doesn't necessarily have to be placed in the center of the image. The focal point can be moved to any position, even in the middle of applying the effect.

- **Transition**: This determines the amount of blur applied to the chromatic aberration as it radiates out from the focal point. At 0%, it will have soft edges, and at 100%, the edges will be hard and defined.

- **Fall off**: This slider controls the distance from the focal point at which the chromatic aberration starts. At 0%, the aberration starts right from the edge of the focal point. At 100%, a large area surrounding the focal point is left unaffected, and the effect starts beyond that radius.

- **Displace**: This mode does not work with a focal point. Instead, it applies chromatic aberration to the entire image and lets you shift it in any direction using your finger. The effects of the **Displace** mode are shown in the following screenshot:

Figure 11.51: Displace mode

The interface of this mode has the following elements:

- **Blur**: This controls the amount of blur applied to your chromatic aberration. At 0%, the edges of the effect are sharp, and as you increase the slider value, they get softer and more blurred.

- **Transparency**: This controls the transparency of the chromatic aberration. At 0% the effect is opaque, while at 100%, it's transparent.

We have now covered all the image effects in the **Adjustments** menu. Next, we will learn about an extremely useful image adjustment tool: **Liquify**.

Warping an image with the Liquify tool

Liquify is a warping tool that lets you stretch and bend pixels to warp your image in a number of different ways. The following screenshots show a possible result of **Liquify**:

Figure 11.52: (a) Original image (b) Liquify applied

Unlike the adjustments we have discussed so far, **Liquify** doesn't have **Layer** and **Pencil** as separate modes of application. It can only be applied by making strokes with your Apple Pencil or finger. **Liquify** is controlled by a toolbar at the bottom of the screen, as shown in the following screenshot:

Figure 11.53: Liquify interface

We are going to look at the different types of controls in the following subsections.

Modes

There are seven types of warping effects that **Liquify** can potentially apply to an image. The tool will behave differently depending on which mode is selected.

In the following points, each mode will be explained and demonstrated:

- **Push**: This mode pushes the pixels of the image in the direction of your stroke. It's the most easily recognizable type of **Liquify**, if you are familiar with other digital art software.

The effects of **Push** are shown in the following screenshot:

Figure 11.54: Push

- **Twirl**: This mode has a left and right option. It twists the image around your stroke in the chosen direction.

The effects of **Twirl** are shown in the following screenshot:

Figure 11.55: Twirl

- **Pinch**: This mode pulls the pixels of the image in toward the stroke.

    The effects of **Pinch** are shown in the following image:

Figure 11.56: Pinch

- **Expand**: This mode creates a ballooning effect by pushing the pixels of the image outward from the stroke.

  The effects of **Expand** are shown in the following screenshot:

Figure 11.57: Expand

- **Crystals**: This mode pushes pixels outward unevenly, so it creates a jagged look.

  The effects of **Crystals** are shown in the following screenshot:

Warping an image with the Liquify tool | 413

Figure 11.58: Crystals

- **Edge**: This mode works by pulling the image in toward a line, creating a "folding" effect.

  The effects of **Edge** are shown in the following screenshot:

Figure 11.59: Edge

- **Reconstruct**: This mode works like an "eraser" for **Liquify**. It removes the effects of **Liquify** and exposes the original image where applied.

> **Important Note**
>
> The strength of **Liquify** depends on how much pressure you apply with your Apple Pencil. You can vary the pressure to observe how the intensity of the effect changes.
>
> When using your finger to apply **Liquify**, it's always at maximum intensity.

Settings

There are several sliders on the toolbar that affect **Liquify**. In this subsection, we will discuss them and understand how they influence the properties of this tool.

Warping an image with the Liquify tool | 415

The following are the settings available in the **Liquify** toolbox:

- **Size**: This slider determines the size of the **Liquify** tool's cursor. It's basically the area each stroke of **Liquify** will affect.

- **Pressure**: This slider determines how much pencil pressure will affect the intensity of Liquify. At low values, pencil pressure will not affect the strength of **Liquify** as much, and vice versa.

- **Distortion**: This setting introduces chaos and randomness to the **Liquify** effect.

- **Momentum**: This setting makes the effect continue even after your pencil has been lifted.

Adjust and Reset

The last two buttons on the top row of the toolbar are **Adjust** and **Reset**.

Tap on **Adjust** to bring up a slider labeled **Amount**, shown in the following screenshot:

Figure 11.60: Amount slider

This slider controls the overall intensity of the **Liquify** effect that has been applied to the image. By default, it rests at the maximum value. It's useful when you want to tune the effect up or down.

Finally, you can reverse all your changes and return to the original image using **Reset**.

In the next and final section, we will discuss the last adjustment tool: **Clone**.

Duplicating objects with the Clone tool

The last tool on the **Adjustments** menu is called **Clone**. This tool allows you to paint one part of a painting over another area. To demonstrate using an example, let's say we want to add a copy of the character to the image. **Clone** will allow us to replicate the character to any other part of the image without having to draw them again by hand. In this section, we'll look at how the **Clone** tool works and how to use it.

The Clone interface

When you select **Clone**, a disc appears at the center of your screen, as shown in the following screenshot:

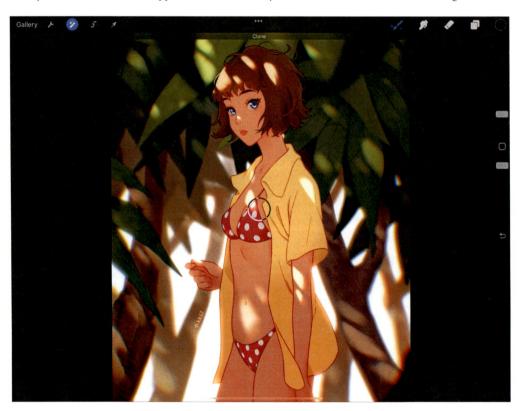

Figure 11.61: Cloning disc

This disc can be moved around. You can reposition it anywhere on the screen. The position of the disc represents the reference point from which your artwork will be cloned.

To use **Clone**, follow these steps:

1. From the **Adjustments** menu, select **Clone**.

   The cloning disc will appear at the center of the screen. You will also notice that the brush icon of the **Paint** tool now has sparkles on it, indicating that it has become a cloning tool.

2. Reposition the cloning disc on the part of the image that you want to clone. For instance, let us clone the character in the previous screenshot, *Figure 11.61*, to add another copy to the empty spot on the right.

3. Start painting on the empty spot. You will notice that the disc mirrors the movement of your brush while recreating whatever area it covers on this new portion of the canvas, as shown in the following screenshot:

Figure 11.62: Cloning follows the brush stroke

4. The cloning brush works exactly like the regular **Paint** tool. This means that you can choose different brushes and change brush size and opacity. All of it will ultimately affect the area affected by **Clone** when you draw.

   The following screenshot shows the same tree cloned using different brushes:

   Figure 11.63: Cloning using different brushes

5. When you're happy with the cloning, tap on the **Adjustments** button or long-press the **Paint** button to finalize the changes and exit **Clone**.

> **Tip**
>
> By default, the cloning disc moves with your brush. This means that every time you lift your pencil, the disc is in a different position. This can make it difficult to clone the same object multiple times since you'll need to manually reposition the disc after each stroke. To help with this, you can lock the cloning disc in one position so that each fresh stroke starts cloning from the same point.
>
> Touch and hold the disc until it pulses. This means that it has been locked. Now the disc won't mirror the movement of your brush, making it much easier to make several clones from the same point.
>
> To unlock the disc, touch and hold it again.

Once you are accustomed to using **Clone**, it will become much easier to create repeating motifs such as forests, visual effects, and clothing patterns.

Now that we have covered the entire **Adjustments** menu, we can go ahead and summarize this chapter.

Summary

The **Adjustments** menu offers a wide range of image editing tools that give an edge to your artwork. In this chapter, we looked at this menu in detail. We started with colour adjustments that make modifications to the existing colours of the image to change its overall appearance. We learned about the three types of blur effects that help add a hint of camera-like realism to your art. Next, the chapter covered image effects that aesthetically enhance an image with filters such as **Noise**, **Chromatic Aberration**, **Halftone**, and many more.

The chapter also discussed the **Liquify** tool, which provides several different ways to warp and distort a picture to achieve interesting effects. Lastly, we learned about the **Clone** tool, which allows you to paint over one part of the image with another part.

Once you are comfortable with using this menu, you will have an extremely powerful set of tools at your disposal, which can have an interesting visual influence on your art.

In the next chapter, you will be introduced to assisted drawing tools available in Procreate.

12
Using Assisted Drawing Tools

Sometimes your artwork requires you to draw within constraints with accuracy. This could mean drawing perfectly straight lines, following a perspective grid, and so on. To help you with these requirements, Procreate has a feature called **Drawing Assist**.

There are a variety of assisted drawing tools, called drawing guides, available for different purposes. With drawing guides, you can easily draw geometrically accurate drawings such as squared grids and isometric diagrams. You can also follow a realistic perspective or draw perfectly symmetrical drawings. We will cover all of them in depth in this chapter.

We're going to cover the following broad topics here:

- Using the Drawing Assist interface
- Drawing squared grids with 2D Grid
- Drawing technical graphics with the Isometric Grid
- Realistic drawing with Perspective Guides
- Symmetrical drawing with Symmetry Guides

By the end of this chapter, you will have learned about the four different types of drawing guides, and when to use them, to draw precisely and accurately.

Using the Drawing Assist interface

To start using drawing guides on a specific canvas, you must activate Drawing Assist on it. This feature allows you to choose and edit which type of drawing guide will be applied to your art. Drawing Assist can be toggled on and off using the **Canvas** tab of the **Actions** menu (the wrench-shaped icon in the top left-hand corner of the screen). To turn it on, follow these steps:

1. Tap the wrench icon to open the **Actions** menu popover, and select the **Canvas** tab, as shown in the following screenshot:

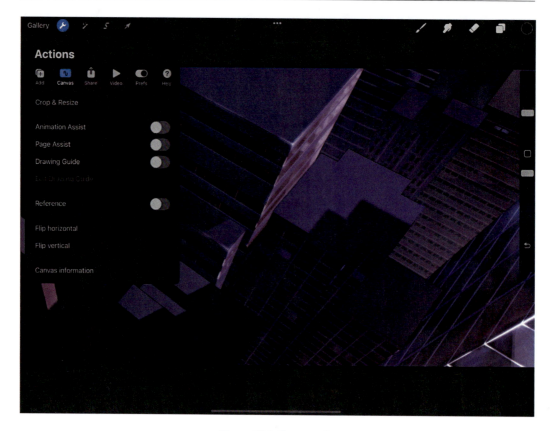

Figure 12.1: Canvas tab

2. Toggle on the **Drawing Guide** option. A square grid will appear over your canvas. This is the 2D Grid, which is the default drawing guide, as shown in the following screenshot:

Figure 12.2: Drawing Assist active

If you've already used another drawing guide on this canvas before, Procreate will load that instead.

1. Notice the option **Edit Drawing Guide** in the **Actions** menu. It was greyed out earlier but is now active. Tap it to bring up the **Drawing Guides** interface, shown in the following screenshot:

424　Using Assisted Drawing Tools

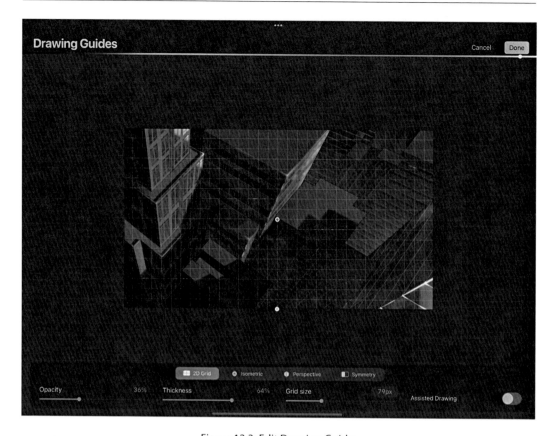

Figure 12.3: Edit Drawing Guide

This interface is where you will be able to select a preferred drawing guide and customize it to suit your needs. We will learn more about each type of drawing guide in later sections of the chapter.

2. The toolbar at the bottom of the screen sports a toggle labeled **Assisted Drawing**. Toggle this to turn it on to make your active layer follow the drawing guide, as shown in the following screenshot:

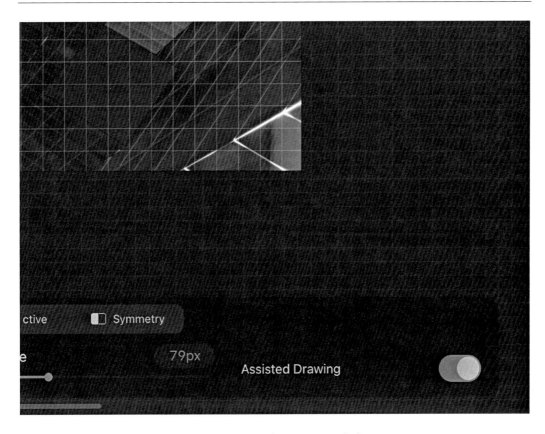

Figure 12.4: Assisted Drawing toggled on

3. Another way to activate it is to tap on a layer to bring up the layer options menu, and select **Drawing Assist**. This is shown in the following screenshot:

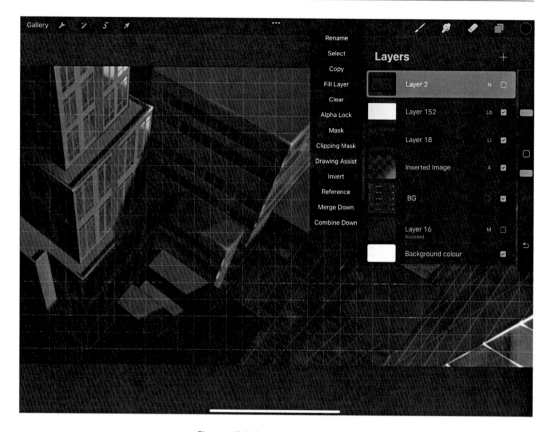

Figure 12.5: Layer options menu

4. Tap on **Done** to commit to changes or **Cancel** to discard them and exit the interface.

> **Important Note**
>
> Multiple layers may have **Drawing Assist** enabled at the same time, but it needs to be enabled on them one at a time. You cannot enable **Drawing Assist** on a layer group, or several layers at once.
>
> Moreover, two types of drawing guides can't be active at the same time on the same canvas, though you may switch between them anytime.

In the following sub-section, we'll go over the basic elements of the **Drawing Guides** interface, which are shared by all the drawing guides.

The Drawing Guides interface

The interface of the **Drawing Guides** screen has certain elements that are common no matter which style of guide you're using. We will look at some of those in this sub-section:

- **Color**: The hue slider at the top of the screen lets you edit the color of gridlines.
- **Nodes**: Each type of grid except **Perspective** has two types of nodes to help manipulate the position and rotation of the grid. The blue (positional node) is used to reposition the grid and the green (rotational node) is used to rotate it, as shown in the following screenshots:

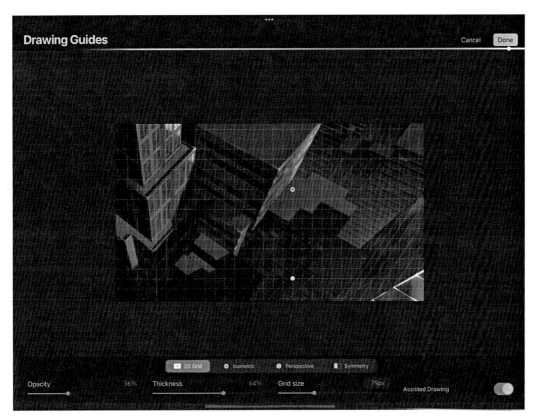

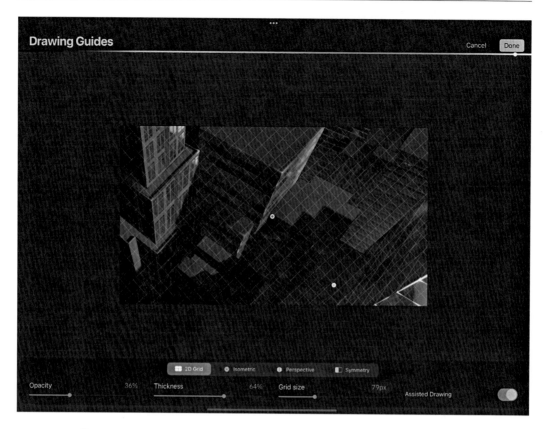

Figure 12.6 (a): Positional node repositions grid (b): Rotational node rotates grid

They also serve functions specific to the type of drawing guide, which we will discuss later in the chapter.

- **Opacity**: This slider controls the opacity of the gridlines.
- **Thickness**: By default, a drawing guide grid has thin lines, but this slider lets you control the line thickness further.

Now that you are familiar with the **Drawing Assist** interface, let us look at the different drawing guide styles.

Drawing squared grids with 2D Grid

The first type of drawing guide on the toolbar is **2D Grid**. This guide helps you draw straight lines in the vertical and horizontal directions. It functions like a ruler that restricts every stroke you draw to a straight vertical or horizontal line. The following screenshot shows rectangular panels, which can be drawn using this guide:

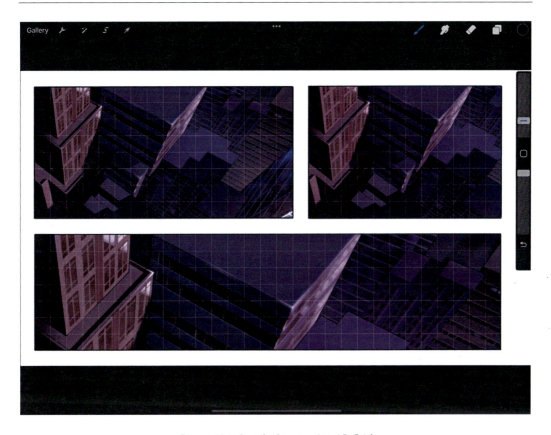

Figure 12.7: Panels drawn using 2D Grid

We will now look at the interface of this guide.

The 2D Grid interface

When **2D Grid** is selected, the toolbar has the interface shown in the following screenshot:

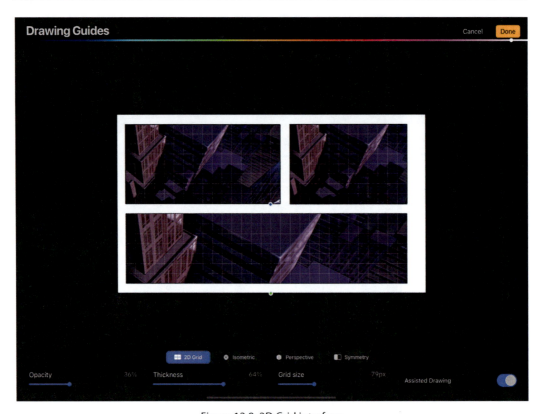

Figure 12.8: 2D Grid interface

These are the elements of this interface:

- **Opacity**: This slider controls the opacity of the gridlines.
- **Thickness**: This slider controls the thickness of the gridlines.
- **Grid size**: This slider controls how large the grid appears on the canvas.
- **Nodes**: This guide has both the positional and rotational nodes. The blue positional node lets you move around the grid, while the green rotational node rotates it.

  Tap on the either of these nodes to bring up a button called **Reset**, shown in the following screenshot:

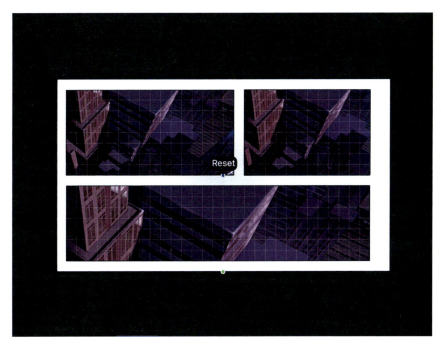

Figure 12.9: Reset grid

Tap it to reset the grid to its original position or rotation.

With this, you will be able to use the 2D Grid guide to draw squared grids. In the next section, we will discuss another similar style of drawing guide.

Drawing technical graphics with the Isometric Grid

The Isometric Grid functions in a way that is similar to the 2D Grid. The Isometric Grid lets you draw straight vertical lines, as well as lines at a 45° angle. This guide is useful for drawing isometric views in technical drawings. Shown below is an isometric diagram that can be drawn using this guide:

432   Using Assisted Drawing Tools

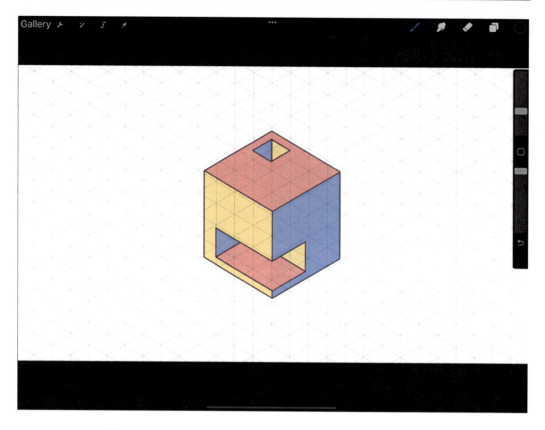

Figure 12.10: Technical graphic drawn with the Isometric Grid guide

We will now look at the interface of this guide.

The Isometric interface

When **Isometric** is selected, the toolbar has the interface shown in the following screenshot:

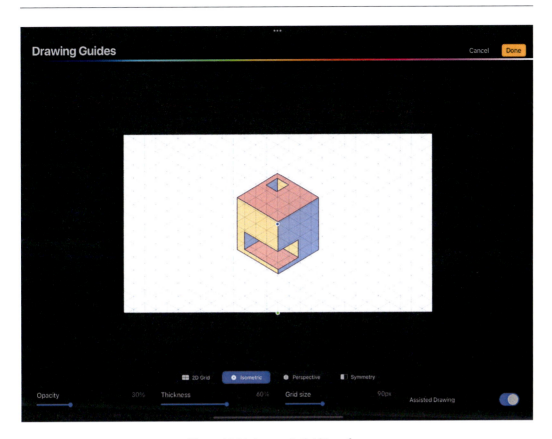

Figure 12.11: Isometric Grid interface

These are the elements of this interface:

- **Opacity**: This slider controls the opacity of the gridlines.
- **Thickness**: This slider controls the thickness of the gridlines.
- **Grid size**: This slider controls how large the grid appears on the canvas.
- **Nodes**: This guide has both the positional and rotational nodes, much like the previous guide. The blue positional node lets you move around the grid, while the green rotational node rotates it.

    Tap on either of these nodes to bring up a button called **Reset**, shown in the following screenshot:

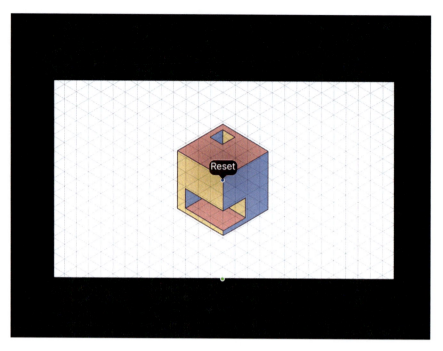

Figure 12.12: Reset grid

Tap it to reset the grid to its original position or rotation.

The next section will introduce the next type of guide, which functions slightly differently from the grid-style guides.

Realistic drawing with Perspective Guides

The **Perspective** guide is a special kind of assisted drawing tool. It helps you draw backgrounds and objects with a realistic perspective by adding up to three adjustable vanishing points. The following screenshots show one-point, two-point, and three-point perspectives that can be drawn using this guide:

Realistic drawing with Perspective Guides 435

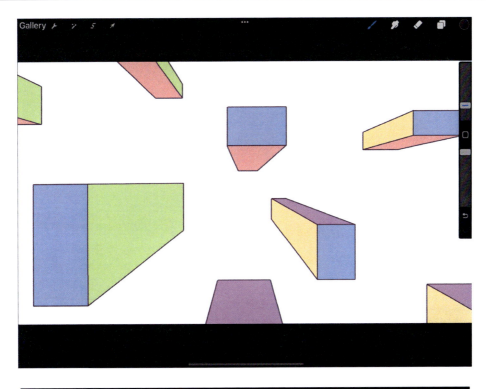

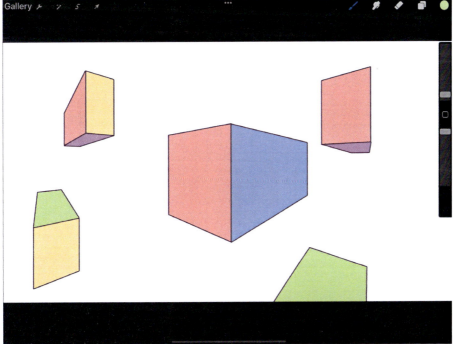

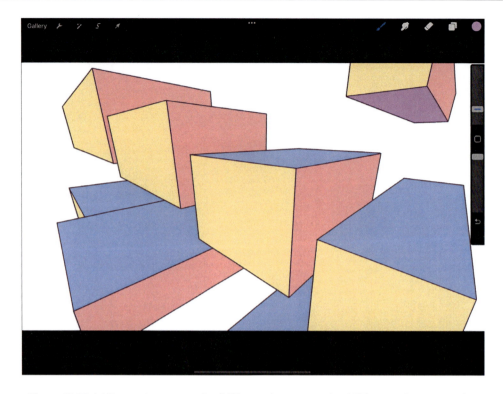

Figure 12.13: (a) One-point perspective (b) Two-point perspective (c) Three-point perspective

To use the **Perspective** guide, follow these steps:

1. Open **Actions** and select **Edit Drawing Guide**.
2. From the toolbar, select **Perspective**.
3. Tap anywhere on the screen to create a vanishing point at that spot. The vanishing point is marked by a blue node, as shown in the following screenshot:

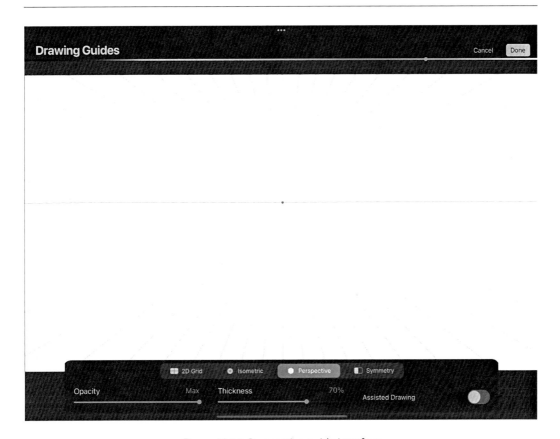

Figure 12.14: Perspective guide interface

This point may be inside or outside the canvas boundaries.

1. Add up to two more vanishing points similarly by tapping on the screen. All these points are adjustable. Place your finger on the node and move it around to reposition it. You will notice the perspective grid re-adjust itself as you move the vanishing points.
2. Tap on a vanishing point to bring up the two options shown in the following screenshot:

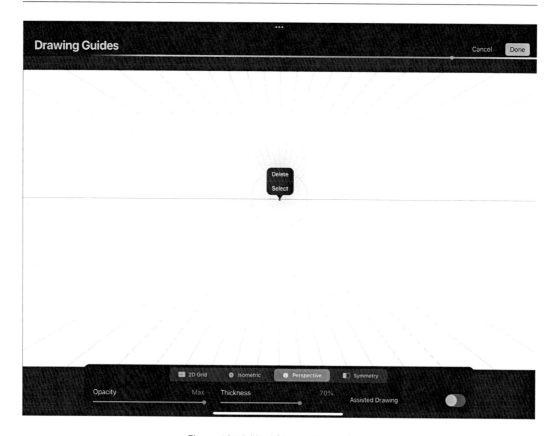

Figure 12.15: Vanishing point options

When you tap on **Select**, all changes made to the color, opacity, or thickness of the guide affect only the perspective lines radiating from that vanishing point. The **Delete** option removes a vanishing point.

3. Once you're happy with the perspective setup, tap on **Done** to exit the **Drawing Guides** interface and go back to drawing. Your lines will now follow this setup.

We will now look at the interface of this guide.

The Perspective interface

When **Perspective** is selected, the toolbar has the interface shown in the following screenshot:

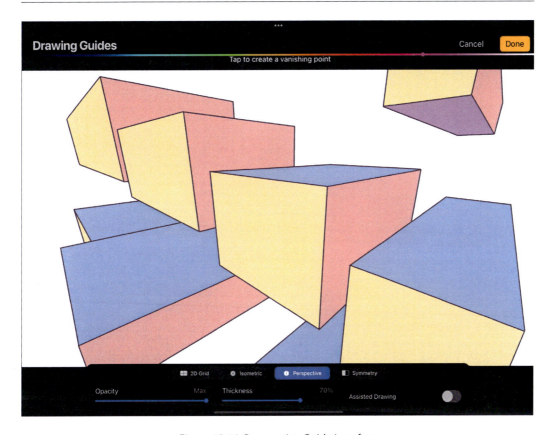

Figure 12.16: Perspective Guide interface

These are the elements of this interface:

- **Opacity**: This slider controls the opacity of the gridlines.
- **Thickness**: This slider controls the thickness of the gridlines.
- **Vanishing points**: These function as nodes that can reposition the guide. They can also be selected and deleted as we learned previously.

This tool will help you easily tackle drawing environments and objects that require knowledge of perspective. The next section will discuss the next and final type of drawing guide.

Symmetrical drawing with Symmetry Guides

The last type of drawing guide is the Symmetry Guide. It is used to draw perfectly symmetrical drawings along four different styles of alignment. The following screenshots show some drawings that can be drawn using this guide:

Using Assisted Drawing Tools

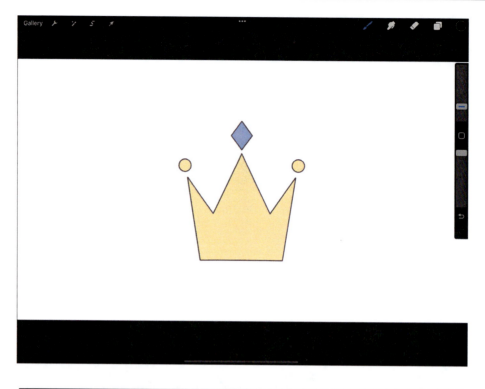

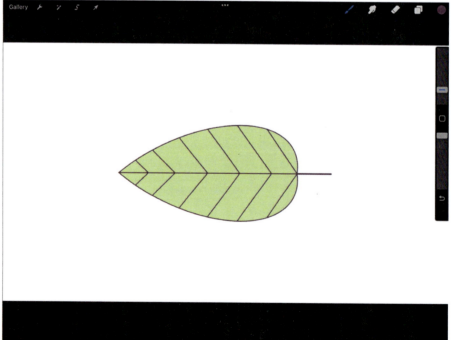

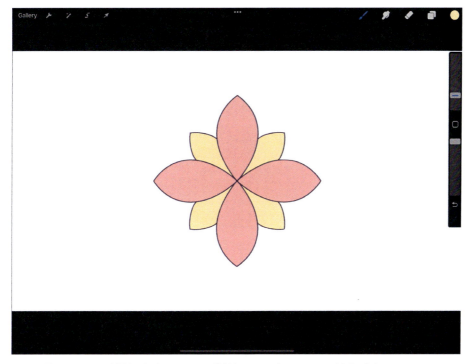

Figure 12.17: (a) Vertical symmetry (b) Horizontal symmetry (c) Radial symmetry

We will now look at the **Symmetry** interface.

The Symmetry interface

When **Symmetry** is selected, the toolbar has the interface shown in the following screenshot:

442 Using Assisted Drawing Tools

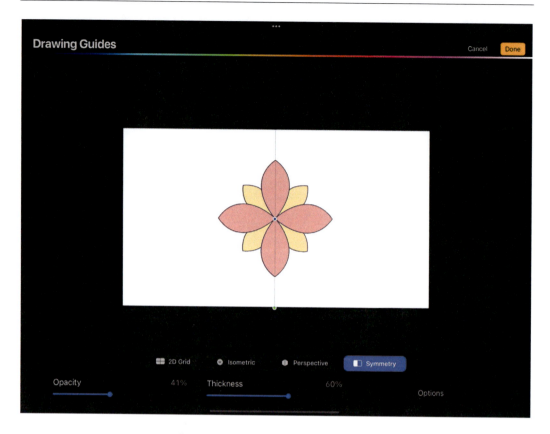

Figure 12.18: Symmetry Guide interface

These are the elements of this interface:

- **Opacity**: This slider controls the opacity of the guide.
- **Thickness**: This slider controls the thickness of the guide.
- **Options**: This button to the right brings up the following menu when tapped:

Symmetrical drawing with Symmetry Guides 443

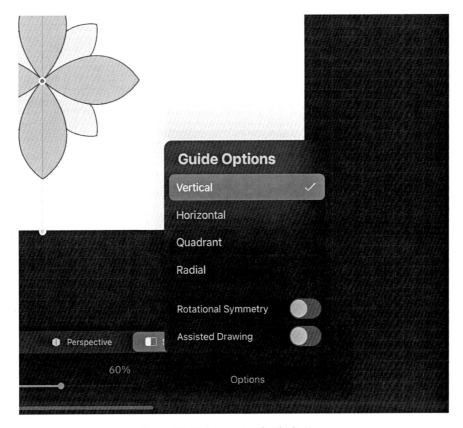

Figure 12.19: Symmetry Guide Options

These are the different styles of symmetry that can be achieved using this guide. We will learn more about them in the next sub-section.

- **Axes and nodes**: Each symmetry style has its own configuration of axes, be it a single horizontal or vertical axis or multiple radial ones. These axes appear on the canvas, along with the positional and rotational nodes like the previous guides.

Next, we will look into the different guide options for **Symmetry**

Guide Options

Tapping on the button labeled **Options** in the **Symmetry** toolbar brings up the following menu:

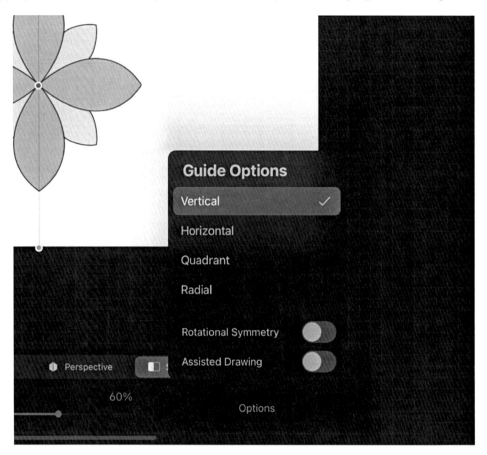

Figure 12.20: Symmetry Guide Options

These are the options available:

- **Vertical**: This option divides the canvas into two halves with a vertical axis. Drawings are mirrored in a left-right direction, as shown in the following screenshot:

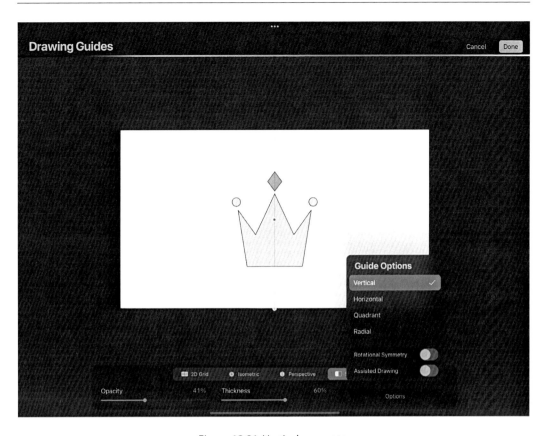

Figure 12.21: Vertical symmetry

- **Horizontal**: This option divides the canvas into two halves with a horizontal axis. Drawings are mirrored in an up-down direction, as shown in the following screenshot:

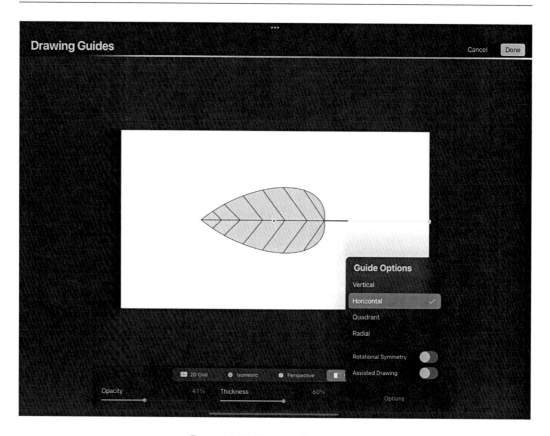

Figure 12.22: Horizontal symmetry

- **Quadrant**: This option divides the canvas into four quadrants with two intersecting vertical and horizontal axes. Drawings are mirrored four ways along each axis, as shown in the following screenshot:

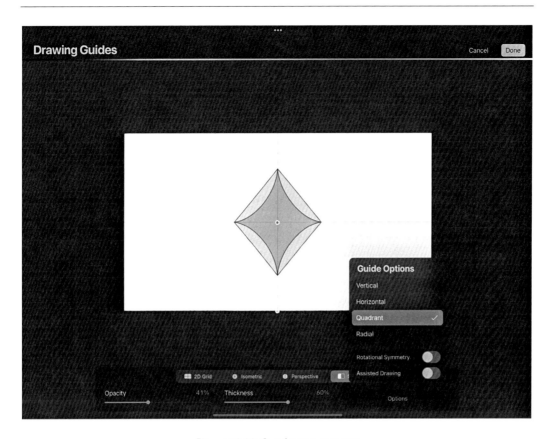

Figure 12.23: Quadrant symmetry

- **Radial**: This option divides the canvas into eight radial portions with four intersecting axes. Drawings are mirrored eight ways along each axis, as shown in the following screenshot:

Using Assisted Drawing Tools

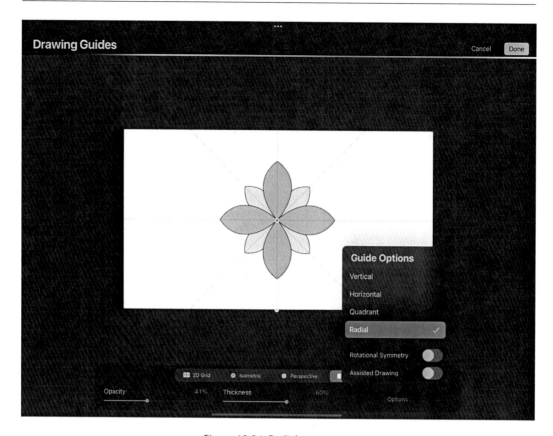

Figure 12.24: Radial symmetry

The next option on the menu is a toggle button called **Rotational Symmetry**. By default, the **Symmetry** Guide uses what is known as **Mirrored Symmetry**. This is when the drawing on one side is flipped once about the axis of symmetry, as shown in the following screenshot:

Figure 12.25: Mirrored Symmetry

Rotational Symmetry is when a drawing is flipped twice— once about the axis, and then along the direction of the axis, as shown in the following screenshot:

Figure 12.26: Rotational Symmetry

It gives rise to interesting results when used in combination with any of the four types of symmetry guides.

This brings us to the end of this chapter, where we discussed the various types of drawing guides available on Procreate. Let's summarize.

Summary

Drawing guides are assisted drawing tools available on the Procreate app. These tools help you draw accurately based on constraints. This chapter introduced you to the different types of drawing guides and how to use them.

We learned about drawing squared grids with vertical and horizontal lines using the **2D Grid** guide. The chapter also introduced how to create isometric technical drawings with the **Isometric** Grid Guide. The **Perspective** Guide makes it easy to incorporate realistic perspective and space into your artwork, using up to three vanishing points. Lastly, the chapter covered using the Symmetry Guide to make mirrored drawings across multiple configurations of axes.

In the next chapter, we will learn how to create animations in Procreate.

13
Using Animation Assist for 2D Animation

Animation works by creating the illusion of motion by placing one drawing after another. Each drawing is called a frame. The drawings change slightly from frame to frame, making the final output appear as if it's moving.

Aside from illustration, Procreate also offers robust tools for 2D animation. These tools are organized under a feature called **Animation Assist**. It works by converting your workspace from an illustration-focused interface to an animation-focused one.

In this chapter, you will be introduced to this feature in detail. This will help you create your own animations on the app. We will learn about the interface of Animation Assist, and how to use its specialized tools for animating.

We're going to cover the following broad topics here:

- Using the Animation Assist interface
- Fine-tuning motion using animation settings
- Editing frames with Frame options

By the end of this chapter, you will have learned how to create 2D animated clips in Procreate.

Using the Animation Assist interface

To start animating on Procreate, you must first switch to the animation interface, by activating something called Animation Assist.

Using Animation Assist for 2D Animation

Animation Assist can be toggled on and off using the **Canvas** tab of the **Actions** menu (the wrench-shaped icon in the top left-hand corner of the screen). To turn it on, follow these steps:

1. Tap the wrench icon to open the **Actions** menu popover and select the **Canvas** tab, as shown in the following screenshot:

Figure 13.1: Canvas tab

2. Toggle on the **Animation Assist** option. A timeline will appear at the bottom of the screen. This timeline houses the frames of your animation, as shown in the following screenshot:

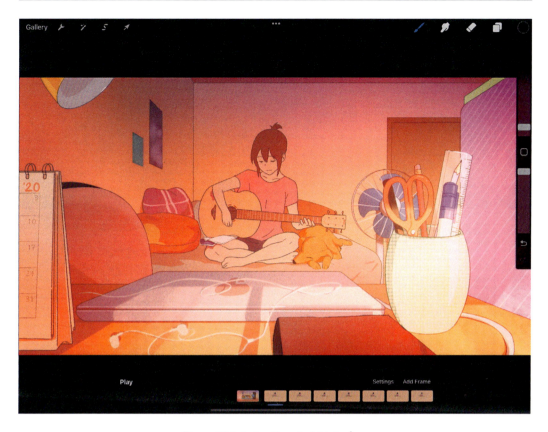

Figure 13.2: Animation Assist interface

3. This will activate Animation Assist on your canvas. This means that the canvas is now all set up for animating.

> **Important Note**
> Each layer is treated as a separate frame of animation. The layers on the bottom appear first on the timeline. If you want to have several elements in one frame, group them into a layer group. Each layer group is treated as a separate frame.

In the following sub-section, we'll go over the basics of how the Animation Assist interface works.

Animation Assist interface

The interface of the Animation Assist screen has the following elements:

- **Canvas**: When Animation Assist is on, the canvas shows only the currently selected frame as a solid opaque layer. This refers to the contents of the selected layer or layer group. This is unlike the regular illustration canvas, which shows all the visible layers. By default, the canvas also has onion skins turned on, which shows colored, transparent versions of the previous and next layers. The following screenshot shows onion skins. Only the lines have been made visible to clearly show the effect:

Figure 13.3: Animation canvas with onion skins

- **Timeline**: The timeline houses the frames of your animation in order. The primary frame, or the one you are working on, is indicated by a blue line underneath. Tap on any frame to jump to it and draw on it. The timeline can also be scrubbed with your finger to preview the animation on the canvas. When the visibility of a layer or group is turned off, its respective frame also disappears from the timeline.

- **Play/Pause** button: In the top-left corner of the animation toolbar, you will find a button labeled **Play**. This button can be used to play or pause your animation preview. When a preview is playing, the button says **Pause**.

- **Add Frame**: This button is placed in the top-right corner of the animation toolbar. It adds a frame right after your primary frame. Every frame gets added as a new layer.

- **Settings**: This button sits next to **Add Frame**. It brings up a popup when tapped, as shown in the following screenshot:

Figure 13.4: Settings

These are the settings that control various attributes of your animation. We will learn more about them later in this chapter.

- **Frame options**: Tap on any frame to bring up frame-specific options, as shown in the following screenshot:

Figure 13.5: Frame options

We will learn more about them further ahead in this chapter.

> **Important Note**
> Animation Assist allows you to import videos into Procreate. When a video clip is imported into the Procreate **Gallery**, the resulting canvas turns on Animation Assist automatically. The frames of the video, in order, make up the frames on the animation timeline, until the layer limit is reached.

Now that you are familiar with the Animation Assist interface, let us look more closely at animation settings.

Fine-tuning motion using animation settings

Animation settings refers to a set of tools that allow you to fine-tune your animation to look how you want it to. These settings also let you choose how your animation preview will appear. To bring up this menu, tap on the **Settings** button in the animation toolbar, as shown in the following screenshot:

Fine-tuning motion using animation settings   457

Figure 13.6: Animation settings

We will now look at the interface of this popup.

Preview settings

The first three options on the panel, **Loop**, **Ping-Pong**, and **One Shot**, control how the preview of your animation plays.

These are the playthrough options:

- **Loop**: This option is selected by default. It plays your animation from beginning to end on a loop until you press **Pause**.
- **Ping-Pong**: This option plays your animation from beginning to end and then in reverse, and repeats this way, going back and forth. Exporting an animation with **Ping-Pong** exports a clip that loops back and forth, just like the preview. For instance, this mode will be useful for animating a pendulum.
- **One Shot**: This option plays your animation from start to finish only once, and then stops until you press **Play** again.

In the next sub-section, we will discuss the next set of animation settings.

Frame settings

The next three options on the panel, **Frames Per Second**, **Onion skin frames**, and **Onion skin opacity**, affect the frames of your animation.

These settings work in the following ways:

- **Frames Per Second**: This option decides how many frames will be played through in 1 second. It is controlled by a slider that runs from 1 to 58 FPS. The higher the frame rate, the more frames you must draw to create a 1-second clip.

- **Onion skin frames**: This option controls how many frames on either side of the primary frame will show up on the canvas as onion skins.

    Onion skin frames are colored, low-opacity frames on both sides of the selected frame, as shown in the following screenshot:

Figure 13.7: Onion skins

This helps you animate accurately since both the initial and final frames are clearly visible. By default, this slider is set to **1**. This means the canvas will show your primary frame at full opacity, as well as onion skins of one frame before it (in red) and after it (in green). Using the slider, you can set this range to include as many frames on both sides as you wish. At **0**, no onion skins show up. At **Max** value, all the existing frames on either side of the primary frame are visible.

- **Onion skin opacity**: Use this slider to determine how solid or transparent the onion skins appear.

In the next sub-section, we will discuss the last two options.

Appearance settings

The last two animation settings, **Blend primary frame** and **Onion skin colors**, have to do with how the frames appear on the canvas.

These settings work in the following ways:

- **Blend primary frame**: By default, the primary frame has a solid appearance. This setting is a toggle, which blends the primary frame, making it transparent like an onion skin.
- **Onion skin colors**: This option controls the colors of the onion skin frames. Tap on it to bring up a color companion popup, as shown in the following screenshot:

Figure 13.8: Onion skin colors editor

The bar at the top left represents the frames prior to the primary frame, and the one on the right represents the frames after. Tap on each bar to edit the color assigned to it. Once happy, tap the arrow to go back to the **Settings** menu, or tap anywhere outside the popup to resume animating.

In this section, we discussed the settings that can be used to control aspects of your animation and fine-tune it.

In the next section, you will be introduced to tools specific to individual frames of animation.

Editing frames with Frame options

Frame options are certain settings that can be applied to each frame individually, without affecting the others. To bring up this popup, tap on the frame you want to edit, as shown in the following screenshot:

Figure 13.9: Frame options

Let's take a closer look at these options:

- **Hold duration**: Timing is important in animation. Sometimes, you may want to hold a drawing for longer than one frame. This slider lets you do so without needing to duplicate a frame, and by extension, without disturbing the layer count.

- **Duplicate**: This option creates a duplicate of the frame after it. This function is different from increasing the hold duration as it creates a fresh new frame on a new layer/group. This layer or group can be edited independently of the original one.

- **Foreground**: The rightmost frame, corresponding to the topmost layer/group of the canvas, can be set as the animation foreground. This means that the contents of that frame will consistently appear as a still frame over the rest of your animation. The **Frame options** popup for only this frame has a toggle labeled **Foreground**, as shown in the following screenshot:

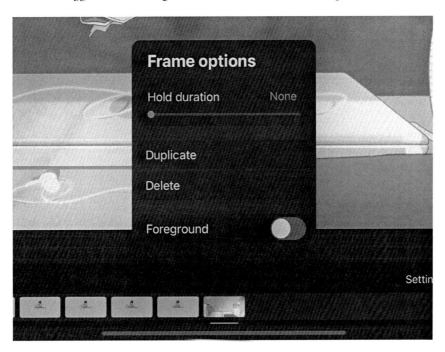

Figure 13.10: Foreground toggle

Once a frame has been made the foreground, it can't be moved from the rightmost spot on the timeline. The layer position is likewise locked to the top. No other frames can be moved past it to the right unless **Foreground** is toggled off. There can't be multiple foreground frames. You may, however, choose to have multiple objects in the foreground, by grouping those layers into a single frame. The following screenshot shows multiple objects in the foreground and their corresponding layer group:

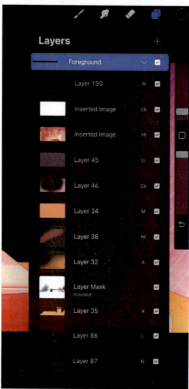

Figure 13.11: (Top) the foreground; (bottom) the foreground layer group

- **Background**: The leftmost frame, corresponding to the lowest layer/group of the canvas, can be set as the animation background. This means that the contents of that frame will consistently appear as a still frame behind the rest of your animation. The **Frame options** popup for only this frame has a toggle labeled **Background**, as shown in the following screenshot:

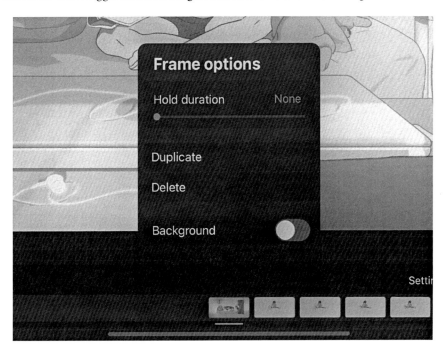

Figure 13.12: Background toggle

Once a frame has been made the background, it can't be moved from the leftmost spot on the timeline. The layer position is likewise locked to the bottom. No other frames can be moved past it to the left unless **Background** is toggled off. There can't be multiple background frames. You may, however, choose to have multiple objects in the background, by grouping those layers into a single frame. The following screenshot shows multiple objects in the background and their corresponding layer group:

Figure 13.13: (Top) the background; (bottom) the background layer group

- **Delete**: This option deletes the frame. If the frame is a layer group consisting of multiple layers, all of those layers will be deleted.

In this section, we learned about the options used to edit frames and give them specific roles, such as **Foreground** and **Background**.

With this, we have covered all the features of Animation Assist. We can now summarize this chapter.

Summary

Procreate is a versatile tool that enables you to draw as well as animate. The Animation Assist interface is optimized to facilitate your needs as a 2D animator. In this chapter, you were introduced to the features of this interface, which allow you to easily animate by making subtle changes in your drawings over time to create smooth and natural motion.

Animation Assist has specialized tools to preview your animation, tweak its settings, and edit individual frames. With animation settings, we discussed how aspects such as frame rate and onion skins are useful while creating an animation. Under **Frame options**, we talked about how each frame can have its own settings and take on specialized roles. At the end of this chapter, you are now familiar with all these tools and are able to use them to create polished 2D animations.

The next chapter will introduce you to a feature similar to Animation Assist, but with a special focus on using Procreate as a sketchbook.

14
Sketchbooking with Page Assist

While most users are familiar with using digital painting software one canvas at a time, Procreate offers a special feature that allows you to work on several canvases at once, like the pages of a sketchbook. This feature, called **Page Assist**, was rolled out with the latest Procreate 5.2 update.

Page Assist helps you create several frames in a single canvas and work on each as a separate page. You can edit and organize the pages of a document, or simply use Procreate as a sketchbook that you can skim through.

We're going to cover the following broad topics here:

- Using the **Page Assist** interface
- Adjusting pages using **Page options**

By the end of this chapter, you will know how to use **Page Assist** to work on several pages in one canvas.

Using the Page Assist interface

To start working with pages on Procreate, you must first activate **Page Assist**.

Page Assist can be toggled on and off using the **Canvas** tab of the **Actions** menu (the wrench-shaped icon at the top left-hand corner of the screen). To turn it on, follow these steps:

1. Tap the wrench icon to open the **Actions** menu popover and select the **Canvas** option, as shown in the following figure:

Figure 14.1: Canvas tab

2. Toggle on the **Page Assist** option. A timeline will appear at the bottom of the screen. This timeline houses frames corresponding to each page, as shown in the following figure:

Figure 14.2: Page Assist interface

This will activate **Page Assist** on your canvas.

> **Important Note**
> Each layer is treated as a separate page. The layers on the bottom appear first on the timeline. If you want to have several elements on one page, group them into a layer group. Each layer group is treated as a separate page.

In the following sub-section, we'll go over the basics of how the **Page Assist** interface works.

Page Assist interface

The interface of the **Page Assist** screen has the following elements:

- **Canvas**: When **Page Assist** is on, the canvas shows only the currently selected page. This refers to the contents of the selected layer or layer group. This is unlike the regular illustration canvas, which shows all the visible layers.

- **Timeline**: The timeline houses the pages of your sketchbook or document in order. The primary page, or the one you are working on, is indicated by a blue line underneath it. Tap on any page to jump to it and draw on it. You may reorder the pages on your timeline by holding and dragging them to the desired position. You may also reorder pages directly from the **Layers** panel.

  When the visibility of a layer or group is turned off, its respective page also disappears from the timeline.

- **New Page**: This button is placed at the top-right corner of the **Page Assist** toolbar. It adds a page right after your primary page. Every page gets added as a new layer.

- **Page options**: Tap on any page to bring up page-specific options, as shown in the following figure:

Figure 14.3: Page options

We will learn more about them further ahead in this chapter.

> **Important Note**
>
> **Page Assist** allows you to import PDF files into Procreate. When a PDF document is imported into the Procreate **Gallery**, the resulting canvas turns on **Page Assist** automatically. The pages of the document, in order, make up the pages on the timeline, until the layer limit is reached. This feature allows you to conveniently import and sign documents or fill in forms on Procreate.

Now that you are familiar with the **Page Assist** interface, let us look more closely at the options available for pages.

Adjusting pages using Page options

Page options provides certain settings that can be applied to each page individually, without affecting the others. To bring up this popup, tap on the page you want to edit, as shown in the following figure:

Figure 14.4: Page options

Let's take a closer look at these options:

- **Duplicate**: This option creates a duplicate of the page after it. It creates a fresh new page on a new layer/group. This layer or group can be edited independently of the original one.
- **Delete**: This option deletes the page.
- **Background**: The leftmost page, corresponding to the lowest layer/group of the canvas, can be set as the background page. This means that the contents of that page will consistently appear as a background behind all the other pages. The **Page options** popup for only this page has a toggle labeled **Background**, as shown in the following figure:

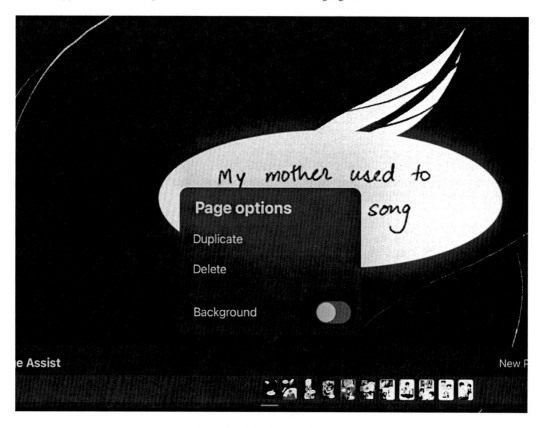

Figure 14.5: Background toggle

Once a page has been chosen as the background, it can't be moved from the leftmost spot on the timeline. The layer position is likewise locked to the bottom. No other pages can be moved past it to the left, unless **Background** is toggled off. There can't be multiple background pages. You may, however, choose to have multiple objects in the background, by grouping those layers into a single page.

> Important Note
> The **Background** feature is useful for several cases. For instance, you may use it when you want a footnote or watermark to appear on all pages of a document, or to set a paper or notebook texture underneath to give your pages a traditional feel.

In this section, we learned about the options used to edit pages and give them a specific **Background** role.

With this, we have covered all the features of **Page Assist**. We can now summarize this chapter.

Summary

In this chapter, we talked about **Page Assist**, a useful tool in Procreate that helps you work on several pages within a single canvas. You learned about the uses of this tool in importing and editing documents, as well as creating multi-page artworks such as sketchbooks and comics.

You learned how to activate **Page Assist** on a canvas, as well as how to import PDF documents directly into Procreate. We also discussed the interface of **Page Assist**, which allows you to sequentially arrange your pages, and edit each of them independently. With **Page options**, this chapter introduced page-specific settings that let you duplicate and delete pages, or set a page as the background.

By now, you should be familiar with the features of **Page Assist** and be able to use it to create your own digital sketchbook.

15
Painting on 3D Models

Through the course of this book, we have explored Procreate as a robust tool for 2D painting. This chapter will cover the final function of the app, which goes beyond a two-dimensional canvas and allows you to paint on 3D objects. In the latest version – Procreate 5.2 – developers introduced a feature that lets you import 3D models into the gallery and paint on top of them.

In this chapter, we will look in depth at what makes 3D painting unique and how the familiar interface of Procreate is modified for a task beyond 2D illustration.

We're going to cover the following broad topics in this chapter:

- Opening a 3D model
- Understanding 3D models
- Using the 3D interface
- Working with layers in 3D
- Transforming graphics on a 3D model
- Modifying the environment using Lighting Studio
- Exporting from a 3D canvas

Opening a 3D model

3D painting canvases work differently from their 2D counterparts. When a 3D model is imported into Procreate, it opens in a 3D canvas, specially designed for this purpose. There are two ways to import 3D models – using the **Import** button in the **Gallery** and by downloading Procreate's own model pack. We will discuss both options in this section.

Importing a 3D model

The **Import** button sits in the top-right corner of the Procreate Gallery, as shown in the following screenshot:

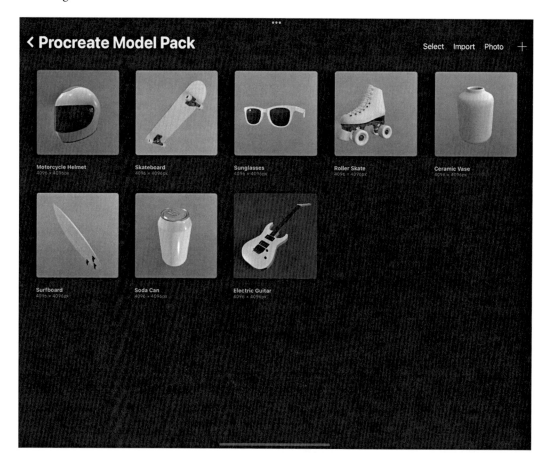

Figure 15.1 : The Import button

Tapping this button will open the **Files** app on your iPad. From here, you can import an external 3D object. Procreate supports .OBJ and .USDZ, two of the most common file types for 3D objects.

You can also drag and drop 3D files directly into Procreate. These files will automatically open in a 3D canvas.

Importing Procreate's Model pack

Procreate offers its own pack of 3D models, consisting of a variety of objects. When you freshly install or update to Procreate 5.2, you will see a welcome screen with a video, as shown in the following screenshot:

Figure 15.2 : The Procreate 5.2 welcome screen

Here, you will find a button that says **Model pack**. Tap on this button to download the pack. These 3D models will directly open in Procreate and don't need to be imported separately. To access this welcome screen anytime, go to **Actions | Help | What's New**. The following screenshot shows this Model pack in Procreate:

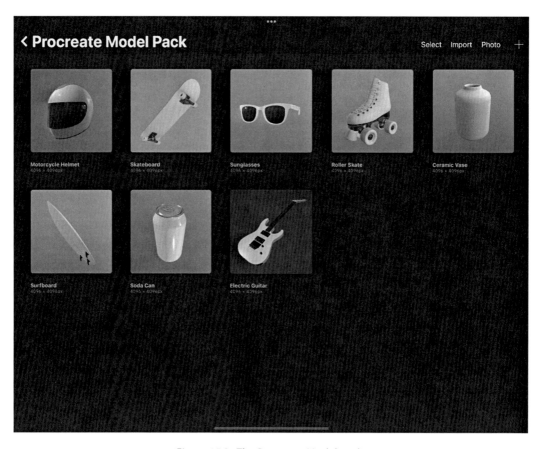

Figure 15.3 : The Procreate Model pack

> **Important Note**
> Make sure the .OBJ or .USDZ file you are trying to import comes with a UV map. The file will be unsupported otherwise. UV maps will be explained in the next section.

In the next section, we will get a basic understanding of how 3D models are composed, especially how painting on them works.

Understanding 3D models

Before getting into the 3D painting features of Procreate, this section will help you form an understanding of how painting on 3D models is made possible. For that, we need to look at painted 3D models as a composite of two parts: the model and the UV map. The presence of a UV map allows you to paint on a 3D model, which would otherwise not be possible. In the following subsection, we will discuss UV maps.

UV maps

3D painting in Procreate requires your 3D model to have an associated UV map. Think of a UV map as a two-dimensional skin that covers all the surfaces of your model like wrapping paper. The following diagram explains how a 2D UV map sits on a 3D model:

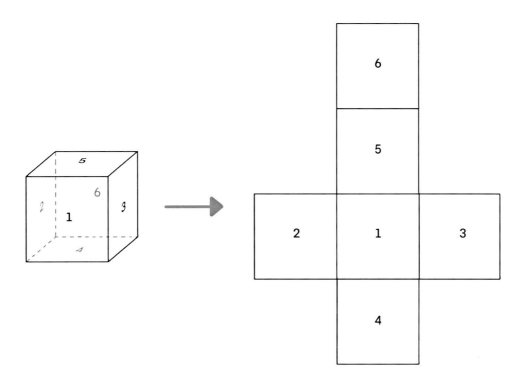

Figure 15.4 : A 3D model versus an unwrapped UV map

UV maps provide a 2D surface to let you paint. This is because 3D models, by themselves, exist in 3D space and can't be painted on. When importing a 3D model into Procreate, consider the following things:

- The model must have an associated UV map. A good way to find out whether a .OBJ or .USDZ file has one is to check whether they have any textures on the model surface. Note that some UV maps may be blank.
- UV maps that contain overlap or leave blank spaces on the model are not suitable for 3D painting, even if they import into Procreate. If possible, try to find models that are specifically created to be painted on.

Once you're familiar with the basics of how 3D painting works, you can start learning about the 3D interface of Procreate.

Using the 3D interface

A 3D canvas is mostly similar to its 2D counterpart. In this section, we will go over the basic interface and gestures that are unique to 3D painting in Procreate.

The workspace

Starting off, we will be looking at the workspace for 3D painting. The following screenshot shows the interface:

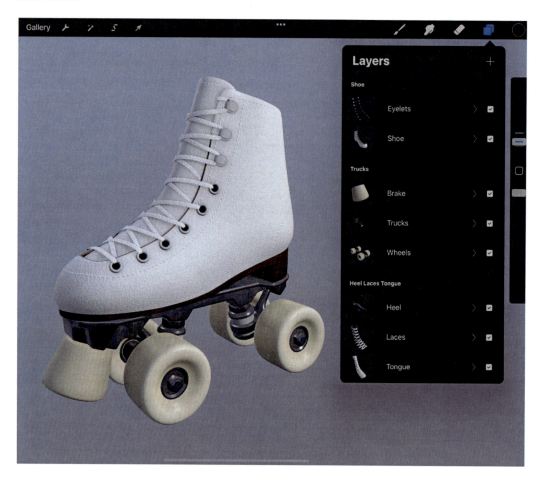

Figure 15.5 : The 3D painting interface

The following are the elements in your workspace:

- The 3D model: Painting on a 3D model works much the same way as 2D painting, except this time, the painted strokes lay on top of a 3D surface (the canvas). This model can be moved and rotated to access different parts of the canvas. For 3D models comprising multiple parts, you can tap on each part to select and draw on.

    Unlike a 2D background, a 3D model exists in an infinite, neutral space. The attributes of a 3D background can be changed using **Lighting Studio**. We'll learn more about it later in the chapter, in the *Modifying the environment using Lighting Studio* section.

- The **Layers** panel: Layers have slightly different features in a 3D canvas. Layers show all the texture sets that make up the separate components of your 3D model. Simple models may have just one or a few texture sets, while complex ones have several. Refer to the *Working with layers in 3D* section to understand more information about layers.

In the next two subsections, we'll discuss the **Actions** menu. In a 3D canvas, the **Actions** menu sports additional features. There is a new option available in the **Reference** companion. You may also notice that the **Video** tab is replaced by a brand new **3D** tab. Let's discuss the first of these additions.

The Reference companion

You may remember learning about the **Reference** companion in *Chapter 4, Using the Actions Menu*. Tap the wrench-shaped icon in the top-left corner of the screen to open the **Actions** menu, select the **Canvas** tab, and toggle on **Reference**. Doing so will open a floating window with a smaller preview of your canvas. This is the **Reference** companion. It allows you to use references while you work, as shown in the following screenshot:

482 Painting on 3D Models

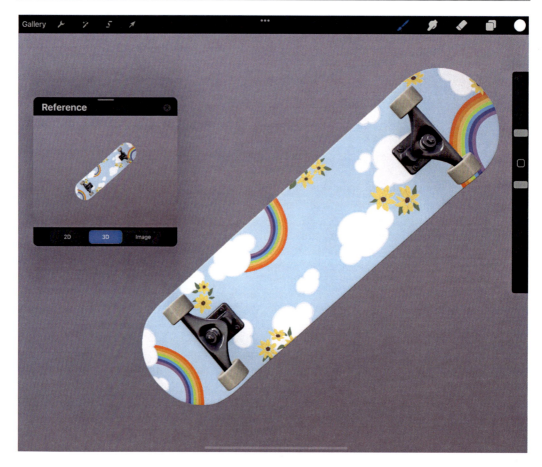

Figure 15.6 : The Reference companion

At the bottom of the **Reference** companion window, there are three options: **2D**, **3D**, and **Image**. They serve the following functions:

- **2D**: When this option is selected, the reference window shows the unwrapped view of the texture map of the currently selected mesh (the 3D component), as shown in the following screenshot:

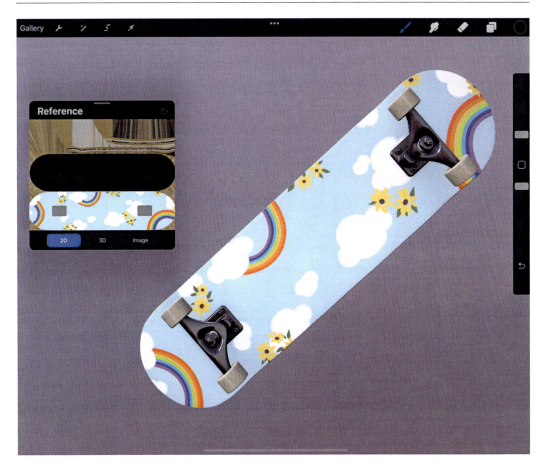

Figure 15.7 : The 2D reference showing a UV unwrap of the Board mesh

Select other layers to observe how the reference changes. Any strokes you make on the model will appear on the 2D reference, corresponding to their location on the UV map.

- **3D**: When this option is selected, the reference window shows a separate view of the 3D model, as shown in the following screenshot:

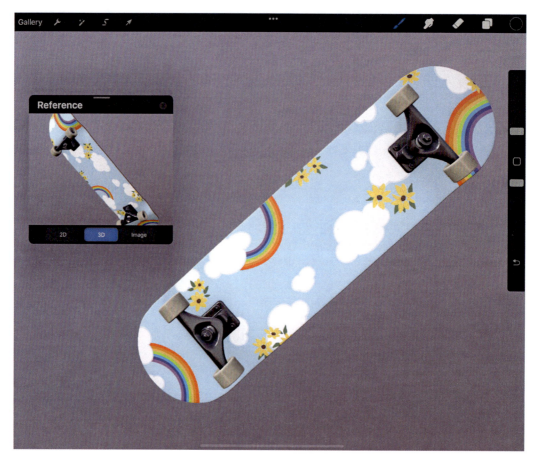

Figure 15.8 : The 3D reference

This view can be moved and rotated independently, while also reflecting any strokes made on the actual model.

- **Image**: With this option, you can import an image from your gallery to use as a reference. Tap on **Import Image** to select a reference picture from **Photos**, as shown in the following screenshot:

Figure 15.9: Reference image

Tap on **Clear** to remove the current reference image. You can also use the eyedropper to pick colors directly from the reference image.

In the next subsection, you will be introduced to the **3D** menu, which is unique to the 3D painting interface.

The 3D menu

The **3D** tab can be found in the **Actions** menu in place of the **Video** tab. It is indicated by a little hexagonal icon, as shown in the following screenshot:

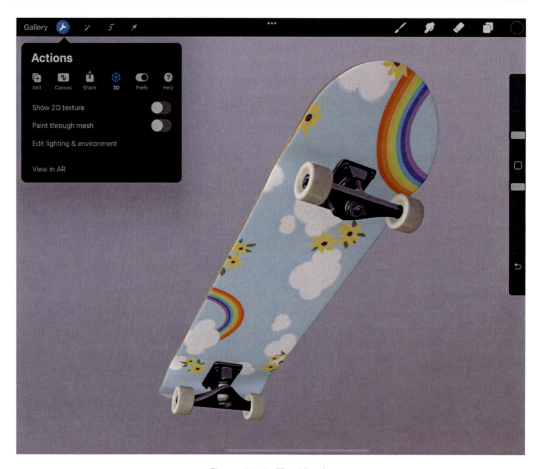

Figure 15.10 : The 3D tab

This menu has utility tools specific to 3D painting, which we'll discuss here:

- **Show 2D texture**: This is a toggle that displays the unwrapped 2D texture on the canvas instead of the 3D model. The canvas will show the UV unwrap of the selected mesh, as shown in the following screenshot:

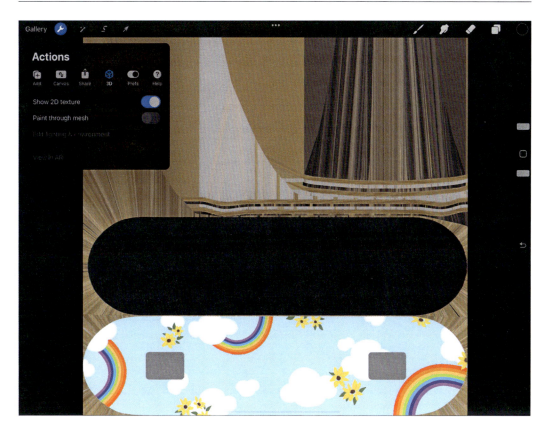

Figure 15.11 : 2D texture

- **Paint through mesh**: This option is helpful when you have overlapping 3D components. Toggling it on lets you paint a continuous image on a mesh even if it has another texture set blocking it. When toggled off, the area blocked off by the overlapping meshes will be left blank. The following screenshots demonstrate the difference between the two:

Figure 15.12 : (a) Paint through mesh active, and (b) Paint through mesh inactive

- **Edit lighting & environment**: This option will take you to Lighting Studio, which is used for setting up the ambient lighting and environment for your model. You will learn more about it in the *Modifying the environment using Lighting Studio* section of this chapter.
- **View in AR**: Use this feature to activate the camera and view your 3D model in the real world using **augmented reality** (**AR**).

With this, we have covered the additional features of the **Actions** menu. The next section is all about the gestures used in 3D painting.

3D gestures

3D painting borrows some regular 2D gestures, even though their effects may look different on a 3D canvas. It also has 3D-exclusive gestures, which we will learn about here.

First, let's look at the basic gestures, as follows:

- **Paint**: By default, you need the Apple Pencil to be able to draw, smudge, and erase on the model. These actions work the same way as 2D. Finger gestures are used for rotating and moving the model.

    However, you can change your painting input to your finger by going to **Actions | Prefs | Gesture Controls | General | Enable 3D painting with finger**.

    Once finger painting has been activated, you will need to hold down the **Modify** button to move and rotate your model:

- **Move the model**: Use a two-finger dragging gesture to move your 3D model around in space.
- **Rotate the model**: Use a one-finger dragging gesture to rotate your 3D model in any direction. A quick one-finger swipe in any direction will make the model spin about its center of focus.
- **Pinch to zoom**: Pinch to zoom in and out of your 3D model.
- **Resize with Quick Pinch**: Make a quick pinching gesture on the screen to fit the 3D model within the screen area. This gesture also works inside the **Reference** companion.

  Note that while Quick Pinch will return the model to its original size, it won't reset any changes in rotation/orientation.

Next, let's look at the more advanced gestures for 3D models:

- **Select mesh**: When you tap on any component of the 3D model, it will flash blue, indicating that the layer corresponding to that mesh has been selected. Your painting will now affect only that component.
- **Select all meshes**: Hold down the **Modify** button and tap on any mesh to instantly select all meshes within that texture set. This is indicated by the texture set flashing blue. Your strokes will now affect all the meshes in the current texture set.
- **Move center of focus**: The center of focus is the point about which a 3D model rotates. By default, it is at its center, but it changes position every time you rotate it. Give your model a quick spin to find out its current center of focus.

This section introduced to you the interface and gestures of 3D painting in Procreate. In the next section, we will discuss the features of 3D layers.

Working with layers in 3D

Layers are an interesting subject when it comes to 3D painting. Although they look similar to those in 2D, 3D layers function differently. In this section, we will familiarize ourselves with the various layer functions in a 3D canvas.

Texture sets

When you open the **Layers** panel in a 3D canvas, you will see layer "groups," corresponding to each separate component of a 3D model. These groups are called texture sets. Each texture set is indicated with a label. The following screenshot shows a model with two texture sets, **Trucks** and **Board**:

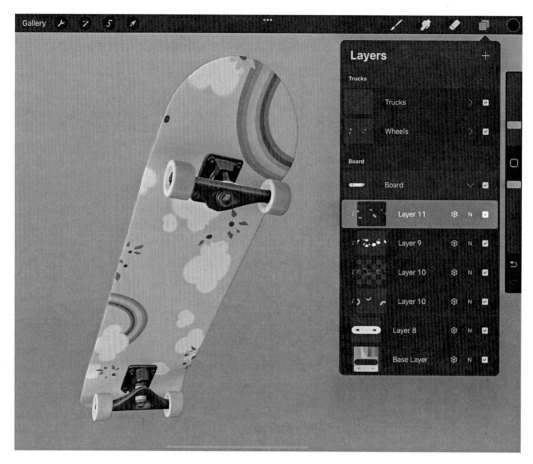

Figure 15.13 : Texture sets

If the model is a simple one, you will find fewer texture sets and vice versa. Components that share the same UV map come under the same set and share a common base layer.

Meshes

Each texture set has associated meshes. You can think of these as "subcomponents." For example, the **Trucks** texture set in the following screenshot has the **Trucks** and **Wheels** meshes under it:

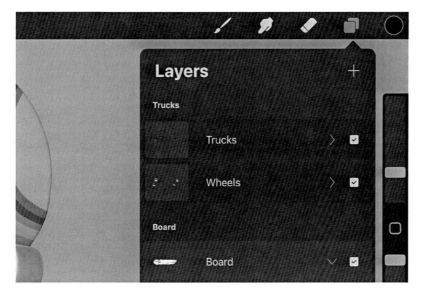

Figure 15.14 : Meshes

Meshes under a single texture set share the same base layer. When a mesh is selected, painting will only affect the part of the base layer being used by that mesh. New layers created on top of the base layer are also shared by all the meshes in the texture set.

Base Layer

When it comes to the Procreate Model pack, you will find that each texture set of each model comes with a Base Layer. This layer contains all the original color and texture information of the 3D model. A Base Layer is shared by all the meshes in the set. The base layer of the **Trucks** set is shown in the following screenshot:

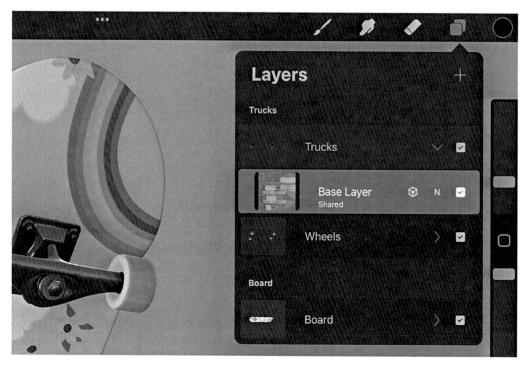

Figure 15.15 : Base Layer

In the **Layers** panel, the base layer appears under whichever mesh is selected, like a floating layer. While it's possible to paint on the base layer, doing so is an invasive process, since you will essentially paint over and lose the original color and texture. To avoid this, it's always a good idea to either duplicate it or create an **Additional Layer** on top of it. A base layer can be set to any blend mode, just like a 2D layer.

> **Important Note**
> Some 3D models may not come with a base layer at all. You can still create new layers for its meshes.

Additional Layers

An Additional Layer is any new layer created within a texture set and shared with all the meshes in it, as shown in the following screenshot:

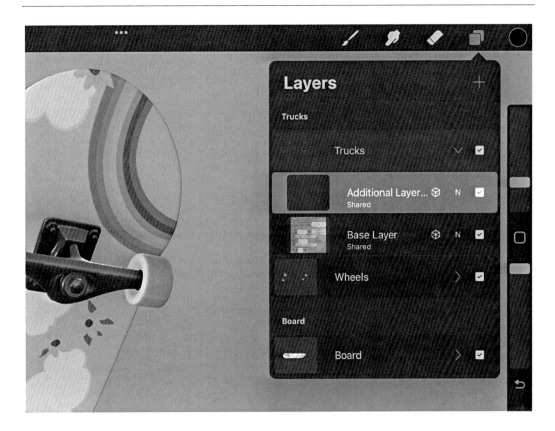

Figure 15.16 : Additional Layer

You can use these layers to paint not only graphics but also materials onto your 3D model. We will discuss materials in the next subsection. All other layer options for additional layers work just like 2D layers. Refer to *Chapter 7, Organizing Your Layers*, for more information on layer options.

Materials

When you paint on a layer, you will see that your stroke covers the surface of the model as an opaque area, erasing all its material and texture information, as shown in the following screenshot:

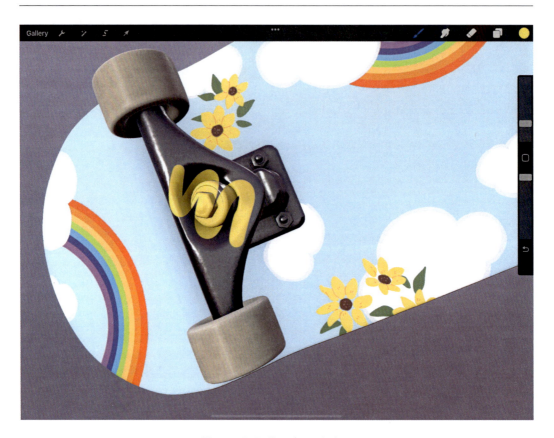

Figure 15.17 : Regular painting

However, each 3D layer has special features that make it possible to paint material properties onto a 3D model. When you alter these properties, the same 3D model can appear to be made of different materials. These properties are called **Colour**, **Roughness**, and **Metallic**. Tap on the little hexagon icon on the layer, called the **Materials** icon, to reveal these layer properties, as shown in the following screenshot:

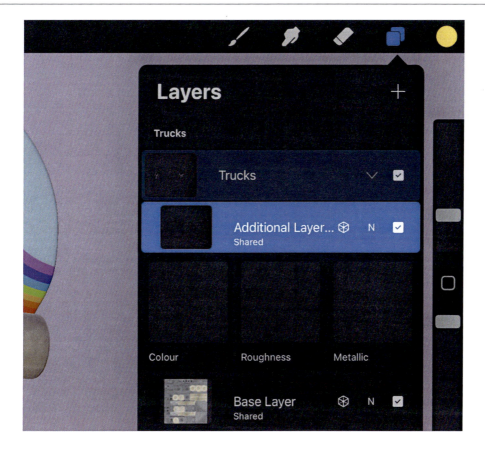

Figure 15.18 : Materials

Each of these can be painted on separately and have different effects on the 3D model. Let's discuss them:

- **Colour**: Tap on the panel labeled **Colour** and start painting. Your strokes will affect only the color of the mesh without changing its texture or material, as shown in the following screenshot:

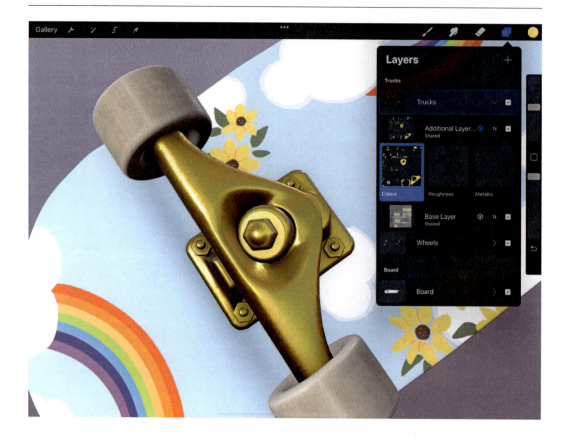

Figure 15.19 : Colour

- **Roughness**: This decides how glossy or matte the surface will look. You can only paint in grayscale on it, much like a layer mask. Different values of gray impart different levels of roughness. Black represents the glossiest finish, and white makes it look matte, as shown in the following screenshots:

Figure 15.20 : (a) Roughness painted with white, and (b) Roughness painted with black

- **Metallic**: This decides whether the surface will look metallic. Here too you can only paint in grayscale. Different values of gray impart different levels of metallic texture. White represents a completely metallic finish, and black makes it look non-metallic, as shown in the following screenshots:

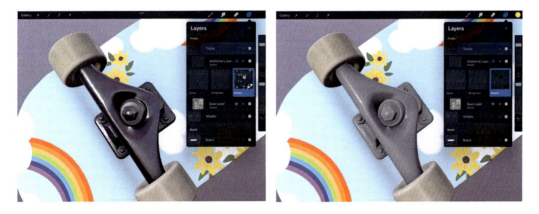

Figure 15.21 : (a) Metallic painted with white, and (b) Metallic painted with black

> **Important Note**
> Some brushes have 3D attributes that allow them to paint **Roughness** and **Metallic** information along with color. To learn more about brush attributes, refer to *Chapter 9, Brush Studio Settings – Editing and Combining Brushes*.

Material options

The three material panels behave like miniature layers and have their very own version of **Layer Options** called **Material Options**, as shown in the following screenshot:

Figure 15.22 : Material Options

Each material has its own menu, so they can be altered separately. In this subsection, we'll discuss all the options in this menu:

- **Select**: This option creates a selection mask with the layer contents, activating the **Selections** tool in the process. This selection can now be drawn in, copied, or transformed.

- **Copy**: This option copies the layer contents and makes them available on the clipboard. These contents can now be pasted in another layer, canvas, or even textboxes that support images, such as those on Twitter.
- **Fill Layer**: This option fills the layer with the currently selected color. For grayscale layers, the layer is filled with a gray of the same value as the active color.
- **Clear**: This option erases the layer contents. This effect can also be achieved by scrubbing the screen with three fingers.
- **Invert**: This option inverts the colors currently painted. This means that every color becomes another color that is diametrically opposite to it on the color wheel. In grayscale images, blacks and whites get interchanged.

With this, we have covered all the layer properties for a 3D layer. In the next section, let's take a look at another common 2D tool that works very differently in a 3D canvas – **Transform**.

Transforming graphics on a 3D model

The **Transform** tool is used to move, rotate, or otherwise modify graphics both in the 2D and 3D contexts. We discussed the 2D transform tool in *Chapter 5, Selecting and Transforming*. In a 3D canvas, the **Transform** tool shares some features with its 2D counterpart. However, it has some unique features.

To activate this tool, tap the arrow icon at the top left of the screen. When working in 2D, the transformation affects all the contents of the layer. However, in a 3D canvas, only the layer contents visible on the screen can be transformed. This means that if you have graphics on the back of the 3D model that were not visible on screen at the time of activating the tool, those graphics won't be included in the transformation. Just like a 2D canvas, you may also use the **Selections** tool to isolate and transform only a specific portion of the graphics.

In the following subsections, we'll delve into the **Transform** tool.

Interface

A toolbar appears at the bottom of the screen when you use **Transform**, as shown in the following screenshot:

Figure 15.23 : The Transform toolbar

The interface has the following elements:

- Bounding halo: When **Transform** is activated, a solid white glowing line surrounds the selection. This is called the bounding halo, as shown in the following screenshot:

Figure 15.24 : The bounding halo

The halo works much like the bounding box in 2D transform. You can tap and drag it to move the selection, as well as pinch to zoom and rotate it.

- **Automatic** mode: At the top of the toolbox, you will notice two options – **Automatic** and **Advanced**. **Automatic** lets you perform the normal move, scale, rotate, and flip functions, similar to 2D transformations.
- **Advanced** mode: This mode helps you perform more 3D-specific transformations. **Advanced** mode allows non-uniform transformation along separate axes and even makes it possible to detach the image from the 3D surface. We will discuss this mode more in the next subsection.
- **Flip**: These buttons flip your drawing vertically or horizontally.
- **Rotate 45°**: Tap on this button to rotate your drawing by 45° clockwise.
- **Projection**: This feature lets you control the direction and depth with which **Transform** can act on a 3D surface. There are two controls under this feature, **Bidirectional** and **Projection depth**, as shown in the following screenshot:

Figure 15.25: Projection

- **Bidirectional** is a toggle. When on, it projects an image identical to the one you are transforming, on a surface that's 180° opposite. Visualize it like two projectors projecting the same image on both sides of a wall.
- **Projection depth** is a slider that lets you control the depth to which your drawing will be transformed. It stretches a 2D image along a third axis. This tool is helpful when transforming across an uneven surface. When you change the slider position, a 3D wireframe box will appear around the image, as shown in the following screenshot:

Figure 15.26: A Projection box

This box will increase or decrease in depth depending on the slider value.

- **Interpolation**: This feature decides how Procreate manages pixels while transforming a drawing. To learn more about **Interpolation**, refer to *Chapter 5, Selecting and Transforming*.
- **Reset**: This option undoes all the transformations you have made so far and resets the selection to its original state.

To apply the changes and exit **Transform**, simply click on any button, such as **Paint** or **Erase**.

In the next subsection, we'll learn about the **Advanced** mode of transformation in more detail.

Advanced transformation

Choosing **Advanced** transformation gives you more options to modify a drawing in a 3D context. In this mode, the drawing is surrounded by a new type of controls, as shown in the following screenshot:

Figure 15.27: Advanced transform

Let's look at these one by one:

- **Uniform scale and rotate**: The ring surrounding the selection can be used to uniformly scale and rotate it. Tap anywhere on the ring and drag inward toward the center to scale down the drawing, and outward to scale it up. Similarly, touching and rotating the ring will let you rotate the selection.

- **Move and detach**: The disc in the middle lets you drag the selection to move it around on the 3D surface. It also allows you to detach the drawing from the 3D canvas and transform it in space.

  To detach the drawing, tap on the disc to bring up the **Detach** option, as shown in the following screenshot:

Figure 15.28: Detach

The disc will change to a dual cone, as shown in the following screenshot:

Figure 15.29 : Dual cone

This means that the selection is now detached from the surface. You may now drag the drawing into 3D space, without it being tethered to the model surface.

Tap on the dual cone again to bring up the **Attach** option, as shown in the following screenshot:

Figure 15.30 : Attach

This will reattach your drawing to the mesh surface.

- **3D rotate**: Hovering over the disc is a blue sphere. It is used to rotate the selection's angle of projection. Tap and drag this sphere to observe how it affects the drawing. This feature is especially useful when the model has sharp edges on its surface.
- **Non-uniform scaling**: Inside the ring, there are two blue cubes. These are used for non-uniformly scaling the selection (stretching and squashing). The cube at the top stretches it in a vertical direction, while the one on the right stretches it in a horizontal direction.

  The scale of the transformation increases the farther you move a cube from the center. As you move it closer to the center, the scale decreases, until the cube crosses the center of the selection. Then, the scale of transformation increases again, as the cube moves away from the center in the opposite direction.

In this section, we covered everything you need to know to use the 3D **Transform** tool. The next section will introduce **Lighting Studio**, which is a simple way to change the environment and lighting conditions for your 3D model.

Modifying the environment using Lighting Studio

Lighting Studio lets you effortlessly adjust the environment and lighting conditions for your model. Lighting can affect the mood and feel of a 3D artwork. To access Lighting Studio, go to **Actions | 3D | Edit lighting & environment**, as shown in the following screenshot:

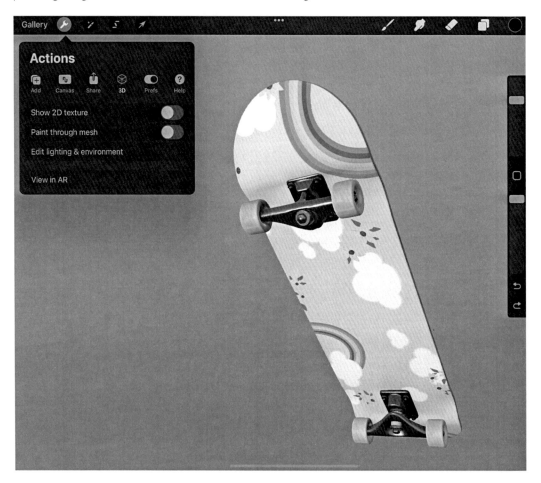

Figure 15.31 : Edit lighting & environment

This will take you to the **Lighting Studio** interface, as shown in the following screenshot:

Modifying the environment using Lighting Studio 509

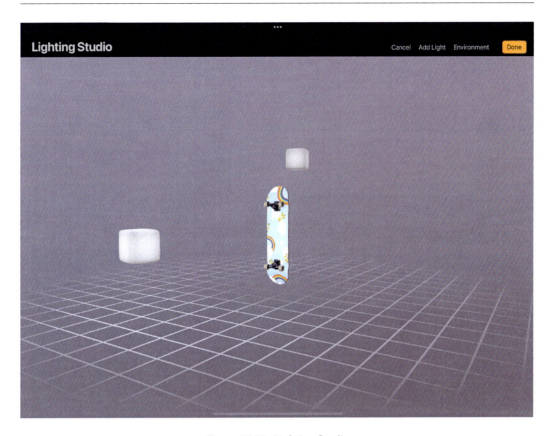

Figure 15.32 : Lighting Studio

Let's look at the interface of **Lighting Studio**.

Overview

The **Lighting Studio** interface has the following elements:

- **Cancel**: Along the buttons in the top-right corner of the screen, the first is **Cancel**. Tap this to exit Lighting Studio without saving any changes.
- **Add Light**: This adds a light source to the environment. You can add a maximum of four lights.
- **Environment**: Adjust and fine-tune the environment and ambient lighting conditions of your 3D model using this option.
- **Done**: Tap this to save the changes you made and exit Lighting Studio.
- **Reference**: A floating **Reference** companion offers a real-time view of how the edits to lighting and environment affect the look of your 3D model.

In the following subsections, we will cover these features in more detail.

Lighting

Light sources in Lighting Studio are represented by cubes. You can add, remove, and edit the properties of these light sources, as well as reposition them to affect your model differently. Lighting Studio allows you to add up to four separate light sources. Tap on a light source to bring up **Light Settings**, as shown in the following screenshot:

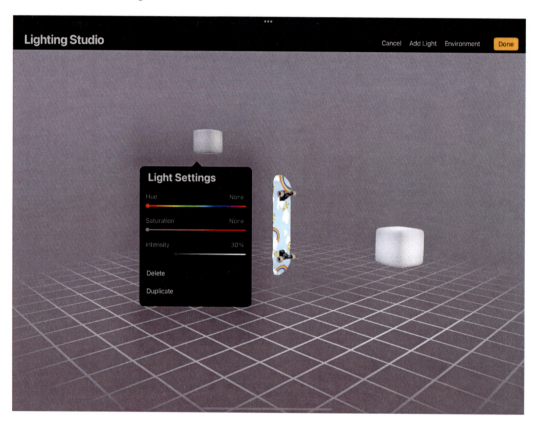

Figure 15.33 : Light Settings

This window has the following settings:

- **Hue**: The **Hue** slider sets the color of light provided by the source.
- **Saturation**: This slider affects how vibrant the chosen hue of light appears. At **0%**, the light is white, while at **100%**, it produces vibrant colored light.

- **Intensity**: This slider controls the brightness of the source. At **0%**, the light is dim, while at **100%**, it has the highest brightness.
- **Delete**: This removes the light source.
- **Duplicate**: This option creates an exact copy of the light source.

Light sources can also be moved around in space. Tap and hold a light source, and then drag to reposition it. You will see a live preview of the 3D model in the **Reference** companion to make sure the lighting is exactly how you want it.

The next subsection will introduce the **Environment** option.

Environment

Aside from direct light sources, **Environment** also provides an ambient lighting condition, which adds a sense of space to your model. Tap on **Environment** to bring up the menu shown in the following screenshot:

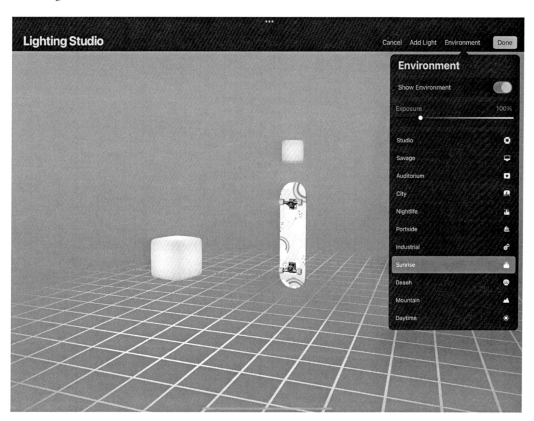

Figure 15.34 : Environment

Let's take look at the **Environment** options:

- **Show Environment**: The first option is a toggle. When turned on, the 3D space around the model shows a blurred representation of an environment. When toggled off, the environment is neutral.

- **Exposure**: This slider mimics the shutter speed and aperture of a camera, which can expand and constrict to let in more or less light. Reducing exposure creates a dark environment and vice versa.

- **Environments**: Procreate offers 11 in-built real-world environments that you can choose from. Although these environments won't be visible in the space around your 3D model, you can see them in the reflections on its surface. A very reflective 3D object can give you a clear view of the current environment. Every environment has a different feel to it and offers unique ambient conditions.

You have now learned how to use Lighting Studio to adjust direct as well as ambient lighting for your 3D model. In the next section, we will discuss how you can export files from a 3D canvas.

Exporting from a 3D canvas

There are several ways to export a 3D model in Procreate. To export, go to **Actions | Share**, as shown in the following screenshot:

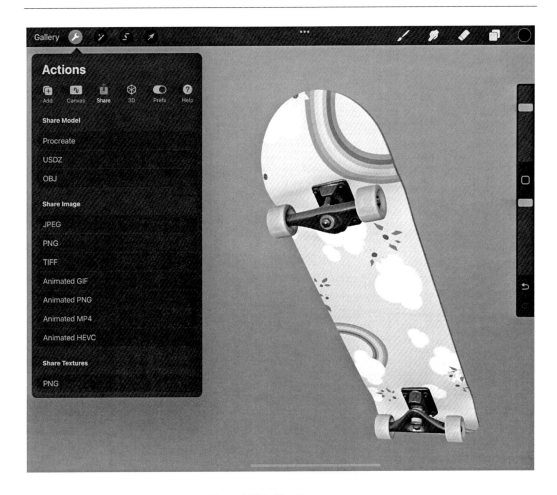

Figure 15.35 : The Share menu

There are three ways by which you can share your model:

- **Share Model**: This option allow you to export the 3D model itself, which can then be opened using 3D software.
- **Share Image**: The options under this heading help you export your 3D model in image or video formats.
- **Share Textures**: The options under this heading help you export your 3D artwork as a flattened image.

In the following subsections, we'll be going over all the formats you can export to from a 3D canvas.

Share Model

The first three options on the list are **Procreate**, **USDZ**, and **OBJ**. These are all formats that allow you to share the 3D model as a whole, which can be transferred to a different location or opened in different 3D modeling software. Let's look at each of these in more detail:

- **Procreate**: Export your 3D model as a `.Procreate` file, which can be opened on the Procreate app.
- **USDZ**: This file type uses the `.USDZ` extension, which can be opened on 3D-modeling software on Apple devices.
- **OBJ**: This is perhaps the most common file type that can be opened by most 3D software.

Share Image

These options export your canvas as a **JPEG**, **PNG**, or **TIFF** image. Animated views of your 3D model also fall under this category, and we will discuss animations later on in this subsection. The following formats are available for image exports:

- **JPEG**: This is the most common format, which compresses the image slightly, resulting in a much smaller file size while still preserving image quality. JPEG is a versatile file type that is supported almost everywhere.
- **PNG**: This format is lossless, which means it preserves the full quality of the resulting image, coupled with a higher file size. A prime advantage of using this format is that it supports transparent pixels. If you wish to export a 3D model in a transparent background, simply open Lighting Studio and toggle off **Show Environment**.
- **TIFF**: This image format also preserves the full quality of the image, with a significantly larger file size. TIFF is a great choice for printing.

Under the **Share Image** umbrella, you will also find several options to export the 3D model as an animation, complete with the lighting and environment. The following formats are available for animated results:

- **Animated GIF**: GIF is one of the most widely used formats for web animations. When trying to export an animated GIF, you will see the following interface:

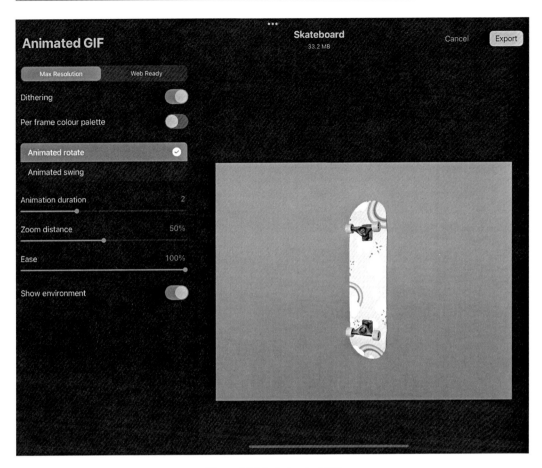

Figure 15.36 : Animated GIF

You will find the following options under **Animated GIF**:

- At the top, you can choose between **Max Resolution** for high-quality output and **Web Ready** for a compressed, smaller file. Compression may cause color banding in your GIF. To reduce this, toggle on **Dithering**.

- **Per frame colour palette** applies a fresh limited color palette to each frame of animation, instead of the whole video, thus increasing file size.

- While exporting an animation, you have the choice to export using either **Animated rotate**, which will make your model rotate in one direction, or **Animated swing**, which will make it 'ping-pong' from side to side.

- **Animation duration** is a slider that determines the duration of one full cycle of an animation.

- **Zoom distance** affects the distance that the model will zoom out to at the farthest point in the animation. At **0%**, the model stays close to the camera throughout. At **100%**, the model moves far away from the camera. Adjust the **Zoom distance** slider to decide which distance suits your needs.

- **Ease** applies a feeling of momentum and naturalness to the motion, by making the animation slow down and speed up at certain points. At **0%**, there is uniform, mechanical motion. At **100%**, the motion appears smoother and more realistic.

- In case you want to export an animation with a transparent background, toggle off **Show environment**. Doing so will reveal another toggle called **Transparent background**. Once it's toggled on, a slider labeled **Alpha threshold** will appear, as shown in the following screenshot:

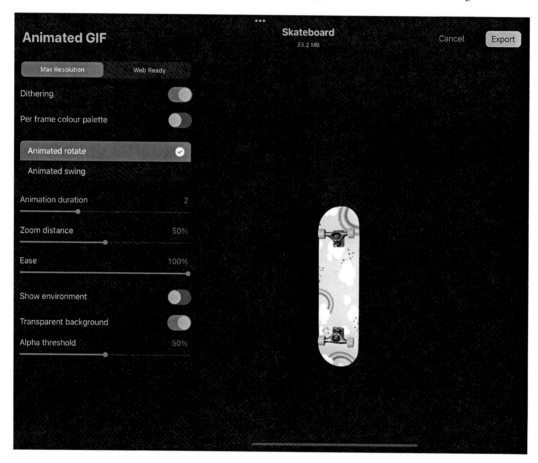

Figure 15.37 : Alpha threshold

This slider helps you reduce any unwanted noise that may appear on the edges of your model. Turn the slider up to **100%** to reduce excess noise.

- **Animated PNG**: PNG is a desirable format when you want to export animations with transparent elements. When trying to export an animated PNG, you will see the following interface:

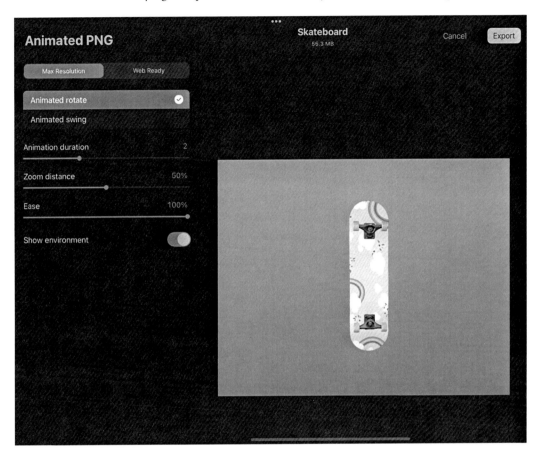

Figure 15.38 : Animated PNG

Since PNG preserves full image quality, you won't find options such as **Dithering** or **Per frame colour palette**. However, all other settings here are identical to **Animated GIF**.

- **Animated MP4**: MP4 offers reasonable video quality at a much smaller file size. It is an extremely versatile format that is supported almost everywhere. When trying to export an animated MP4, you will see the following interface:

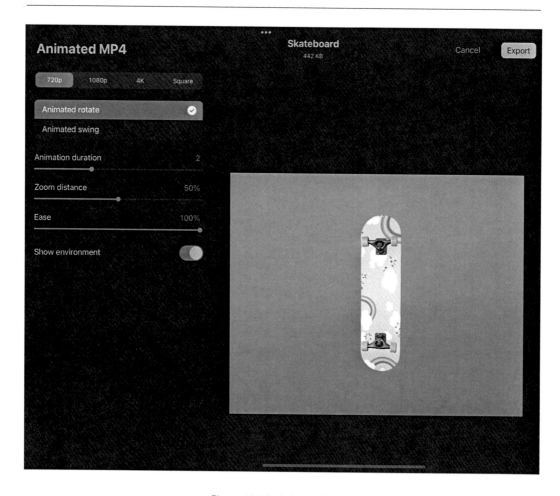

Figure 15.39 : Animated MP4

At the top, you will see four options: **720p**, **1080p**, **4K**, and **Square**. These are the different resolutions you can choose to export with. The rest of the settings are the same as we have previously learned. MP4 lacks the **Alpha threshold** slider, since MP4s can't have transparent backgrounds.

- **Animated HEVC**: HEVC is similar to MP4, but it can also have a transparent background. The file size also tends to be smaller than animated GIFs or PNGs. When trying to export an animated HEVC, you will see the following interface:

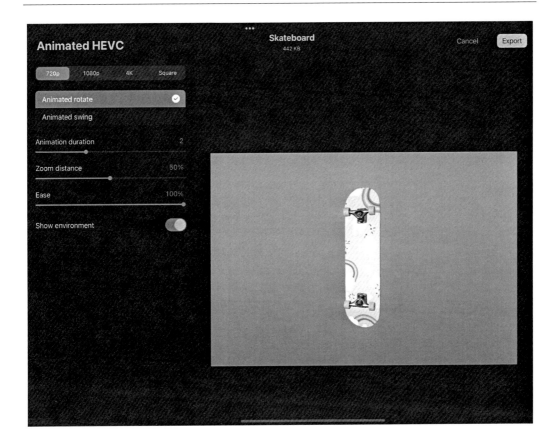

Figure 15.40 : Animated HEVC

This interface is almost identical to that of MP4, with the added **Alpha threshold** feature.

This covers all the animated export formats available in a 3D canvas. In the next subsection, we will cover how to export flattened textures.

Share textures

This kind of export flattens each individual texture into an image and exports them all together. To share textures, go to **Actions | Share | Share Textures | PNG**.

Every texture set is exported as five separate PNG images, each corresponding to the following properties:

- **Ambient Occlusion**
- **Color**

- **Metallic**
- **Normal**
- **Roughness**

Even though properties such as **Ambient Occlusion** and **Normal** can't be edited on Procreate itself, these images can be imported into other 3D software for further editing.

We have now covered all the features of 3D painting in Procreate, so let's summarize.

Summary

This chapter covered the details of 3D painting on Procreate. We learned how to import 3D models into the app from external sources as well as Procreate's own Model pack. The chapter introduced the concepts behind 3D painting and how UV maps facilitate it. Then, we discussed the interface of a 3D canvas in depth, talking about how it is different from its 2D counterpart, as well as introducing the common gestures used.

Next, we took a closer look at layers in a 3D context, specifically how each texture set works as a separate layer and how a layer has its own material properties. We also talked about the versatile **Transform** tool, which helps us adjust the way a drawing is moved, scaled, and projected on a 3D surface.

The chapter then explored Lighting Studio, which lets you adjust the lighting and environment that affect the overall look and feel of your 3D model. Finally, you learned about the various ways a 3D model can be exported – as a model, image, video, or textures.

3D painting is a relatively new addition to Procreate, opening users up to an entirely new way to explore their creativity. The app's versatile 3D tools, as well as easy integration with existing 3D software and conventions, make 3D painting a fascinating experience.

In the next and final chapter, we will look at a simple drawing tutorial that will help you apply your knowledge to your art.

Part 3: Illustration Tips

This final part of the book will focus on a step-by-step breakdown of my illustration process to showcase real-world usage of the app's features.

This section comprises the following chapter:

- *Chapter 16, Rendering Objects Using Blend Modes*

16
Rendering Objects Using Blend Modes

If you are reading this chapter, congratulations! You have made it through all the features of Procreate, tinkered with them by yourself, and hopefully, you're now getting the hang of it. There is a lot to this app that makes it a versatile and useful tool. In this final chapter, we will get hands-on practice and make a finished artwork using this knowledge.

If you remember *Chapter 7*, *Organizing Your Layers*, it introduced the concept of blend modes. Blend modes can add extra personality to your layers and make them useful for a variety of artistic effects. In this chapter, we are going to look at how to use common blend modes to render an object from scratch. For this tutorial, let's use this cute little alarm clock:

Figure 16.1: A reference photograph of an alarm clock

This clock is perfect for demonstration purposes since it sports different kinds of materials to render. The final goal is a stylized study of the clock, as shown in the following diagram:

Figure 16.2: The goal of the stylized study

In this chapter, we're going to break the clock down into its components, under the following broad topics:

- Clock body
- Clock face
- Metal parts
- Finishing touches

Clock body

Before we can start rendering our clock, we need to have it flat filled and prepared, as follows:

Clock body 525

Figure 16.3: Flat filling

In this artwork, the glossy red clock body is the main attention grabber. It needs the most time and care to render. The body is made of painted stainless steel. We are aiming for a shiny, yet non-metallic finish, just like the reference photograph. Let's begin with the shading.

Shading using Multiply mode

Multiply mode is commonly used to shade objects. The blend layer in **Multiply** darkens the base layer; the results vary depending on the colors of the involved layers. To begin, create a layer on top of the flat fill layer, create a clipping mask, and set its blend mode to **Multiply**, as follows:

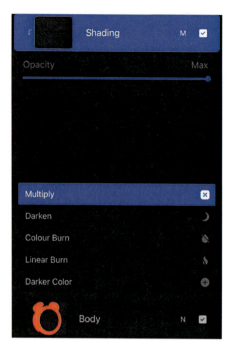

Figure 16.4: New Multiply layer

In this case, we will be using purple for the blend layer, to lay down the basic shading, as shown in the following figure:

Figure 16.5: Basic shading using Multiply

Notice how the base color (red) and the blend color (purple) both affect the resulting color of the shading. Play around with the colors in the **Multiply** layer to observe how your painting changes character.

In the next step, let's push the shading one step further by adding some more detail. In the same **Multiply** layer, we are now using a lighter purple to enhance the three-dimensional appeal of our clock, as follows:

Figure 16.6: Adding detail using Multiply

Notice how using a lighter blend color has also resulted in lighter shading. This effect is especially obvious around the bells, as shown in the following image:

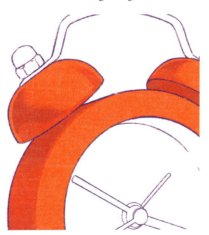

Figure 16.7: Details of shading near the alarm bells

Switching up values while shading can be very useful when you're aiming for a three-dimensional look. For reference, if the **Multiply** layer was set to **Normal** instead, it would appear as follows:

Figure 16.8: Shading viewed in Normal mode

It's fascinating to observe how blend and base colors interact to produce the final effect. In the next section, we will be adding light to the object.

Adding light using Screen mode

Just as **Multiply** darkens the base layer, **Screen** has the opposite effect and is an essential blend mode for adding light. For this step, we will create a new layer on top of the previous one, clip it, and set it to **Screen**, as follows:

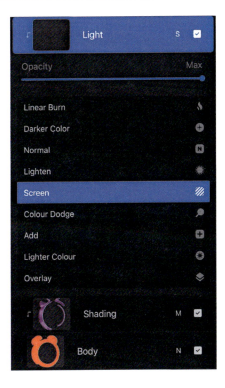

Figure 16.9: New Screen layer

This layer will be used to draw the reflection of the white background on the clock body. Since the background has a cool hue, we will use a medium value sky blue to paint on the **Screen** layer, as follows:

Figure 16.10: Adding light using Screen

Notice how the **Screen** layer affects both the base layer and the **Multiply** layer under it. The sky blue of the **Screen** layer and the purple of the **Multiply** layer create a composite bluish effect on the clock body. Blend modes interact with all layers underneath, so combining different modes can create a variety of interesting effects.

For reference, if the **Screen** layer was set to **Normal**, it would appear as follows:

Figure 16.11: Light reflections viewed in Normal mode

> **Important Note**
>
> Even though we are painting lighter areas, notice the use of a medium value color such as this sky blue. **Screen** has a lightening effect in itself, so using an already light color in **Screen** mode would be too bright for this artwork. While using blend modes, it's a good practice to be deliberate with your choice of blend colors.

With the basics in place, we can now add the shine factor to our artwork.

Drawing specular reflections using Add mode

When a light source directly reflects on a surface, it's called specular reflection. These are the brightest of all and are commonly called "highlights." **Add** is a blend mode that is the most appropriate when it comes to drawing these reflections.

As usual, we'll create a new **Add** layer and clip it to our base layer, as follows:

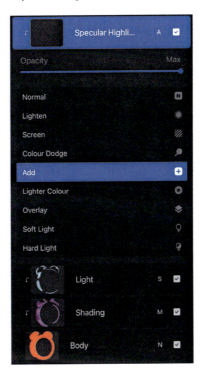

Figure 16.12: New Add layer

We can then paint the specular reflections, as follows:

Figure 16.13: Specular reflections using Add

These highlights were painted using a light blue to stay true to the cool light used in the photograph, as shown in the following image:

Figure 16.14: Specular reflections viewed in Normal mode

However, since we are aiming for an almost white shine, any light color used in **Add** mode will do the trick. In some cases, an artwork might need a specific color of specular reflections, where the color choice is more important.

In the next section, we'll give the artwork a contrast boost.

Drawing dark shadows using Multiply mode

This is a simple step where we fill in the areas of dark shadow with a dark color in **Multiply** mode. Create a new **Multiply** layer, as follows:

Clock body

Figure 16.15: New Multiply layer

In this artwork, dark shadows occur on the undersides of the bells, which we'll block in with a dark purple in **Multiply**, as follows:

Figure 16.16: Dark shadows using Multiply

In **Normal** mode, this layer would appear as follows:

Figure 16.17: Dark shadows viewed in Normal mode

In the next section, we will start getting creative.

Adding color effects using Hard Light mode

Though the reference photograph has no warm lighting, we are attempting to do a stylized study, not necessarily a realistic one. This section will demonstrate how you can add some more visual richness to a study.

To do so, follow these steps:

1. Create a new **Hard Light** layer between the **Screen** and **Add** layers, as follows:

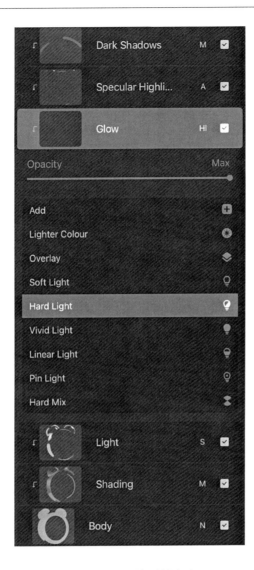

Figure 16.18: New Hard Light layer

2. Using a soft brush and a light yellow, we will add a soft warm glow to some parts of the clock body, as follows:

Figure 16.19: Warm glow using Hard Light

The difference might not be obvious at first glance, but when compared to the last step, it becomes clearer, as shown in the following images:

Figure 16.20 (a): Before the warm glow; (b) After the warm glow

This step isn't essential, but it lends a subtle personality boost to the artwork, as we wrap up the rendering of the body. For reference, this layer will look like the following in **Normal** mode:

Figure 16.21: Warm glow viewed in Normal mode

In the next section, we'll focus on the clock face.

Clock face

In this section, we'll tackle a different kind of material. The clock face has a matte white finish that can be rendered simply using the **Multiply** and **Screen** modes.

Adding cast shadow using Multiply mode

The clock is lit with direct light from the upper-right corner, which makes the body cast a shadow over the clock face. Additionally, the hands of the clock cast their own shadows. The shadows will be painted on a **Multiply** layer on top of the clock face, as follows:

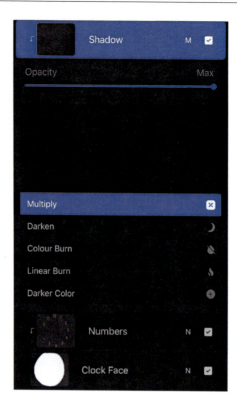

Figure 16.22: New Multiply layer

We will paint the shadows blue, as follows:

Figure 16.23: Casting a shadow using Multiply

Next, using a lighter blue, we can add finer details to the variations within the shadow, as follows:

Figure 16.24: Detailed shading using Multiply

In **Normal** mode, this shading will look as follows:

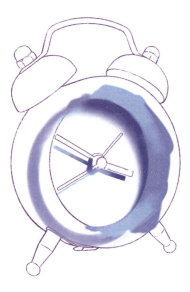

Figure 16.25: Shading viewed in Normal mode

You might be concerned that the shading is spilling over the edges. However, it's clipped to the base layer of the clock face, so the final result looks clean.

In the next section, we will proceed to add a hint of light to the clock face.

Adding light using Screen mode

In the previous step, you might have noticed that the numbers printed on the clock face look disjointed, as though they're not part of the same surface. This happens because the color of the print is dark enough that the **Multiply** layer fails to cause a noticeable change. This makes it look like the lighting doesn't affect the print.

This issue can be simply solved by subtly lightening the rest of the clock face further using a **Screen** layer, as follows:

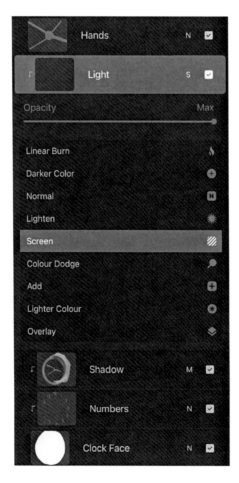

Figure 16.26: New Screen layer

Since **Screen** affects dark colors more noticeably, brightening the non-shadow areas can help unify the print with the surface of the clock face. This effect is shown in the following image:

Figure 16.27: Brightening the non-shadow areas using Screen

This **Screen** layer will look like the following in **Normal** mode:

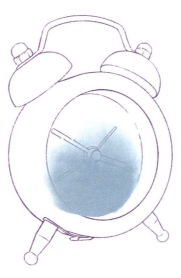

Figure 16.28: Brightened area viewed in Normal mode

This brings us to the end of rendering the clock face. Note how there are no speculars here since it's a matte surface.

In the next section, we'll get into the last material making up this object.

Metal parts

The tiny stainless steel parts provide a fair bit of visual appeal to the clock. They enhance the contrast between the different materials and textures composing the object. To render these bits, we will be aiming for a shiny metallic finish. The first step is to add the shading.

Shading using Multiply mode

Metal surfaces are highly reflective, so they tend to show contrasting dark and light "bands." However, for the purpose of our artwork, we want to focus more of our attention on the clock body, so we can downplay the contrast on the metal a little.

Create a clipped **Multiply** layer on top of the base, as follows:

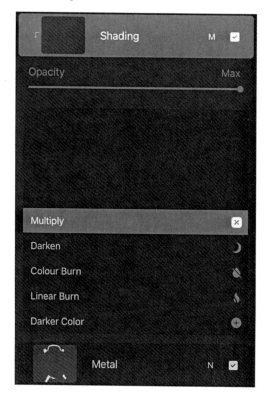

Figure 16.29: New Multiply layer

Next, block in the shading with blue, as follows:

Figure 16.30: Basic shading using Multiply

At this stage, the finish looks relatively matte, so we can create some of those finer reflections within the shadow area using a lighter blue, as follows:

Figure 16.31: Detailed shading using Multiply

Now that the "bands" are clearer, the surfaces are starting to appear more metallic. The shading layer in **Normal** mode would appear as follows:

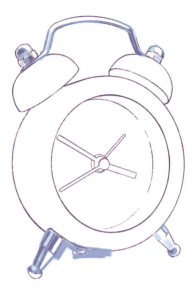

Figure 16.32: Shading viewed in Normal mode

The shininess of the steel will be played up further in the next subsection.

Adding light using Add mode

Metallic surfaces tend to show super bright reflections, so instead of using **Screen** like the previous sections, we're going to use an **Add** layer to paint them, as follows:

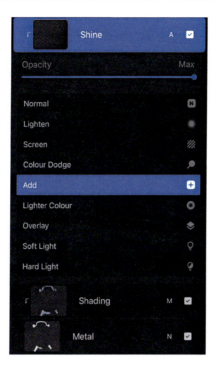

Figure 16.33: New Add layer

Using a light blue in the **Add** layer, we'll draw in the reflections as follows:

Figure 16.34: Reflections using Add

This **Add** layer in **Normal** mode appears as follows:

Figure 16.35: Reflections viewed in Normal mode

In the next section, we'll give the artwork an additional bit of visual information to give it a proper finished look.

Finishing touches

We have finally arrived at the very last stage of the study. In the previous steps, we carefully rendered the individual materials and "built up" the clock. In this last section, we're ready to give it the final push to make it a complete, appealing study.

Adding reflection using Screen mode

The first thing we have to consider is the glass covering the clock face, which we haven't paid attention to up until this point. The presence of a transparent surface can be easily suggested by adding a reflection.

For this, create a **Screen** layer just underneath the clock body layers, as follows:

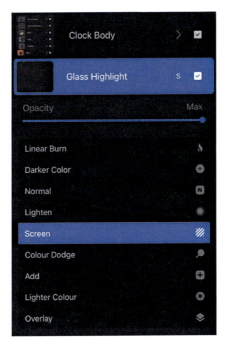

Figure 16.36: New Screen layer

In this layer, using sky blue, draw in a reflection on the upper-right side of the face, as follows:

Figure 16.37: Glass reflection using Screen

Note how doing so immediately suggests the presence of a transparent sheet in front of the clock face. In **Normal** mode, this layer appears as follows:

Figure 16.38: Glass reflection viewed in Normal mode

Even though this reflection isn't present in the reference, it adds believability to our study. When doing a stylized study, it's always fun to experiment with creative liberties and observe how it affects the art.

Next, we'll up the presence of this reflection a bit more dramatically. To do so, duplicate the **Screen** layer and move it to the very top, above the line art, as follows:

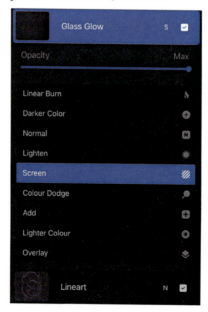

Figure 16.39: A duplicate Screen layer

Your artwork will now look like this:

Figure 16.40: Screen layer copied

This layer is not clipped or hidden by anything, so we need to trim it down to match the shape of the clock face, as follows:

Figure 16.41: Trimming the Screen layer

It doesn't have to be super clean because now we're going to blur it slightly to achieve a glowing effect, as follows:

Figure 16.42: Glow using a blurred Screen layer

Notice how this alone adds so much personality to the little clock. It's now the main character of the canvas.

To finish off, we can add a simple shadow, as follows, and our study is now complete:

Figure 16.43: The complete artwork

Now that we have completed the artwork, let's summarize the chapter.

Summary

In this chapter, we focused on three commonly used modes, namely **Multiply**, **Screen**, and **Add**, as well as a brief mention of **Hard Light** mode. These were used to render different types of surfaces in different ways. Usually, **Multiply** is used to darken the base layer, while **Screen** is used to lighten, and **Add** is used when we want bright specs of light. In this specific study, we also used **Hard Light** to add a soft warm glow to the clock body.

If you have been following along on your own, you will have hopefully started to grasp the uses of blend modes. You'll realize that these techniques can be applied to a wide variety of contexts, be it characters, landscapes, or any other subject. Procreate offers a variety of other blend modes, each with its unique effects. Based on your knowledge from this chapter, you will now be able to explore all of these modes in many different contexts.

Index

Symbols

2D Grid
  about 428
  elements 430
  interface 429, 431
  used, for drawing squared grids 428
3D canvas
  exporting from 512
  layers, working with 489
3D interface. *See also* 3D canvas
  3D gestures 488, 489
  3D menu 485-488
  about 480
  Reference companion 481-485
  workspace 480
3D model
  about 478
  environment, modifying with Lighting Studio 508
  graphics, transforming 499
  importing 476
  opening 475
  Procreate's Model pack, importing 477, 478
  UV map 479

3D model, exporting
  Share Image option 513-519
  Share Model option 513, 514
  Share Textures option 513, 519, 520
3D Transform tool, advanced option
  uniform scale and rotate 504
  move and detach 505
  3D rotate 507
  non-uniform scaling 507

A

accessibility gestures
  single touch gesture, activating 164-166
  using 164
Actions 46-50
active colour
  about 328, 329
  functions 330
active layer 194
Add menu
  about 55, 56
  clipboard tools 62
  file, inserting 56, 57
  photo, capturing 58
  photo, inserting 57, 58
  text, adding 59, 60

Index

Add mode
  used, for adding light 544-546
  used, for drawing specular reflections 530, 532
Adjustments 50, 52
Adjustments actions
  about 358
  options 359
Adjustments interface
  exploring 353
Adjustments menu 354
advanced feature, gestures
  Eyedropper tool 176, 177
  QuickMenu tool 178-181
  QuickShape tool 177, 178
advanced features, Procreate workspace
  about 45
  Actions menu 46-50
  Adjustments menu 50
  Gallery 46
  Selection tool 52
  Transform tool 52
Animated GIF format 514
Animated HEVC format 518
Animated MP4 format 517
Animated PNG format 517
Animation Assist
  about 72, 451
  elements 454-456
  interface 454
  interface, using 451-453
animation settings
  about 456
  appearance settings 459, 460
  frame settings 458
  preview settings 457
  used, for fine-tuning motion 456, 457

anti-aliasing 290
appearance settings
  about 459, 460
  blend primary frame 459
  onion skin colors 459
Apple Pencil 101, 306
Apple Pencil, settings
  Pressure 307
  Size compression 307
  Tilt 307
Artifact effect
  about 393
  settings 394
Assisted Drawing tool 175, 176
augmented reality (AR) 488

B

basic gestures
  about 151
  double-tap undo gesture 153, 154
  four-finger tap gesture 159
  pinch gesture 152
  precise slider control gesture 164
  QuickShape gesture 159-163
  three-finger scrub gesture 155, 156
  three-finger swipe down gesture 156, 157
  three-finger tap redo gesture 154, 155
Blaze 368
blend modes
  about 193, 210
  Add 218
  Color 233
  Color Burn 212
  Color Dodge 217
  Darken 211
  Darker Color 214

Difference 227
Divide 230
Exclusion 228
Hard Light 222
Hard Mix 226
Hue 231
Lighten 215
Lighter Color 219
Linear Burn 213
Linear Light 224
Luminosity 234, 235
Multiply 210
Overlay 220
Pin Light 225
Saturation 232
Screen 216
Soft Light 221
Subtract 229
Vivid Light 223
Bloom interface 388
Bloom interface, sliders
　burn 391
　size 391
　transition 391
blur effects
　Gaussian Blur 376
　Motion Blur 377
　Perspective Blur 378
　working with 376
Brush Library 244-256
Brush Library, features
　brush sets and brushes 245, 246
　pinned brushes 258, 259
　recent brushes 256
Brush opacity slider 43
Brush Size Memory 43, 242, 243
Brush size slider 42, 43

Brush Studio
　about 260, 261
　advanced brush settings 264-266
　brush attributes 267
　interface 262, 263
Brush Studio, settings
　about 310-315
　Apple Pencil 306, 307
　Color dynamics 302-304
　Dynamics 304, 305, 306
　exploring 269
　Grain 291-298
　Materials 309
　Properties 307-310
　Rendering 299, 300
　Shape 278-290
　Stabilisation 273-276
　Stroke path 269-272
　Taper 276-278
　Wet mix 301, 302

C

canvas
　creating 3
　creating, with Import 4, 5
　creating, with Photo 5, 6
　deleting 14, 15
　duplicating 14, 15
　files, sharing by dragging into
　　intended destination 9, 10
　files, sharing by dropping into
　　intended destination 9, 10
　multiple canvases, sharing 8
　ordering 10
　renaming 11, 12
　selecting 14, 15
　sharing 6

single canvas, sharing 6-8
stacking 12, 14
Canvas Information
  about 79
  artwork 79
  colour profile 81, 82
  dimensions 80
  layers 80, 81
  statistics 83, 84
  video settings 82
Canvas menu
  about 63
  Animation Assist 72
  Canvas Information 79
  crop and resize 63, 66, 68
  Crop and Resize 65
  Drawing Guide 74
  Flip Canvas 78, 79
  Page Assist 73
  Reference companion 75
Canvas properties tab 32
cast shadow
  adding, with Multiply mode 537-540
channel buttons 386
channel buttons, controls
  additive 386
  multi 386
  single 386
Chromatic Aberration
  about 397, 404, 405
  perspective mode 405
Classic interface 338, 339
Classic taper 278
clipboard tools 62
clipboard tools, functions
  copy 62
  copy canvas 62

cut 62
paste 62
clock body
  about 524
  color effects, adding with Hard Light mode 534-537
  dark shadows, drawing with Multiply mode 532-534
  light, adding with Screen mode 528, 530
  Multiply mode, shading 525-528
  Multiply mode, shading with 525
  reflection, adding with Screen mode 546-551
  specular reflections, drawing with Add mode 530, 532
clock face
  about 537
  cast shadow, adding with Multiply mode 537-540
  light, adding with Screen mode 540-542
Clone interface
  about 416
  usage 417-419
Clone tool
  about 416
  used, for duplicating objects 416
CMYK color profile 28, 30
color adjustments
  Colour Balance 361, 363
  Curves tool 363-367
  gradient map 368-375
  Hue, Saturation, and Brightness (HSB) 360, 361
  used, for tweaking colours 360
color disc
  about 337
  interface 337

ColorDrop threshold
  activating 330, 331
Color dynamics 302
Color dynamics, settings
  Color pressure 304
  Color tilt 304
  Stamp color jitter 303, 304
  Stroke color jitter 304
color effects
  adding, with Hard Light mode 534-537
color profile
  CMYK 28, 30
  importing 30, 31
  RGB 27
  selecting 27
Colour Balance 361, 363
Colour button 39, 40
ColourDrop
  about 330
  Recolour 331, 333
Colour Points 372
colours
  tweaking, with color adjustments 360
Colours panel
  about 327
  active colour 328
  Colour selection interface 328
  default palette 328
  History section 328
  invoking 328
  primary colour 328
  reticle 328
  secondary colour 328
colour, terms
  about 323
  hue 324
  saturation 324, 326
  value 326

Copy & Paste menu 156
Crop and Resize 63
Curves tool 363-367
custom canvas
  creating 6, 23, 24
  dimensions 25
  resolution 25, 26
custom preset
  Usual Landscape 24

D

dark shadows
  drawing, with Multiply mode 532-534
directional blur 379
displace mode, elements
  blur 406
  transparency 406
Diverge effect
  about 396
  settings 397, 399
Dots Per Inch (DPI) 65
double-tap undo gesture 153, 154
drag and drop export
  used, for exporting layers 236, 237
Drawing Assist
  about 421
  interface, using 421-426
Drawing Guide
  about 74
  interface 427, 428
Dual Brush
  combine mode 318, 319
  creating 316, 317
  editing 317
  uncombine mode 319, 320
Dynamics 304

Dynamics, settings
    Jitter 305
    Speed 305

E

Erase tool 38, 175, 239, 242
Eyedropper tool 176, 177, 335, 336

F

Fit Canvas 168
Flip Canvas 78, 79
four-finger tap gesture 159
frame option
    background 463
    delete 465
    duplicate 461
    foreground 461
    hold duration 461
    used, for editing frames 460
frames
    editing, with frame option 460
frame settings 458
full screen gesture 181, 182

G

Gallery 3, 46
Gaussian Blur
    about 376
    usage 376
gestures
    advanced feature 176
    customizing 173, 174
    full screen gesture 181, 182
    general options 186-188
    layer content gesture 182
    painting 174, 176
gestures, 3D interface
    about 488
    advanced gestures 489
Glitch interface
    about 391, 392
    Artifact effect 393
    Diverge 396
    Signal effect 395
    Wave effect 394
gradient map 368-375
Grain 291
Grain Editor
    using 296-298
Grain, settings
    3D Grain Behavior 295
    Grain behavior 294, 295
    Grain Filtering 295
    Grain Source 291-293
graphics
    transforming on 3D model, with
        Transform tool 499

H

Halftone interface
    about 399-401
    full colour 402
    newspaper 403
    screen print 403
Hard Light mode
    used, for adding color effects 534-537
Harmony
    about 340
    colors, selecting 342
    interface 340

modes 341, 342
reticles 340
Help menu
  about 104
  advanced settings 105-108
  customer support 112
  features 108, 110
  Procreate Folio 112
  Procreate functionality 111
  Procreate Handbook 110
  restore purchases 105
  Review, writing 113, 114
hexadecimal (hex) codes 343
histograms 367
hue 324
Hue, Saturation, and Brightness
    (HSB) 360, 361

I

image effects
  applying 383
  Bloom interface 388
  Chromatic Aberration interface 404, 405
  Glitch interface 391, 392
  Halftone interface 399-401
  Noise 385
  Noise interface 383
image effects, types
  Adjustments 354
  Filters 354, 355
image warping
  adjust and reset button 415, 416
  modes 408
  settings 414
  with Liquify tool 407, 408
Import
  used, for creating canvas 4, 5

interface elements, Transform tool
  bounding box 130, 131
  bounding box adjust node 131
  rotation node 132
  transformation nodes 131
Isometric Grid
  elements 433
  interface 432
  used, for drawing technical
    graphics 431-434

L

Layer and Pencil modes
  about 355, 358
  functions 356
layer content gesture
  about 182
  Clear Layer 182, 183
  Copy & Paste 183, 184
  Layer Select 184-186
layer gestures
  exploring 168
  inch to merge layer 170
  layer, selecting 168
  two-finger hold to select layer contents 172
  two-finger swipe right for
    alpha lock 171, 172
  two-finger tap for layer opacity 170, 171
layer limits 26
Layer Options menu
  Alpha Lock option 206
  Clear option 206
  Clipping Mask option 207
  Combine Down option 210
  Copy option 205
  Drawing Assist option 209

exploring 204
Fill Layer option 206
Invert option 209
Mask option 206, 207
Merge Down option 210
Reference option 210
Rename option 204
Select option 205
layers
    deleting 202, 203
    duplicating 202, 203
    grouping 197, 199
    grouping, with gestures 198
    grouping, with Layer Options 198
    grouping, with multiple layers selection 197
    locking 202, 203
    moving 199
    organizing 194
    selecting 194-197
    sharing 235
    sharing, with drag and drop export 236, 237
    sharing, with Share Layers menu 237
    transferring, between canvases 200-202
layers, 3D canvas
    additional layers 492, 493
    base layer 491, 492
    material options 498, 499
    materials 493-497
    meshes 491
    texture sets 489, 490
Layers icon 39
Layers interface
    about 190
    background color 193
    blend mode 193
    layer, creating 191
    layer name 192
    Layer Options menu 194

layer thumbnail 192
layer visibility 193
primary layer 192
Lighting Studio 481
    environment, modifying with 508
    environment options 511, 512
    interface 509
    light settings 510
    light sources 510
Liquify tool
    about 407
    used, for image warping 407, 408

M

material properties
    colour 495
    metallic 497
    roughness 496
Materials 309
Materials, settings
    Metallic 310
    Roughness 310
Metal parts
    about 542
    light, adding with Add mode 544-546
    Multiply mode, shading with 542-544
Mirrored Symmetry 448
modes, image warping
    about 408
    Crystals 412
    Edge 413
    Expand 411
    Pinch 410
    Push 408
    Reconstruct 414
    Twirl 409

Modify button 43, 44
motion
  fine-tuning, with animation settings 456, 457
Motion Blur
  about 377
  usage 378
Move
  about 168
  feature 168
multiple canvases
  sharing 8
Multiply mode
  about 525
  shading with 525-528, 542-544
  used, for adding cast shadow 537-540
  used, for drawing dark shadows 532-534

N

nodes 364
Noise interface
  about 383
  billows 385
  clouds 385
  ridges 385
Noise interface, sliders
  octaves 385
  scale 385
  turbulence 385

O

objects
  duplicating, with Clone tool 416

P

Page Assist
  about 73
  elements 469, 470
  using 467-469
Page options
  about 471, 473
  used, for adjusting pages 471, 473
painting tools, Procreate workspace
  about 35, 36
  Colour button 39, 41
  Erase tool 38
  Layers icon 39
  Paint tool 36, 37
  Smudge tool 37
Paint tool 36, 37, 239, 240
Palette Capture
  about 349
  from camera 349, 350
  from files 350
  from photos 351
palette library
  about 348
  features 348, 349
palettes
  about 344
  creating 348
  deleting 349
  duplicating 349
  importing 351
  reordering 349
  setting, as default 348
  sharing 349-352
  swatches 344
Palettes
  swatches 346, 347

Perspective Blur
  about 378
  usage 380-383
Perspective Blur, types
  directional blur 379
  positional blur 378
Perspective guide
  elements 439
  interface 438
  realistic drawing 434-438
perspective mode, Chromatic Aberration interface
  displace 406
  fall off 406
  focal point 405
  transition 405
Photo
  used, for creating canvas 5, 6
pinch gesture 152
pinch gesture, type
  pinch and twist to rotate 153
  pinch to zoom 152
  quick pinch 153
positional blur 378
PPI (Pixels per Inch) 26
precise slider control gesture 164
Prefs (Preferences) menu
  about 94
  gesture controls 102
  interface toggles 95, 98
  legacy stylus, connecting 98, 99
  pressure and smoothing 99, 101
  Rapid Undo Delay 102
  Selection Mask Visibility 103, 104
presets
  4K 19
  4 x 6 Photo 21

  A4 20
  about 17
  Comic 22, 23
  Paper 21, 22
  Screen Size 18
  Square 19
Pressure taper 277, 278
preview settings
  about 457
  frames per second 458
  loop 457
  one shot 457
  onion skin frames 458, 459
  onion skin opacity 459
  ping-pong 457
primary colour 328
primary layer 192, 194
Procreate's Model pack
  importing 477, 478
Procreate workspace
  left panel 42
  painting tools 35
  top-left panel 45
  top-right panel 35
Properties, settings
  Brush behavior 309
  Brush properties 308

Q

QuickMenu tool 178-181
QuickShape gesture 159-163
QuickShape tool 177, 178

R

realistic drawing
  with Perspective guide 434-438

Recolour
  using 331, 333
Redo button 45, 166
Reference companion
  about 75
  canvas 76
  face 78
  image 77, 78
Reference companion, 3D interface
  about 481
  options 482-485
Rendering 299
Rendering, settings
  Blending 300
  Rendering mode 299, 300
Resample canvas
  about 68
  grid overlay, dragging 68, 69
  grid overlay, scaling 68, 69
  values, entering 69, 70
reset grid 430
reticle 328
RGB color profile 27
Rotation 71, 72
Rotational Symmetry 448

S

saturation 324, 326
saturation disc
  about 337
  Snap 338
  Zoom 338
Screen mode
  used, for adding light 528, 530, 540-542
  used, for adding reflection 546-551
scrub 155
secondary colour 328

secondary layers 195
selection mask 127
Selections tool
  about 115, 116
  Add button 121, 122
  Automatic selection 116, 117
  Copy & Paste 124
  edits, committing 129
  edits, finalizing 129
  Ellipse 120, 121
  Feather 125
  Freehand selection 118, 119
  Invert 123, 124
  Layer contents, selecting 128, 129
  Rectangle 120, 121
  Remove button 122
  Save & Load 126
  secondary tools 116
  Selection mask visibility 127, 128
  selection modes 116
Shape 278
Shape, settings
  Shape behavior 282-286
  Shape filtering 290
  Shape Source 279-282
Share Image 85, 86
Share Image options
  formats 514-519
Share Layers
  about 86
  Animated GIF 87
  Animated HEVC 87
  Animated MP4 87
  Animated PNG 87
  export options 87, 88, 89
  PDF 86
  PNG files 87

Share Layers menu
　about 237
　used, for sharing layers 237
Share menu
　about 84, 85
　Share Image 85, 86
　Share Layers 86
Share Model options 514
Share Texture options 519
sidebar, Procreate workspace
　about 42
　Brush opacity slider 43
　Brush size slider 42, 43
　Modify button 43, 44
　Redo button 45
　Undo button 45
Signal effect
　about 395
　settings 396
single canvas
　sharing 6-8
single touch gesture
　activating 164-166
　Fit Canvas 168
　Move 168
　Undo and Redo 166
　Zoom 166
Smudge tool 37, 174, 239-242
Snapping 70, 71
specular reflections
　drawing, with Add mode 530-532
Split View 9
squared grids
　drawing, with 2D Grid 428
Stabilisation 273, 274
Stabilisation, settings
　Motion filtering 276
　Streamline 276

stack 12
stroke 269
Stroke path 269, 270
Stroke path, settings
　Fall off 272
　Jitter 271, 272
　Spacing 270, 271
SwatchDrop 333, 335, 347
swatches
　about 344
　Cards 346
　Compact 344
　creating 347
　deleting 347
　reordering 347
　setting, to current colour 347
symmetrical drawing
　with Symmetry guide 439, 441
Symmetry guide
　elements 442, 443
　interface 441
　symmetrical drawing 439, 441
Symmetry guide, options
　about 444, 450
　horizontal 445
　quadrant 446
　radial 447
　vertical 444

T

Taper
　about 276
　Classic taper 278
　Pressure taper 276-278
　Touch taper 276, 278
technical graphics
　drawing, with Isometric Grid 431-434

three-finger scrub gesture 155, 156
three-finger swipe down gesture 156, 157
three-finger swipe down gesture, options
   Copy 158
   Copy All 158
   Cut 158
   Cut & Paste 158
   Duplicate 158
   Paste 158
three-finger tap redo gesture 154, 155
Time-lapse Recording 91, 92
Time-lapse Replay 90, 91
time-lapse video 31, 32
Time-lapse video
   exporting 92, 93, 94
Touch taper 278
Transform 52
Transform tool
   about 61, 115, 129, 130, 499
   Advanced transformation 504-507
   Distort 136, 137
   edits, committing 147
   edits, finalizing 147
   Fit to Screen 144, 146
   Flipping tools 143
   Freeform 133, 134
   interface 130, 499-503
   Interpolation 146, 147
   Reset 147
   Rotate 45° 143
   Snapping 141, 142
   Uniform 135
   Warp 138, 140

U

Undo button 45, 166
Usual Landscape preset 24

V

Value
   about 342
   interface 343
video length 83
Video menu
   about 89, 90
   Time-lapse Recording 91, 92
   Time-lapse Replay 90, 91
   Time-lapse video, exporting 92-94

W

Wave effect
   about 394
   settings 395
Wet mix 301
Wet mix, settings
   Attack 302
   Blur 302
   Blur jitter 302
   Charge 302
   Dilution 301
   Grade 302
   Pull 302
   Wetness jitter 302
workplace, 3D interface
   3D model 481
   Layers panel 481

Z

Zoom
   about 166
   feature 166

Packt.com

Subscribe to our online digital library for full access to over 7,000 books and videos, as well as industry leading tools to help you plan your personal development and advance your career. For more information, please visit our website.

Why subscribe?

- Spend less time learning and more time coding with practical eBooks and Videos from over 4,000 industry professionals
- Improve your learning with Skill Plans built especially for you
- Get a free eBook or video every month
- Fully searchable for easy access to vital information
- Copy and paste, print, and bookmark content

Did you know that Packt offers eBook versions of every book published, with PDF and ePub files available? You can upgrade to the eBook version at packt.com and as a print book customer, you are entitled to a discount on the eBook copy. Get in touch with us at customercare@packtpub.com for more details.

At www.packt.com, you can also read a collection of free technical articles, sign up for a range of free newsletters, and receive exclusive discounts and offers on Packt books and eBooks.

Other Books You May Enjoy

If you enjoyed this book, you may be interested in these other books by Packt:

Adobe Illustrator for Creative Professionals

Clint Balsar

ISBN: 978-1-80056-925-6

- Master a wide variety of methods for developing objects
- Control files using layers and groups
- Enhance content using data-supported infographics
- Use multiple artboards for better efficiency and asset management
- Understand the use of layers and objects in Illustrator
- Build professional systems for final presentation to clients

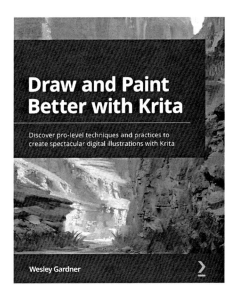

Draw and Paint Better with Krita

Wesley Gardner

ISBN: 978-1-80107-176-5

- Use layers, layer management, and layer blending modes to make images pop
- Understand Krita's default workspace and customize it
- Understand the terminology of digital visual communication (dots per inch, resolution, and more)
- Explore color in a digital space, such as RGB profiles and Look-Up-Tables (LUTS)
- Discover the color wheel for painting and learn how digital color (light and alpha channels) works as opposed to traditional painting materials
- Focus on proper layer management for easy, non-destructive manipulation of art pieces quickly

Packt is searching for authors like you

If you're interested in becoming an author for Packt, please visit `authors.packtpub.com` and apply today. We have worked with thousands of developers and tech professionals, just like you, to help them share their insight with the global tech community. You can make a general application, apply for a specific hot topic that we are recruiting an author for, or submit your own idea.

Hi!

I am Samadrita Ghosh, author of *Get Set Procreate 5*. I really hope you enjoyed reading this book and found it useful for increasing your productivity and efficiency in Procreate.

It would really help me (and other potential readers!) if you could leave a review on Amazon sharing your thoughts on *Get Set Procreate 5*.

Go to the link below or scan the QR code to leave your review:

`https://packt.link/r/1800563000`

Your review will help me to understand what's worked well in this book, and what could be improved upon for future editions, so it really is appreciated.

Best Wishes,

Samadrita Ghosh